GLOBAL
ACCOUNTING & CONTROL

A Managerial Emphasis

SIDNEY J. GRAY

University of New South Wales

STEPHEN B. SALTER

University of Cincinnati

LEE. H. RADEBAUGH

Brigham Young University

Acquisitions Editor: Mark Bonadeo
Marketing Manager: Clancy Marshall
Senior Designer: Dawn L. Stanley
Production Management Services: Suzanne Ingrao

This book was set in New Baskerville by Nesbitt Graphics and printed and bound by Hamilton Printing. The cover was printed by Lehigh Press.

This book is printed on acid-free paper.

L.C. call no.   Dewey Classification No.   L.C. Card No.
ISBN 0-471-12808-2

Printed in the United States of America

10 9 8 7 6 5 4 3 2 1

ABOUT THE AUTHORS

Sidney J. Gray, BEc (Sydney), Ph.D. (Lancaster), FCCA, CPA, ACIS, MIMgt

Professor Gray received his economics degree from the University of Sydney and his Ph.D. in international accounting from the University of Lancaster. He teaches and researches international accounting, international business strategy, and cross-cultural management at the University of New South Wales, Sydney, Australia, where he is a Professor and Head of the School of International Business. He was formerly a Professor at the University of Warwick in England and the University of Glasgow in Scotland.

Sid Gray has published in many leading journals around the world including *Journal of Accounting Research, Abacus, Journal of International Business Studies, Journal of International Financial Management and Accounting, Accounting and Business Research, European Accounting Review, International Journal of Accounting,* and the *Journal of Business Finance and Accounting.* He is the author/co-author of more than 20 books and monographs and 100 articles. His books include *International Accounting and Multinational Enterprises* (John Wiley & Sons) with Lee H. Radebaugh and *Financial Accounting: A Global Approach* (Houghton Mifflin) with Belverd E. Needles Jr.

He is active in many academic and professional organizations. He has served as President of the International Association for Accounting Education and Research (IAAER), Chairman of the British Accounting Association, and Secretary General of the European Accounting Association. He has served as a member of the Accounting Standards Committee for the U.K. and Ireland and as a member of the Consultative Group to the International Accounting Standards Committee. In 1994, he received from the American Accounting Association's International Section the award of "Outstanding International Accounting Educator." He is currently a Vice-President of the Australia-New Zealand International Business Academy.

Stephen B. Salter, BSc, (UMIST), MBA (Windsor), Ph.D. (South Carolina)

Dr. Salter is an Associate Professor in the College of Business Administration, University of Cincinnati. In addition, he is the Academic Director for Global Business Programs at the University of Cincinnati. He has a Ph.D. in International Accounting from the University of South Carolina. Dr. Salter is also an Associate Editor of *Advances in International Accounting.* He previously taught at Texas A&M University in College Station, Texas. He has been an invited lecturer at universities in the United Kingdom, France, Canada, Singapore, and Australia. Prior to entering academia, he worked for a large Canadian bank in the Far East, and was a partner in Ernst & Young Management Consultants in Trinidad, West Indies.

Stephen Salter has written over 20 articles in the area of International Accounting. These have been published in journals such as the *Journal of International Business Studies, Journal of International Accounting Auditing and Taxation, British Accounting Review, Journal of Teaching International Business, International Journal of Accounting Education and Research,* and *International Studies of Management and Organization.* He is a contributor in two books and is currently co-author of two others. He has also made presentations at over 30 conferences.

His research interests currently focus on the impact of culture on management control and accounting. His teaching interests are in the global dimension of Management Accounting and Control. Dr. Salter is a member of the American Accounting Association, the Canadian Academic Accounting Association, the European Accounting Association, and the Academy of International Business. He has served as both Secretary and Treasurer of the International Accounting Section of the American Accounting Association.

Lee H. Radebaugh, MBA, DBA. (Indiana)

Professor Radebaugh is the Director of the School of Accountancy and Information Systems and KPMG Professor of Accounting at Brigham Young University. In addition, he is the Executive Director at the BYU Center for International Business Education and Research (CIBER). He received his MBA and Doctorate from Indiana University. He previously taught at Penn State University from 1972 to 1980. In 1975 he was a visiting professor at Escuela de Administración de Negocios para Graduados (ESAN), a graduate business school in Lima, Peru. In 1985, he was the James Cusator Wards visiting professor at Glasgow University in Scotland. He was Associate Dean of the Marriot School of Management from 1984 to 1991.

Lee Radebaugh is the author of *International Business Environments and Operations* (Addison-Wesley, 9th edition) with John D. Daniels, *International Accounting and Multinational Enterprises* (John Wiley & Sons, 4th edition) with Sidney J. Gray, *Introduction to Business: International Dimensions* (South-Western Publishing Company) with John D. Daniels, and is the co-editor of seven book on Canada-U.S. trade and investment relations. He has also published several other monographs and articles on international business and international accounting in journals such as the *Journal of Accounting Research,* the *Journal of International Business Studies,* the *Journal of International Financial Management and Accounting,* and the *International Journal of Accounting.*

His primary teaching interests are international business and international accounting. He is an active member of the American Accounting Association, the European Accounting Association, and the Academy of International Business, having served on several committees, and as the President of the International Section of the AAA and the Secretary-Treasurer of the AIB. He is also active with the local business community as former President of the World Trade Association of Utah and member of the District Export Council. In 1998, he was named the "Outstanding International Accounting Educator" of the International Section of the American Accounting Association and "International Person of the Year" by the World Trade Association of Utah.

PREFACE

The global challenges of doing business in the twenty-first century require managers and accountants who are more aware of the international financial complexities involved and who have knowledge and understanding relevant to solving problems arising from the ever-increasing pace of international business, finance, and investment.

Target Audience. Our aim in writing this book is to contribute to the development of internationally competent business people. The target audience at undergraduate level includes both business and accounting students. At Master's level it is students in MBA and executive general management programs as well as specialist accounting students looking to broaden their horizons. In addition, this book should be helpful to practicing managers, accountants, and consultants becoming involved in the international aspects of accounting and control.

A Managerial Emphasis. This book is designed to help students tackle accounting and control issues in a global context from a managerial perspective (rather than a technical or preparer perspective). Our emphasis is on the needs of users of financial and accounting information across borders with the aim of enhancing their understanding of how to use information and make more informed decisions in an increasingly complex and dynamic international business environment.

Contents on the Book. Drawing on the leading text *International Accounting and Multinational Enterprises* by Lee Radebaugh and Sid Gray, this book emphasizes the international business context of international accounting and financial decision making. A succinct and balanced coverage is provided of issues relevant to users at both the internal and external levels of international business activity:

- Chapter 1 examines the global business context of accounting and control.
- Chapter 2 provides an introduction to the fundamental issue of dealing with foreign currencies and evaluating questions of foreign exchange risk management.
- Chapter 3 outlines how strategic and organizational changes in the multinational enterprise are reflected in changes in control systems and the need for accounting information.
- Chapter 4 looks at the practice of management control across borders and explores the variety of national and cultural influences at work.
- Chapter 5 examines some of the special problems of planning and performance evaluation in the multinational enterprise with particular reference to the complexities of foreign exchange and transfer pricing.

- Chapter 6 deals with the challenges of coping with the complexities of taxation across borders and need for effective tax planning.
- Chapter 7 focuses on the use of financial statements across borders by managers and investors alike and the problems of understanding the meaning of financial information in different national contexts.
- Chapter 8 examines issues associated with corporate transparency and disclosure in a global context and the pressures for both traditional as well as more market-oriented approaches to disclosure.
- Chapter 9 deals in some detail with the problems and impact of foreign currency accounting in an environment of changing exchange rates.
- Chapter 10 concludes the book with an examination of auditing issues relevant to the multinational enterprise.

Chapter Materials. Each chapter concludes with a summary of the main points of the chapter. In addition, discussion questions, exercises, and cases are provided. Some useful Internet Web sites are also listed. Throughout the book, reference is made in the text to relevant research and items of special interest are highlighted either in tables or in the international bulletins.

Instructors' Manual This book is accompanied by an instructors' manual that includes: (1) suggested course outlines, (2) solutions for the discussion questions, exercises, and cases, and (3) transparency masters.

Acknowledgments. We would like to thank our many colleagues from around the world for their contributions to the international business and accounting literature. Their research has been of great benefit to us and has helped to ensure the relevance and reliability of the subject matter. Many individuals have been helpful in the process of producing the book. We especially would like to thank Grace Setiawan at the University of New South Wales and Mark Bonadeo and his team at John Wiley & Sons for their assistance.

Sidney J. Gray
Stephen B. Salter
Lee H. Radebaugh

CONTENTS

CHAPTER 1   GLOBAL BUSINESS: ACCOUNTING AND CONTROL ISSUES   1

Introduction 1
Doing Business in the Global Economy 1   Trade 1   Strategic
Alliances and Collaborative Arrangements 2   Foreign Direct Invest-
ment 2   Portfolio Investment 3

Choosing a Method of Business Involvement in the Global Economy 3
Trade 3   Strategic Alliances and Collaborative Arrangements 3
Moving to Foreign Direct Investment 4

Multinational Enterprises 5
What Are Multinational Enterprises and How Important Are
They? 5   Unique Issues for the Multinational 6

Accounting and Control in Global Business 6
Accounting, Control, and Corporate Global Involvement 7

Conclusions 9
Summary 9
Discussion Questions 9
Exercises 10
References and Further Reading 10
Some Useful Internet Web Sites 11

CHAPTER 2   FOREIGN CURRENCIES AND EXCHANGE RISK MANAGEMENT   12

Introduction 12
Foreign Exchange Risks and Solutions 12   Exporting Problems 12
Derivative Markets (Forward Contacts, Futures, and Options): What
Is a Derivative? 15   Forward Contracts and Forward Market 16
Futures 18   Foreign Currency Swaps 18   Options 18

Foreign Exchange Risk and the Multinational Enterprise 20
Classifying Risk and Exposure 20

Conclusions 21
Summary 22
Discussion Questions 22
Case: Barings Bank 23
References and Further Reading 25
Some Useful Internet Web Sites 25

CHAPTER 3   GLOBAL ORGANIZATION, COORDINATION, AND CONTROL   26

Introduction 26
Organizational Structure 26
      Domestic Structure 27   International Division Structure 27
      Global Structure 28
Centralization versus Decentralization 30
Firm Structure and the Accounting Function 33
      Centralization, Strategy, and the Accounting Function 33   The Use
      of Informal Controls 34
Management Information Systems and the Global Firm 35
      Theories and Realities of Global Information Processing 36   MNEs
      and Transborder Data Flows 37   Management Information Systems
      and the Strategy of the Firm: Some Final Thoughts 37
Conclusions 39
Summary 39
Discussion Questions 40
Exercises 40
Case: Procter & Gamble 2005 41
References and Further Reading 44
Some Useful Internet Web Sites 44

CHAPTER 4   COMPARATIVE INTERNATIONAL MANAGEMENT ACCOUNTING   46

Introduction 46
      What Is Management Accounting? 46   Management Control 47
      Does Management Accounting Mean Management Control? 47
Culture, Markets, and Control 48
      An Introduction to Culture 48   Culture and Control 49
Empirical Studies of Differences in Management Accounting and
   Control Practices across Nations 52
      Setting Objectives: A Global Overview 52   The Budget Process
      across Countries: Basics 55   Cross-National Studies of Participation
      in Budgeting 55   Other Issues in the Budgeting Process 56
Conclusions 58
Summary 59
Discussion Questions 59
Case: The Ameripill Company 59
References and Further Reading 69
Some Useful Internet Web Sites 70

CHAPTER 5   PLANNING AND PERFORMANCE EVALUATION IN MULTINATIONAL ENTERPRISES   71

Introduction 71
The Strategic Control Process 71

Challenges of Control in the Global Firm 72
Planning and Budgeting Issues 72   Ways to Bring Foreign
Exchange into the Budgeting Process 74   Budget and Currency
Practices 79   Capital Budgeting 80

Intracorporate Transfer Pricing 80
Matching Price to Market Conditions 81   Allocation of Overhead 82   Cross-National Allocation of Expenses 82

Costing 83
Target Costing 84

Quality 85

Performance Evaluation Issues 86
Separating Managerial and Subsidiary Performance 87   Properly
Relating Evaluation to Performance 88   Emerging Trends in
Performance Evaluation 88

Economic Value Added 89

Conclusions 90

Summary 90

Discussion Questions 91

Exercises 91

Case: Niessen Apparel 92

References and Further Reading 93

Some Useful Internet Web Sites 94

CHAPTER 6   TAXATION AND THE MULTINATIONAL ENTERPRISE   95

Introduction 95

Direct Taxes 95
Corporate Income Tax 95   What Income Is Taxable? 96
Determination of Expenses 97   Withholding Tax 97

Indirect Taxes 98
Value-Added or Goods and Services Taxes 98

The Avoidance of Double Taxation of Foreign Source Income 98
Credits and Deductions 98   Tax Treaties 100

Minimizing Global Tax 100
Tax Haven Concept 100   Tax Incentives 101   The Controlled
Foreign Corporation 102

Tax Dimensions of Expatriates 102

Intracorporate Transfer Pricing 102
Tax Considerations in Transfer Pricing Decisions 103   U.S.
Rules 103

Tax Planning in the International Environment 105
Choice of Methods of Servicing Foreign Markets 105   Transfer
Pricing 106

Conclusions 106

Summary 107

Discussion Questions 108

Exercises 108

Case: Midwest Uniforms 109
References and Further Reading 113
Some Useful Internet Web Sites 113

CHAPTER 7   GLOBAL FINANCIAL STATEMENT ANALYSIS   114

Introduction 114
Environmental Influences on Financial Reporting 116
Classification of Financial Reporting Systems 118
    Nobes Model 118   Gray Model 119
Financial Reporting Values and International Classification 121
Major Differences in Financial Reporting 122
    Format 122   Measurement 125
Impact of Accounting Differences 126
    Conservatism and SEC Form 20-F 127
Global Harmonization 129
Conclusions 133
Summary 135
Discussion Questions 135
Exercises 136
Case: British Telecom 137
References and Further Reading 139
Some Useful Internet Web Sites 140

CHAPTER 8   GLOBAL TRANSPARENCY AND DISCLOSURE   141

Introduction 141
Disclosure in Corporate Reports 141
    Importance of Information Disclosures 143   Managerial Incentives
    to Disclose Information 143   Costs of Information Production 144
    Competitive Disadvantage of Disclosure 144   Managerial Attitudes
    to Voluntary Disclosures 145
International Disclosure Regulation and Reporting Trends 146
    Corporate Review 150   Operations Review 154   Financial Re-
    view 155
Segmental Reporting 155
    Users and Uses of Segmental Information 155   Benefits of
    Segmental Reporting 156   Costs of Segmental Reporting 156
    U.S. Requirements 157   U.K. Requirements 157   Requirements
    Around the World 158   IASC Requirements 158
Conclusions 163
Summary 164
Discussion Questions 164
Case: Nestlé 165
References and Further Reading 167
Some Useful Internet Web Sites 168

CHAPTER 9 FOREIGN CURRENCY ACCOUNTING AND EXCHANGE RATE CHANGES   169

Introduction 169

Accounting for Foreign Exchange Transaction Risk 169
Aloha Company Problem 171   Comparative National
Differences 171   Hedging and Derivatives for Foreign Currency
Transactions 172   Accounting for Hedges and Derivatives:
U.S. Approach 173   Comparative National Practices 174
International Accounting Standards 174

Accounting for Foreign Exchanges Translation Risk 174
Translation Methodologies: Overview 175   Temporal Method 175
Current Rate Method 175   Translation Process: Temporal
Method 176   Translation Process: Current Rate Method 179

Translation Process: Global Overview 181
United States 181   Europe in General 182   United Kingdom 182
Canada 183   International Accounting Standards 184

Conclusions 184

Summary 184

Discussion Questions 185

Exercises 185

Case: Piparo International 186

Case: Yarmouth Woolens 186

References and Further Reading 198

Some Useful Internet Web Sites 198

CHAPTER 10   AUDITING AND THE MULTINATIONAL ENTERPRISE   199

Introduction 199

The Global Audit 199
Services of the Global Audit Firm 199

Challenges to Auditing the Multinational Enterprise 200
Audit Challenges: Local Business Practices and Customs 200   Audit
Challenges: Currency, Language, and Law 201   Audit Challenges:
Distance and Organization for Providing Audit Services 202
Audit Challenges: Audit Impediments from Cross-National Diversity,
Availability, and Training for Auditors 203

Global Audit Firms 206
Introduction 206   Strategies of the Global Audit Firm 206   Structure of the Audit Industry 207

IFAC and the External Auditor 209

Conclusions 210

Summary 210

Discussion Questions 211

Case: Bell Canada Enterprises 212

References and Further Reading 214

Some Useful Internet Web Sites 215

INDEX   217

CHAPTER ONE

GLOBAL BUSINESS: ACCOUNTING AND CONTROL ISSUES

INTRODUCTION

Just pick up a local business paper or magazine and you will realize that business has become increasingly global. Involvement in the world economy takes place in a variety of forms, including:

- Trading goods or services across borders (exporting and importing)
- Establishing a strategic alliance or collaborative arrangement such as a franchise or joint venture with companies from other countries
- Investing in majority ownership of assets and companies overseas
- Investing directly or indirectly in the shares and bonds of companies based in other countries

DOING BUSINESS IN THE GLOBAL ECONOMY

Trade

Trade is by far the most important international business activity, usually providing a significant percentage of the annual income of wealthy countries such as the United Kingdom, United States, Canada, France, Germany, or Sweden. Many major corporations earn a significant portion of their living outside their home country. Procter & Gamble (P&G), producer of many well-known brands, while based in the United States, makes over half its sales from markets outside North America. Table 1.1 gives an example drawn from the Segmental Reporting note of the 1999 P&G *Annual Report*.

World trade has grown dramatically since the 1950s and has accelerated in recent years with the lowering of trade barriers. As of 1970, total world trade (the sum of imports and exports) had grown to around 600 billion U.S. dollars per year. In the period from 1970 to 1998, it had grown from 600 billion U.S. dollars to over 10,500 billion U.S. dollars per year.

Table 1.1   Procter & Gamble 1999 Segment Analysis

		North America	Europe, Middle East, and Africa	Asia	Latin America	Corporate and Other	Total
Net Sales	1999	$18,977	$11,878	$3,648	$2, 825	$797	$38,125
	1998	18,456	11,835	3,453	2,640	770	37,154
	1997	17,625	11,587	3,573	2,306	673	35,764
Net Earnings	1999	2,710	1,214	279	318	(758)	3,763
	1998	2,474	1,092	174	274	(234)	3,780
	1997	2,253	956	275	256	(325)	3,415
Identifiable	1999	11,390	6,286	2,793	1,577	10,067	32,113
Assets	1998	11,063	5,998	2,499	1,519	9,887	30,966
	1997	10,280	5,433	2,726	1,389	7,716	27,544
Capital	1999	1,484	905	265	174	—	2,828
Expenditures	1998	1,433	686	266	174	—	2,559
	1997	1,163	547	287	132	—	2,129

Note: In 1999, the Company was organized and managed on a geographical basis, with four operating segments: North America, which includes the United States and Canada; Europe, Middle East, and Africa; Asia; and Latin America.

Strategic Alliances and Collaborative Arrangements

In addition to expanding abroad by exporting and importing, companies can grow by one of several types of strategic alliances. The term *strategic alliance* tends to be used to describe a wide variety of arrangements between actual or potential competitors, including cross-shareholding deals, licensing, franchising, joint ventures, and informal cooperative agreements. The choice of the type of strategic alliance depends on a variety of influences but the motives often include the aim of gaining access to new markets. Corning from the United States and Samsung from Korea, for example, teamed up to provide TV sets to the Korean market, with Corning's glass technology and Samsung's market knowledge and local production management combining to good effect.

Foreign Direct Investment

Trade and strategic alliances are not the only business activities that have grown. Ownership of assets and companies through *foreign direct investment* (FDI) emerged from the 1980s as a major component of international business. FDI is the direct investment by a company from one country in a second country. It can include mergers and acquisitions, that is, the purchase of an existing local company by one from outside the country (e.g., the purchase of Chrysler in the United States by Daimler-Benz from Germany) or the setting up of a completely new operation, that is, a greenfield site, by a business from one country in another country (e.g., the building of BMW plants in the United States, or Nissan plants in the United Kingdom).

Since the early 1980s, FDI flows have increased three times faster than the growth of exports and four times the growth of world trade, constituting a major portion of capital flows around the globe. Total global foreign direct investment flows in 1999 totaled US$830 billion. In addition, cross-border mergers totaled US$1,100 billion in 1999. The total stock of investments by companies in locations outside their home was US$9,860 billion at the end of 1999. It is interesting to note that many of the major investing countries such as the United States and United Kingdom are also major recipients of inward investment. However, the share of developing countries relative to developed countries increased during the 1990s.

Portfolio Investment

A more recent phenomenon is the flow of capital, particularly equity capital, between countries for the purpose of investing in a small percentage of the shares of a company. A private investor usually carries this out by purchasing a mutual fund or unit trust that specializes in a particular country, region, or global investment portfolio.

CHOOSING A METHOD OF BUSINESS INVOLVEMENT IN THE GLOBAL ECONOMY

Trade

Why do businesses move outside their own countries for trade and investment? Trade is fairly easily explained. Companies often sell abroad because they need a larger market over which to spread costs. This may be because of high fixed costs or research and development costs (e.g., in aircraft production or automobiles). The local market is just too small to achieve economies of scale.

In other cases, companies sell goods abroad to use up excess production capacity. Finally, companies and countries may enjoy a natural comparative advantage in terms of price or access to raw materials or labor vis á vis other competitors.

In the last twenty years the prospects of such a global trading strategy succeeding have been enhanced by the trade liberalization efforts of the World Trade Organization (WTO) and the creation of several regional economic *free trade* zones. Some of the better-known free trade zones are the European Union (EU), the North American Free Trade Agreement (NAFTA), and MERCOSUR in South America.

Strategic Alliances and Collaborative Arrangements

Strategic alliances include a variety of collaborative arrangements ranging from joint ventures to contractual agreements. Firms may ally themselves with others for a number of reasons. First, an alliance may facilitate entry into foreign markets, just as it did for Corning in Korea following its alliance with Samsung. Second, it may also help to share the costs and risks of developing new products or processes. Third, an alliance may bring together complementary skills that would be difficult for each partner to develop on its own. At the same time, alliances are not without their disadvantages. A competitor may use alliances to obtain access to new technology and markets at the expense of its partners. The important thing is to be aware of the risks and to try to ensure that an alliance is a success for all of the parties involved. In this respect, partner selection, alliance structure, and alliance management are critical factors.

Moving to Foreign Direct Investment

While global trade can be explained largely through economic theories of *comparative advantage,* motives for foreign direct investment are less clear. In a perfect world, companies would simply trade the goods and services in which they have a comparative advantage. Most of the theories that explain investment by a firm outside its own country include seeking something not available there. These theories include following the customer, seeking raw materials, circumventing barriers to trade, and taking advantage of patents and technology.

More recent theories attempt to explain both FDI and the existence of multinational enterprises. These theories center on interaction between the external environment (e.g., legal and economic conditions) and certain firm-specific elements or strengths. A company's decision to produce outside its own borders depends on how effectively management assesses two different but interactive dimensions: (1) the external environment (environmental opportunities and constraints); and (2) the internal capabilities of the firm (firm-specific advantages). Some countries, for example, might have location-specific advantages such as a key natural resource; the availability of a plentiful, cheap labor supply; or the presence of a large market. Any or all of these advantages are reasons why a firm might want to invest in a particular location. These country-specific advantages would exist as incentives, rather than barriers, to investment.

Firm-specific advantage, also called *ownership-specific advantages,* relate primarily to the intangible assets that the firm possesses. Firm-specific advantages may include a unique market niche, a patent, or a unique product capability. Typically, competitors cannot easily duplicate these firm-specific advantages, except in the long run or at very high costs. Thus, as Professor Alan Rugman explains, "the core skill of the MNE can be some element of its management structure, marketing techniques, or overall strategic planning that leads to a firm-specific advantage. These firm-specific advantages are modeled as endogenous to the MNEs, since their internal markets permit the MNEs to control them" (Rugman et al., 1985:104).

A firm with a set of firm-specific advantages that wishes to do business outside its own country has a variety of options available for its productive use including trade, strategic alliances, and FDI. The firm could exploit this advantage through exports. Exports may be a good starting point. However, tariff and nontariff barriers to exports may lead the firm to explore other options.

Renting out or selling the firm-specific advantage through licensing, franchising, or strategic alliances with another firm is a possibility, but the gains from the sale would not be as high as they would be if the firm were to use the firm-specific advantage internally. There may, however, be gains from the country-specific knowledge or capital and other resources of franchises and partners. Further, in some countries the only available options may be to transfer firm-specific advantages to local firms or joint ventures. Malaysia, for example, requires that all firms include an indigenous *bumiputra* partner.

Finally, a firm can decide to use its firm-specific advantages through FDI. In this situation the firm is said to have made a decision to *internalize* the firm-specific advantages. There are two major objectives to internalization: "(1) to provide channels for the transfer of this knowledge at lower costs than via external modes and (2) to avoid or slow down dissipation of this knowledge to competitors" (Calvert, 1981:48). The latter point is important because in many industries, innovation is the key to remaining competitive and firms need to guard their technological lead as a barrier to entry.

MULTINATIONAL ENTERPRISES

What Are Multinational Enterprises and How Important Are They?

In the previous sections we have used the expression *multinational enterprises* (MNEs). The time has come to formally define and discuss these entities. Multinational enterprises are entities that do a significant portion of their business in more than one country. Traditionally, a rough benchmark has been that sales outside of the home country will constitute over 25 percent of total sales. Multinationals are the prime users of internationalization as a strategy and often think of themselves not so much as national companies doing business abroad but as global companies that produce goods in multiple locations. With some exceptions these companies provide products that are universally recognized and may often be thought of as local products, such as Coca-Cola or Shell gasoline.

Although a smaller company can be an MNE, the level of investment and time required to effectively manage a global strategy is likely to exclude very small companies. Globally, in the 1990s, more than 37,000 parent MNE companies existed. These MNE parents, in turn, controlled over 200,000 affiliates. However, much of the power, investment, and employment was the preserve of a select group of 100 very large companies. As Table 1.2 shows, the United States, the European Union, and Japan are home to most of the world's largest multinationals. The 20 most multinational enterprises are listed in Table 1.3, from which it can be seen that European multinationals are the dominant group.

Table 1.2   The Worlds Largest Multinationals

Country/Block	Number of MNEs in 1998
United States	185
European Union	156
Japan	100
Canada	12
Switzerland	11
South Korea	9
Australia	7
China	6
Brazil	4
Others	10
Total	500

Source: Adapted from *"The Fortune Global 500,"* *Fortune,* August 1999.

Table 1.3   The World's Most Multinational Enterprises

Rank	Company Name	Home Country	Index of Transnationality
1	Nestlé	Switzerland	94.0
2	Thomson Corporation	Canada	93.3
3	Holderbank Financière	Switzerland	92.1
4	Seagram Company	Canada	89.7
5	Solvay	Belgium	89.6
6	ABB Asea Brown Boveri	Switzerland	88.6
7	Electrolux	Sweden	88.3
8	Unilever	UK/Netherlands	87.1
9	Philips Electronics	Netherlands	85.4
10	Roche Holdings	Switzerland	85.1
11	SCA	Sweden	79.7
12	Northern Telecom	Canada	78.4
13	Glaxo Wellcome	UK	76.5
14	Cable and Wireless	UK	75.6
15	Volvo	Sweden	73.8
16	News Corporation	Australia	73.5
17	Shell, Royal Dutch	UK/Netherlands	73.0
18	Grand Metropolitan	UK	72.4
19	Petrofina	Belgium	70.4
20	Saint-gobain	France	69.7

Source: Adapted from United Nations, *World Investment Report,* 1997. Data are for 1995.

Unique Issues for the Multinational

In a sense, business may be thought of as a discipline with common rules. Multinational business adds complexity to what is already a fairly complex activity. Farmer and Richman (1965) demonstrated in their important book that companies moving abroad often encounter patterns of educational, sociocultural, legal, political, and economic environment different from those with which they are familiar. In this regard, International Bulletin 1.1 provides some examples of problems with using product and company names across borders.

ACCOUNTING AND CONTROL IN GLOBAL BUSINESS

Given the previously described challenges, what unique accounting issues appear as a firm becomes more global? Accounting and control issues for the global firm can be broadly divided into two types:

1. Issues that directly affect the firm in its day-to-day management of the risks of multinationality

2. Issues that arise as the firm prepares its external financial reports or analyzes the financial reports of firms from other countries

International Business Blunders

Today, more and more firms are initiating research in hopes of avoiding costly and embarrassing mistakes. Even the largest and most sophisticated firms are not immune to the difficulties of product-name interpretation. For example, when the Coca-Cola Company was planning its strategy for marketing in China in the 1920s, it wanted to introduce its product with the English pronunciation of "Coca-Cola." A translator developed a group of Chinese characters that, when pronounced, sounded like the product name. These characters were placed on the cola bottles and marketed. Was it any wonder that sales levels were low? The characters actually translated to mean "a wax-flattened mare" or "bite the wax tadpole." Since the product was new, sound was unimportant to the consumers; meaning was vital. Today Coca-Cola is again marketing its cola in China. The new characters used on the bottle translate to "happiness in the mouth." From its first marketing attempts, Coca-Cola learned a valuable lesson in international marketing. . . .

General Motors was faced with a somewhat similar problem. It was troubled by the lack of enthusiasm among the Puerto Rican auto dealers for its recently introduced Chevrolet Nova. The word *nova* means "star" when translated literally. However, when spoken, it sounds like "no va" which in Spanish means "it does not go." This obviously did little to increase consumer confidence in the new vehicle. To remedy the situation, General Motors changed the automobile name to Caribe and sales increased. . . .

Of course, not all companies have been forced to change their names. In fact, some of them have traveled quite well. Kodak may be the most famous example. A research team deliberately "developed" this name after carefully searching for a word that was pronounceable everywhere but had no specific meaning anywhere. Exxon is another such name that was reportedly accepted only after a lengthy and expensive computer-assisted search.

Source: David A. Ricks, *Blunders in International Business,* Cambridge, MA: Blackwell, 1993, pp. 34–35, 43–44.

Both of types of accounting issues may operate simultaneously and unfold as the firm increases its commitment to the global market.

Accounting, Control, and Corporate Global Involvement

As discussed earlier in the chapter, an MNE often follows a strategy of gradual engagement with the world outside its home base. Such a strategy will likely begin with foreign trade. Over a period of time, there will be moves to enter strategic alliances or make foreign direct investments. Eventually, global listing of its shares or [*possibilty*] a global structure of production will emerge. Not all firms follow this approach; firms may skip a step or simply stop at one or another of the stages of the process.

Assuming the firm follows the classic cycle, its first exposure to international accounting usually occurs as a result of an import or export opportunity. In its earliest trading opportunity a domestic company may receive an unsolicited inquiry or purchase order from a foreign buyer. Assuming the domestic company desires to make the sale, it needs to investigate the foreign buyer, particularly when the buyer asks for an extension of credit. This procedure is often not as easy as it appears.

When the foreign company offers a balance sheet and income statement for analysis, several things become immediately evident. First, the language and currency are different. Second, the terminology is different. Third, the types and amount of information disclosed are likely to be different. Also, the procedures that were followed to arrive at the final figures are likely to be different. Differences in valuation and income measurement often render the financial statements meaningless unless the analyst is familiar with the foreign country's accounting system.

The second aspect of foreign trade is the domestic accounting impact of foreign currency receivables (accounting for foreign exchange). A simple export sale or foreign purchase will lead to a receivable/payable being created in a foreign currency. Since most countries prepare financial statements in their own domestic currency (e.g., dollars in the U.S., pounds in Britain), the export receivable/import payable will have to be converted to the domestic currency to record the initial transaction. Since the amount receivable/payable remains in foreign currency, the value of these items in the domestic currency will change as the rate of exchange between the domestic and foreign currency changes. These changes, which are essentially current value or *mark-to-market* valuations, must be accounted for within the framework of the current financial reporting system which, in most countries, assumes historic cost and the constant value of money. The typical impact of such value changes will be to cause a restating of the value of the receivable and possibly a gain or loss in the current period. There are solutions that are discussed in Chapter 2.

As a firm moves through exporting to FDI, corporate strategies and control systems are impacted by the need to operate in a number of countries. As discussed in Chapters 3, 4, and 5, management control systems must be appropriate to the needs and sophistication of individual countries, and yet they must also satisfy the needs of the corporation as a whole for global coordination. A key element of this will be ensuring that control achieves the objectives laid out in the strategic plan.

Firms with significant FDI must deal with multiple tax authorities. As Chapter 6 notes, a typical MNE has to file tax returns in each of the foreign locations in which it operates. In addition, if its parent country taxes worldwide income it must be prepared to integrate the numbers developed in the foreign tax returns into a consolidated domestic tax return. Depending on the rules of the various countries, this situation presents opportunities to minimize global taxes. The other side of this issue, of course, is that lack of knowledge or inappropriate procedures can lead to a multinational paying tax on the same income in multiple countries. One issue that a multinational with global production must face here is transfer pricing. The MNE will expect to transfer either raw material, semifinished, or finished products between its subsidiaries. The price at which goods are transferred, which has relatively few tax implications within a domestic framework, becomes a complex matter in the international environment.

As a firm moves through exporting to FDI, it must also develop financial statements in each of the countries where it has operating subsidiaries, according to the laws of those countries. Furthermore, financial statements must be prepared consistent with accounting standards and practices in its home country. Chapters 7, 8, and 9 examine some of the main differences involved and the reasons for them as well as recent trends in accounting and disclosure practice. These statements also need to be audited, and in this respect a number of global audit firms have arisen from the former loose alliances of national firms. Chapter 10 discusses the differences in national audit professions and the strategy and character of the emerging global audit profession.

There are potentially many situations that require some understanding of international accounting. This book emphasizes a management approach, that is, that managers must understand accounting and control issues as firms cross borders. The objective is to draw from those accounting systems the information that will help managers to meet existing strategic objectives and develop/refine different strategies. Public accountants will also increasingly need to provide international accounting services to companies with international operations. Finally, as global capital markets continue to broaden, all users of financial statements, be they managers or financial analysts, investors, or others, need to understand international accounting in order to better understand company financial reports from around the world.

CONCLUSIONS

The world has always been an interdependent entity. What has changed in the last fifty years is that much larger portions of the business community have begun to realize that domestic business is just a subset of global business. This has created significant questions of global strategy, including where to produce; how to service markets; what makes these markets different; and how to use a firm's unique ability to service those markets. Since the role of accounting is to provide useful information to firms and other entities around the world, it is perhaps hardly surprising that accountants have faced a series of challenges in providing information on a firm's global operations. In the next chapters we will explore these challenges. We will also examine the different accounting environments faced by accountants in a variety of countries as they report to external authorities and analyze financial statements.

SUMMARY

1. There is considerable evidence that firms are increasingly operating in a global marketplace.

2. As a firm leaves its purely domestic roots, it begins to face challenges both of different national environments and unique international problems. Examples include different currencies and cultures.

3. A number of theories explain why and how firms enter the international arena.

4. Management control systems need to be locally appropriate but also to facilitate global coordination.

5. Many of the factors that impact on the conduct of international business also result in unique accounting problems (e.g., the need to deal in foreign currencies results in foreign exchange accounting).

6. One key problem for the users of financial information is the wide variety of national accounting and financial reporting practices around the world.

DISCUSSION QUESTIONS

1. What are some of the major reasons why a business or accounting student should be interested in international business?

2. What are the major reasons why companies become involved in international business?

3. What are some of the different ways in which a firm can get involved in international business?

4. Why are Japanese companies among the largest in the world?

5. What are some of the environmental constraints a company must consider as it develops its global strategy?

6. What are firm-specific advantages, and how do they influence a company's global strategy?

7. Why have strategic alliances and joint ventures become a popular way of growing internationally?

8. What is it that differentiates MNEs from domestic corporations and gives rise to differences in accountability?

9. Discuss the importance of access to international securities markets to the development of multinationals.

10. How important is an appreciation of cultural differences in doing business internationally?

EXERCISES

1. Prepare a list of multinational firms that operate in your city. A good guide might be a firm that recruits on campus. Try to find their Web sites on the Internet and list where they have manufacturing facilities around the globe.

2. Visit a local supermarket and make a list of ten products manufactured outside your country.

3. Visit a Web site for currencies and make a list of currencies and rates of exchange with your own home currency.

4. Plan a study term abroad. What would you want to learn and why? How would this change if you were a business?

5. Extract the annual report of a Fortune Global 500 company from a country different from your home country; use the site www.glgc.com/g600.html, or http://www.pathfinder.com/fortune/global500/index.html. How different is the format of the annual report compared with that of a major company from your own country?

REFERENCES AND FURTHER READING

Calvert, A. (1981). "A Synthesis of Foreign Direct Investment Theories and Theories of the Multinational Firm." *Journal of International Business Studies* (Spring–Summer).

Dunning, J. (1988). "The Eclectic Paradigm of International Production: A Restatement and Some Possible Extensions." *Journal of International Business Studies* (Spring).

Farmer, R. and B. Richman. (1965). *Comparative Management and Economic Progress.* Homewood, IL: Irwin.

Hill, C.W. (2000). *International Business: Competing in the Global Marketplace,* 3rd ed. Homewood, IL: Irwin.

Hofstede, G. (1980). *Culture's Consequences: International Differences in Work-Related Values.* Beverly Hills: Sage.

Hout, T., M. Porter, and E. Rudden. (1982). "How Global Companies Win Out." *Harvard Business Review* (September–October), 98–108.

Radebaugh, L. and S. Gray. (1997). *International Accounting and Multinational Enterprises,* 4th ed. New York: John Wiley & Sons.

Rugman, A., D. Lecraw, and L. Booth. (1985). *International Business: Firm and Environment.* New York: McGraw Hill.

United Nations. (1997). *World Investment Report 1997: Transnational Corporations, Market Structure and Competition Policy,* New York: UN.

SOME USEFUL INTERNET WEB SITES

1. *http://www.pathfinder.com/fortune/global500/index.html*
   This site contains a lead-in to a data card on each of the Fortune Global 500 companies; each card usually has a link to the latest annual report.

2. *http://www.glgc.com/g500.html*
   This site contains links to Web sites for most of the Fortune Global 500 companies.

3. *http://www.visuallink.com/money.htm*
   This Web site will convert foreign currencies.

4. *http://www.stat-usa.gov/itabems.html*
   This Web site has links to the big emerging markets (BEM) for products. This site would be helpful for any student of international business. It would also be helpful for accounting students to focus on the possible countries/accounting standards they could be dealing with in the future.

5. *http://www.cba.bgsu.edu/amis/cpafirms/cpabigo.html*
   This Web site has all of the Big Five accounting firms' links. It also has links to the history of accounting and other related accounting sites.

6. *http://www.pg.com/doceurocareers/operations/locations/*
   This web site has a list of links to Proctor & Gamble's international locations.

7. *http://www.odci.gov/cia/publications/nsdo/factbook/ag.htm*
   This Web site has links to all countries. Each link connects to the home page of each country. This is a good site for overall international business purposes.

8. *http://www.worldbank.org/*
   This site provides valuable financial statistics and country information.

9. *http://www.decima.com/publicns/report/wr9710.htm*
   This Web site has an article on global/domestic brands. Any international business student would find this site interesting.

10. *http://www.msm.byu.edu/c&i/cim/*
    This Web site has links to descriptions of accounting standards and annual reports in several countries.

11. *http://www.craig.csufresno.edu/*
    This Web site has accounting links such as the CPA home page, accounting jobs, accounting resources, cost accounting, and other related links.

12. *www.worldculture.com/*
    This Web site has world cultural links about communication, nonverbal cues, language, and other cultural topics. This is a good site for the international business student.

CHAPTER TWO

FOREIGN CURRENCIES AND EXCHANGE RISK MANAGEMENT

INTRODUCTION

In order to understand the financial complexity of managing the multinational enterprise (MNE), it is important to first understand the organization and dynamics of the foreign exchange market. This chapter explains the terminology of foreign exchange products, the major types of foreign exchange risk, and some alternative approaches to foreign exchange risk management.

FOREIGN EXCHANGE RISKS AND SOLUTIONS

Exporting Problems

Let's start our introduction to foreign exchange with a problem not unfamiliar to persons in stage one of international activity, that is, the import or export of goods. Consider a simple scenario. Your firm, Alamo Computers of San Antonio, Texas, in the United States wishes to buy some computer motherboards. A quick survey of the Web tells you there are three main suppliers, all of whom will deliver to your door. These are Suntech, based in California, Changi Boards, based in Singapore, and Mcboards, based in Edinburgh, Scotland. All of the boards are priced in local currency (i.e., U.S. dollars, Singapore dollars, and British pounds). The prices are US$105, Singapore $170, and £64. Since the boards are of equal quality you must make the final choice on price alone. What do you do next?

Given that the prices are in three different currencies, you first need to calculate the price in a common currency. Since you are in San Antonio, the U.S. dollar would probably be a good basis. To work out the purchase price you need the price in local currency and the exchange rate between U.S. dollars and the non-U.S. currencies. The *exchange rate* is the amount of one currency that must be given to acquire one unit of another currency. If the rate is quoted for immediate currency transactions it is called the *spot rate*. In 2000, approximately 40 percent of all foreign exchange transactions took place in the spot market.

Exchange rate quotes can be obtained from a number of sources, such as the *Wall Street Journal* (United States) and the *Financial Times* (United Kingdom). On

Table 2.1 U.S. Dollar Exchange Rates in Number of Foreign Currency Units per Dollar, Thursday, October 7, 1999

Country	Today	Country	Today
Argentina Peso	0.9998	Japan Yen	107.26
Australia Dollar	1.5196	1-month forward	106.77
Austria Schilling	12.845	3-months forward	105.16
Bahrain Dinar	0.377	6-months forward	102.04
Belgium Franc	37.657	Jordan Dinar	0.7108
Brazil Real	1.934	Kuwait Dinar	0.3032
Britain Pound	0.6054	Lebanon Pound	1502
1-month forward	0.6054	Malaysia Ringgit	3.8001
3-months forward	0.6051	Malta Lira	0.3953
6-months forward	0.6053	Mexico Peso (Float)	9.465
Canada Dollar	1.4709	Netherland Guilder	2.0572
1-month forward	1.4699	New Zealand Dollar	1.9275
3-months forward	1.4669	Norway Krone	7.729
6-months forward	1.4644	Pakistan Rupee	51.83
Chile Peso	530.85	Peru new Sol	3.4575
China Renminbi	8.2778	Philippines Peso	40.5
Colombia Peso	1994.5	Poland Zloty	4.0775
Czech. Rep. Koruna	34.3	Portugal Escudo	187.15
Denmark Krone	6.9435	Russia Ruble	25.795
Ecuador Sucre (Float)	14600	Saudi Arabia Riyal	3.7505
Euroland (Euro)	0.9334	Singapore Dollar	1.6783
Finland Markka	5.5503	Slovak Rep. Koruna	40.42
France Franc	6.1233	South Africa Rand	6.055
1-month forward	6.1088	South Korea Won	1202
3-months forward	6.0636	Spain Peseta	155.32
6-months forward	5.9809	Sweden Krona	8.1427
Germany Mark	1.8258	Switzerland Franc	1.4868
1-month forward	1.8214	1-month forward	1.4816
3-months forward	1.8079	3-months forward	1.4665
6-months forward	1.7833	6-months forward	1.438
Greece Drachma	306.62	Taiwan Dollar	31.75
Hong Kong Dollar	7.7686	Thailand Baht	39.92
Hungary Forint	241.04	Turkey Lira	464480
India Rupee	43.55	United Arab Dirham	3.6729
Indonesia Rupiah	7775	Uruguay New Peso (Financial)	11.65
Ireland Punt	0.735	Venezuela Bolivar	630.13
Israel Shekel	4.2641	SDR	0.7222

the Web you can access the travel guide site *http://www.mytravelguide.com/tools/ currencyconverter.asp* or the Canadian Bank of Montreal economics site at *http://www.bmo.com/economic/*. Table 2.1 shows October 7, 1999, rates provided by Prof. Werner Antweiler, through his Web site *http://pacific.commerce.ubc.ca/xr/* at the University of British Columbia, Vancouver, Canada. These rates are the number of foreign currency units per U.S. dollar, often referred to as *indirect* or European rates. These rates are updated daily.

Table 2.2 Pricing a Motherboard Using U.S. Dollar Exchange Rates, Thursday, October 7, 1999

Company	Country	Local Currency Price (A)	Number of Foreign Currency Units per $(B)	US$ Price (A/B)
Suntech	United States	$105	1	$105
Changi Boards	Singapore	Sin $170	1.6783	$101.29
Mcboards	British pounds	£64	0.6054	$105.71

To compute the U.S.-dollar cost of the motherboard you should divide the foreign currency cost by the exchange rate. The results of this are shown in Table 2.2. Clearly, the Singaporean supplier is cheaper and if you were paying cash that would be your choice. However, since you are placing an order for 100,000 boards the British supplier is prepared to give you six months' credit at 0 percent. Neither the U.S. nor Singaporean supplier offers any credit at all. Borrowing money is not a problem but your current interest rate is 1 percent per month simple interest, so the British proposal could be attractive. Since the price of any import is the foreign currency price converted into your currency, you are naturally concerned about the exchange rate. Will it stay the same? If it changes, what will it be in six months' time? How can you protect yourself from this and still enjoy the credit terms? We will address this in the next section.

International Bulletin 2.1

What Is the Euro?

What Is the Euro?
It is the European Union's future single currency, adopted by the Treaty on European Union and ratified on behalf of the people by the parliaments of the member states.

When Will it Arrive?
For most people it will become part of their everyday lives from January 1, 2002 at the latest when coins will become available. However, the Euro began as a legal currency from January 1, 1999, enabling it to be used in financial markets and for a range of company activities.

Did All Countries in the EU Adopt the Euro from January 1, 1999?
The 11 member countries of the Euro area are Austria, Belgium, Finland, France, Germany, Italy, Ireland, Luxembourg, The Netherlands, Portugal, and Spain. Denmark, Greece, Sweden, and the United Kingdom will not participate in the first phase.

How Does it Work?
On December 31, 1998, all of the currencies listed below were irrevocably locked into the exchange rates also listed below in terms of Euro. Thus, while one may see a quotation for the franc in the newspaper, in fact the franc no longer trades but represents 1/40.33399 or 0.02479 of whatever the Euro traded for on that day.

Currency	Number of Local Currency per Euro
Belgian franc	40.3399
Deutsche mark	1.95583
Spanish peseta	166.386
French franc	6.55957
Irish pound	0.787564
Italian lira	1936.27
Luxembourg franc	40.3399
Dutch guilder	2.20371
Austrian schilling	13.7603
Portuguese escudo	200.482
Finnish markka	5.94573

How Has it Done as a Currency?

Many experts thought the Euro would be a significant challenge to the dollar. Given that it was heavily weighted toward the rock-solid German mark, this was not an unreasonable expectation. Regrettably, this has not proved to be the case, as the chart below shows.

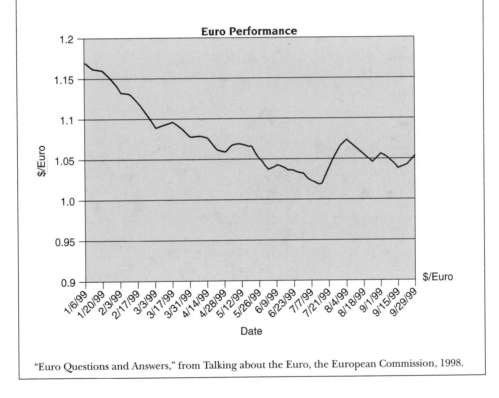

"Euro Questions and Answers," from Talking about the Euro, the European Commission, 1998.

Derivative Markets (Forward Contracts, Futures, and Options): What Is a Derivative?

The one thing about foreign exchange rates that you can be certain of is that they will change. Figure 2.1 is a graph of the value of the British pound over the nine months ending September 30, 1999. As you can see, the exchange rate varied quite

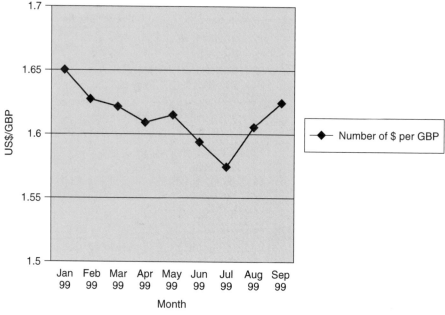

Figure 2.1   The British Pound in 1999, Monthly Average Value in $/GBP

(handwritten margin note: can buyers do this too?)

a bit over that time. One of the solutions that are available to a firm that needs foreign currency for a future payment is to use one of the main derivative products: a future forward or option to lock in the exchange rate between currencies.

A derivative is a contract whose value changes in concert with the price movements in a related or underlying commodity or financial instrument, such as the value of a foreign currency. Whereas the spot market deals in foreign currency transactions that take place almost immediately, the foreign currency derivatives markets deal with foreign currency transactions that will take place in the future. In 2000, derivatives accounted for 60 percent of transactions on foreign exchange markets. While derivatives markets offer an unlimited variety of sometimes quite exotic combinations of risks, we will deal here with basic "plain vanilla" forwards, swaps, and options. Persons wishing to get involved in more complex products should first consult their auditors and/or financial advisors.

Forward Contracts and the Forward Market

A *forward contract* is a contract between a foreign currency trader and client for the future sale or purchase of foreign currency. The majority of the transactions in the forward market are 30 to 180 days into the future, but contracts of other maturities are possible. The *forward rate* is a contractual rate between the foreign exchange trader and his or her client for a certain amount of one currency that must be given to acquire one unit of another currency for delivery at a fixed date in the future. Forward contracts must be completed and usually form part of a firm's line of credit. Forwards are probably the product most often used by companies to cover exposure even though they are a relatively small percentage of the overall foreign currency market.

Forward rates are almost never the same rate as the spot rate on the day the contract is made, and it may or may not be the same as the spot rate in effect when the forward contract is completed. The forward contract is a derivative because its future value is based on the current spot exchange rate adjusted for future expectations. The difference between the spot and forward rate is known as the spread. In Table 2.1, for example, the spot and ninety-day forward rates quoted for British pounds per U.S. dollar were:

Britain pound spot	0.6054
1-month forward	0.6054
3-months forward	0.6051
6-months forward	0.6053

Thus the spread in the British pound between spot and six months forward as calculated by the forward rate minus the spot rate was –.0001 (.6053 – .6054). The negative sign indicates that the U.S. dollar, which is the denominator, is weakening and as such the U.S. dollar is said to be trading at a discount. Some prefer to use the reciprocal or direct quote of US$/£. In this case the rates would be as follows:

Britain pound spot	$1.6518
1-month forward	$1.6518
3-months forward	$1.6526
6-months forward	$1.6521

The (forward-spot) calculation is now positive at .0003, indicating that it will cost more U.S. dollars to buy a British pound for future delivery. If we apply this information to our motherboard purchase, the results as demonstrated in Table 2.3 indi-

Table 2.3 Pricing a Motherboard Using U.S. Dollar Forward Exchange Rates, Thursday, October 7, 1999

Company	Country	Local Currency Price (A)	Number of Foreign Currency Units per $ (B)	US $ Price A/B	Cost of 100,000 Units	Interest for Six Months @ 1% per Month Simple Interest	Total Cost
Suntech	United States	$105	1.00	105.00	$10,500,000	$630,000	$11,130,000
Changi Boards	Singapore	170	1.68	101.29	$10,129,000	$607,740	$10,736,740
Mcboards	UK	64	0.6054	105.71	$10,571,000	$634,260	$11,205,260
Mcboards payment in 6 months using £/$	UK	64	0.61	105.73	$10,573,269	$0	$10,573,269
Mcboards payment in 6 months using £/$	UK	64	1.639344	105.73	$10,573,269	$0	$10,573,269

cate that even though the initial British price is higher, with the addition of a deferred payment option locked in with a forward contract, the British product often becomes a great deal more attractive, even though the British pound costs more to purchase for delivery in six months than now.

Futures

A *future* is a highly standardized foreign exchange contract written against the exchange-clearing house for a fixed number of foreign currency units and for delivery on a fixed date. Because of the high level of standardization, futures contracts can be traded readily in a secondary market such as the Chicago Mercantile Exchange (*www.cme.com*).

Foreign Currency Swaps

A *swap* is a simultaneous spot and forward transaction. For example, assume that a U.S. company has just received a dividend from a French subsidiary, but it has no use for the French francs for thirty days. It could take the French francs and deposit them in a French bank for thirty days to earn interest, or it could enter into a swap transaction. In a swap, the U.S. company would take the French francs to its bank and convert them into U.S. dollars to use for thirty days in the United States. At the same time, it would enter into a forward contract with the bank to deliver dollars in thirty days in exchange for French francs at the forward exchange rate. Swaps are the largest part of the overall foreign currency market, taking up 50 percent of the currency market.

Options

Another derivative is an option, which is the right but not the obligation to trade foreign currency at a given exchange rate on or before a given date in the future. Options that operate during a stipulated period are called *American options*. Those that end at a specified end date are called *European options*. An up-front fee (option premium or commission) is paid for the right to *buy* (call option) or *sell* (put option) a fixed amount of foreign currency. This premium is expressed in U.S. cents per foreign currency unit. This is in addition to the actual cost of the foreign currency at the agreed rate. Options operate similarly to insurance; in this case the option locks in a fixed rate for a fee without the firm having to commit to completing the deal. The option market quotes a number of prices at which one can obtain the right to buy or sell foreign currency at a particular point in time. Because options are market traded they cover standardized amounts of foreign currency and, unlike forward contracts, can be purchased for any amount. Thus a firm may well find itself in the situation of having option contracts for an amount that is more or less than it is trying to cover. Options can be traded at an exchange, such as the Chicago Mercantile Exchange, or with a financial intermediary, such as an investment banker like Goldman Sachs.

Let us once again compute the cost of our motherboards using a British pound call option for delivery in six months' time. Table 2.4 gives the option rates from the Chicago Mercantile Exchange (*http://www.cme.com/market/quote.html*).

Table 2.4 Foreign Exchange Options, Rates, and Premiums for October 7, 1999, for Call to Expire in June 2000

Strike Price \$/£	Premium \$/£	Sum = Total \$ Cost Per £
1.58	0.0862	1.6662
1.6	0.0724	1.6724
1.62	0.0602	1.6802
1.64	0.0494	1.6894
1.68	0.0322	1.7122

Source: Chicago Mercantile Exchange (*http://www.cme.com/market/quote.html*).

Since no April rates were quoted we used the nearest contract, which expires in June, and can be called at any time prior to that.

We will not be able to buy exactly the pounds we need because pounds contracts come in multiples of £31,250. However, if we assume that we sell off the rest of the pounds at breakeven including recovery of the option premium, our cost per pound at its lowest is \$1.6662 per pound or \$1 = £0.600268. As Table 2.5 shows, using options is considerably more expensive than a forward, although to be fair, our forward calculation assumes no additional fees. This additional amount is the result of having the freedom to walk away from this transaction should the pound be worth less and settling at spot. As we know, there is no free lunch.

Table 2.6 shows how to compute the option expense and the actual cash that would have to be paid as premium on day one.

Table 2.5 Pricing a Motherboard Using a British Pound Option, Thursday, October 7, 1999

Option Premium	Country	Local Currency Price (A)	Number of Foreign Currency Units per \$ (B)	US \$ Price	Cost of 100,000 Units	Interest/ Option Costs for Six Months @ 1% per Month Simple Interest	Total Cost
Suntech	United States	\$105	1.00	105.00	\$10,500,000	\$630,000	\$11,130,000
Changi boards	Singapore	170	1.68	101.29	\$10,129,000	\$607,740	\$10,736,740
Mcboards	UK	64	0.6054	105.71	\$10,571,000	\$634,260	\$11,205,260
Mcboards payment in 6 months using a forward contract	UK	64	0.61	105.73	\$10,573,269	\$0	\$10,573,269
Mcboards payment in 6 months using an option	UK	64	0.632911	105.73	\$10,112,000	\$551,680	\$10,663,680

Table 2.6   Cost of the Motherboards Using Options

Number of pounds needed for 100,000 boards	£6,400,000.00
Standard market size of contract	£31,250.00
Number of contracts needed	204.8
Total cost for the pounds	$10,663,680.00
Option cost adjusted for resale	$551,680.00
Option Premium	
Premium rate in $/GBP	0.0862
Cost per contract (31250 • premium rate in $/GBP)	$2,693.75
Total option premium (205 contracts • $2,693.75 per contract)	$552,218.75

FOREIGN EXCHANGE RISK AND THE MULTINATIONAL ENTERPRISE

As the simple example above shows, the right choice of price and foreign currency product can make for considerable saving. In the example above, the saving is approximately 5 percent of the highest price. This amount is equal to the net margin of many companies, and if applied to the revenue of a large multinational such as General Motors would save US$3.4 billion (enough to hire nearly 50,000 new MBAs at current U.S. salaries). MNEs care a great deal about the impact of foreign exchange differences on their cross-border operations. Exchange rate movements impact on all business decisions, ranging from the most basic such as the location of facilities to the day-to-day management of the risk of having accounts receivable in more than one country.

[handwritten: Because you can save considerable amounts of money if you make wise decisions]

Classifying Risk and Exposure

Movements in exchange rates between the home and other currencies lead to three types of foreign exchange exposure: *transaction, translation,* and *economic.*

   Transaction exposure results from unhedged contracted future cash flows. Transaction exposure arises from:

1. Purchasing, or selling on credit, goods or services whose prices are stated in foreign currencies
2. Borrowing or lending funds when repayment is to be made in a foreign currency
3. Being a party to an unperformed foreign exchange forward contract
4. Otherwise acquiring assets or incurring liabilities denominated in foreign currencies (e.g., a lease.)

Transaction exposure arises because we do not have a method of accounting for multiple currencies. In other words, eventually we need to account for items in our own currency. As Wolk et al. (1997) note:

> In non-barter economies, money serves as the medium of exchange. As a result, money has also become the principal standard of value and is subject to the measurement process. Thus financial statements are expressed in terms of the

monetary unit of their particular nation. (Wolk, Francis, and Tearney, *Accounting Theory*, p. 120.)

To cope with the risk inherent in transactions a separate budget for international cash flows may be prepared to assess if the volume of unhedged cash flows is significant. Such a budget will facilitate planning, controlling, and evaluating hedging activities and policies. While this can be done at the local level, the vast majority of companies appear to do this at global or regional treasury offices. Such treasury offices will plan a hedging strategy. However, hedging expenses will need to be included in the income and expense budgets prepared both for the company as a whole and for the divisions. The dangers of not managing transactions are discussed in our case, Barings Bank.

Translation exposure describes the situation where assets and liabilities in one currency have to be reexpressed in another currency. Balance sheet and income statement items, whose value remains constant in local currency, will change as they are translated into the currency of the parent company. Accounting for translation exposure has been a significant source of discord between the financial regulators and the business community. This discord is particularly strong because translation accounting is often seen as an accounting issue that provides little real business information but causes managers to take real actions to protect against paper gains and losses. This translation effect also influences budgets. First, in budgetary planning an initial rate must be chosen to prepare projected statements. This may be the current rate at the time the budget is prepared, a forward rate for the beginning or end of the budget, or some series of multiple rates. During the period for which the budget has been prepared, exchange rate variances occur. In addition, depending on the method chosen for translation accounting, assets acquired through operations to the end of the year will be subject to an additional effect from exchange rate movements.

Economic exposure is the third impact of foreign exchange rate variations on corporations and corporate budgeting. It involves uncontracted and unplanned changes in future cash flows generated from operations and foreign investments as a result of a change in exchange rates. Decisions involved in dealing with this type of exposure are primarily long term and include choosing market and production facility locations. Other decisions include pricing strategy, sales mix, how operations are financed, and personnel rewards. The impact of each of these decisions will clearly be a part of the profit planning and control structures. In the case of budgeting, if the budget is to be at all realistic, these economic impacts of foreign exchange variations should determine the base assumptions and decisions, which in turn generate the most basic numbers for the budget.

CONCLUSIONS

If you ask any multinational manager what differences there are between domestic and global business, there may be many answers but at least one of them would be foreign exchange. In the period after World War II and up until the 1970s, many suppliers came to regard currencies as relatively stable. In the period since then, one of the constant themes in international business has been a complete lack of stability. During that period, for example, the British pound has ranged from as high as $2.80 to lows of close to $1.00 and as of 2000 stands at approximately $1.60. Other currencies have been equally volatile. While there is some hope for more stability with the coming of the Euro in Europe, the period since the 1997 Asian currency crisis shows the need to be ever vigilant. As one currency stabilizes others become destabilized. The arrival of many and varied derivatives, many of which involve foreign exchange, is also stretching the ability of the current accounting model to provide useful information. It is perhaps not unreasonable to argue that accounting for derivatives and currency movements will be the defining issue for accounting regulators into the new millennium. The accounting issues will be addressed in a later chapter. All in all, the new millennium promises to be an interesting time.

SUMMARY

1. An exchange rate is the amount of one currency that must be given to acquire one unit of another currency. The spot rate refers to a quote on current transactions.

2. Foreign exchange is quoted direct (the number of units of your currency for one unit of the foreign currency) or indirect (the number of units of the foreign currency for one unit of your currency).

3. A derivative is a contract, the value of which changes in concert with the price movements in a related or underlying commodity, such as foreign exchange.

4. The most important foreign currency derivatives are forwards, swaps, futures, and options.

5. A forward contract is a contract between a foreign currency trader and client for the future sale or purchase of foreign currency. A swap is a simultaneous spot and forward transaction. A futures contract is similar to a forward contract except that it is traded on an exchange rather than with a bank. An option is the right, but not obligation, to trade foreign currency in the future at an agreed-upon rate.

6. Transaction exposure results from unhedged contracted future cash flows.

7. Translation exposure describes the situation where assets and liabilities in one currency have to be reexpressed in another currency.

8. Economic exposure is the impact of foreign exchange rate variations on future cash flows from foreign operations and foreign investments.

DISCUSSION QUESTIONS

1. Explain the difference between spot and forward exchange rates.

2. Find a currency of your choice. How has its value changed against the U.S. dollar over the last ninety days? What about since January 3, 1975?

3. What kinds of foreign exchange risk would a U.S. company face that is exporting goods to Mexico? What kinds of things would you monitor to determine what will happen to the value of the Mexican peso?

4. You have just been asked to conduct an executive program for the international controller's office of a company from your home country that is becoming increasingly involved in exports to countries in Europe, Asia, and Latin America. Because the company has only recently begun to expand abroad, none of the staff members are familiar with accounting for foreign currency transactions. The only hedge instrument that the company uses is forward contracts. What are the topics that you would include in your discussion? How would you recommend the company account for its forward contracts?

CASE

Barings Bank

Barings Debacle: A High-Finance Thriller
Could a single trader upset world's financial markets?
Source: Marcus Eliason, Associated Press, March 1995.

Singapore

The Barings desk on the trading floor is abandoned. The computer screens are dead. The little Union Jack that was sitting on one of the terminals a few days ago has mysteriously vanished. This little island of silence amid the hordes of roaring, gesticulating traders is a melancholy symbol of how the mighty have fallen—Barings, the old paragon of British investment banking, and Nick Leeson, the ambitious futures whiz from London who is being blamed for breaking the bank.

Barings, which was founded 232 years ago and helped finance the British Empire, is broke. Leeson, who spent his 28th birthday hiding out in Borneo last week, is in a German jail fighting extradition to Singapore. The global financial industry has been shaken, and questions are being asked about whether the breakdown of controls at Barings could happen elsewhere.

How did it come to this?

The first inklings came in September, when traders who follow the futures market noticed big bets being placed by Barings on the movements of the Nikkei average, the leading Japanese stock measure. Market-watchers began paying close attention to a tall, bespectacled trader and amateur soccer player named Nicholas William Leeson, who was doing extraordinarily big business in the futures pit at the Singapore International Monetary Exchange, the SIMEX.

Who was backing his multimillion-dollar gambles? "By December the speculation began to get feverish," said Mike Kokalari, vice president of Paribas Capital Markets Ltd. in Tokyo. Knowing Barings to be a bank that plays the market for clients, rather than for itself, most traders assumed Leeson had netted a big customer. A senior futures executive in Singapore, who spoke off the record, ruefully recalls how envious he was and how he badgered his own traders to get a piece of Leeson's action. In fact, as it later became shatteringly clear, there never was any client. Leeson was playing the futures market with Barings' own money, and his wrong guesses had gutted the bank—by losing an estimated $1 billion. Initially the gamble seemed sound.

Leeson was using a complex system called "straddling," based on the assumption that the 225-stock Nikkei index would stay steady and not stray far from the 19,000-point level. Japan looked like it was pulling out of its long recession, and the Nikkei was stable. Moreover, Leeson had done well for Barings since he was posted to Singapore three years ago. The Singapore futures executive said Leeson showed an impressive understanding of the Nikkei and the Japanese economy. But on Jan. 17, an earthquake struck the Japanese port of Kobe. Six days later, when damage estimates rocketed to $100 billion, the Nikkei plunged 1,054.73 points in a single day—its biggest drop in more than four years, Leeson doubled his bets—5,158 futures contracts in Osaka, Japan, on Jan. 25; 7,775 the next day; and by Feb. 21, Barings was holding 20,076 Nikkei futures in Osaka. Paribas, its nearest rival, had just 2,710.

Rather than cut his losses, Leeson piled more money into Nikkei futures, apparently believing he could move the index upward by sheer weight of trading. It moved, but not enough. In Singapore, traders who watched Leeson at the futures pit saw a man being driven deeper into a corner. As one of them observed, it is hard to take on an earthquake that has knocked out a Japanese commercial hub. The plasterer's son from the housing projects of Watford, England, had created a monster that was about to devour him. The countdown to disaster was well along.

On Feb. 23—the day Barings says it first learned of the problem—Leeson and his 23-year-old wife left their fifth-floor condo, and Leeson drove over the bridge across the Johore Strait into Malaysia, reportedly in a white rented Mercedes. The apartment showed signs of a hurried departure. Blue and white business shirts were still hung out to dry on the balcony. Two sports bicycles leaned against a wall.

Meanwhile, in London, bank chairman Peter Barings was about to get the shock of his life. Instead of the profits and bonuses he was planning to announce, he was discovering his bank was in deep trouble. At about noon the next day, Barings phoned the Bank of England. The central bank soon determined that Barings could stay in business that day, but would have to be saved before the Asian markets opened the following Monday.

End of Vacation

To complicate things, the governor of the Bank of England, Eddie George, had just left for a skiing vacation in Avoriaz, France. As George walked into his Alpine lodge, the phone rang. The governor left his family playing in the snow and flew to England on a standby ticket. When he got into his London suburban house, he said he first had a drink, then settled in to see whether Barings could be saved. As he worked the phones, "Steady Eddie" George knew two things: He wanted Barings saved because it was such a pillar of British banking; and he was not going to spend taxpayers' money bailing it out.

Emergency Meetings

Over the next 48 hours, the heads of Britain's leading banks huddled at the headquarters of "the old lady of Threadneedle Street," as the Bank of England is known. One option was to find the traders who had taken Leeson's bets, and cut a deal with them. It proved impossible. There were simply too many. At one point George went into his private office, sat at his leather-bound desk lined with computer screens, and phoned the Bank of Japan to ask if it would help square Barings' futures positions. The Bank of Japan asked the Japanese Ministry of Finance for advice. "Legally speaking, it is impossible," was the reply.

With time running out last Sunday, Eddie George contacted the Sultan of Brunei, the world's richest man and an old friend of Britain who had helped out its finances before. The sultan was asked to underwrite half of a $960 million bailout. The sultan was interested at first, but then backed out. At 8:35 p.m., a dejected George walked into a room full of bankers to say all hope was gone.

That night, a High Court judge went to Barings' office to place the bank under administration of the Ernst & Young international accounting firm. It was the coup de grace. Barings was officially broke.

Questions

1. What type of instruments was Leeson trading?

2. What risks should his firm have been aware of?

3. What controls should the directors of the bank have put in place to prevent such a situation from happening?

4. Although Mr. Leeson's losses were large they do not seem huge compared with the assets of most banks. Why did Barings go bankrupt?

5. Why did Mr. George allow Barings to go bankrupt?

6. What lessons are there in this case for other multinationals?

7. Can you find any examples of similar situations where misunderstood options caused significant losses?

REFERENCES AND FURTHER READING

Allen, D. (1999). "Foreign Currency Risk." *Chartered Accountants Journal of New Zealand* 78(3):16–18.

Allen, D. (1998). "Currency Risk: The Plot Thickens." *Management Accounting* 76(10, Nov.):29.

Anonymous. (2000). "SEC Mulls Expanded Role for Risk Modeling." *Journal of Accountancy* 189(1, Jan.)21–23.

Colerick, C. (2000). "Embracing the Euro." *Credit Management* (Feb):24–26.

Eiteman, D.K., A.I. Stonehill, and M.H. Moffett. (1998). *Multinational Business Finance*. Reading, MA. Addison Wesley.

Janowski, D. (1999). "Global Pricing/Risk Management Techniques." *TMA Journal* 19(5, Sept./Oct.):20–29.

Kawaller, I. (1998). "Capitalizing on Change: Preparing for the Euro." *TMA Journal* 18(5, Sept./Oct.):32–35.

Lessard, D.R. and J.B. Lightstone. (1986). "Volatile Exchange Rates Can Put Operations at Risk." *Harvard Business Review* (July/Aug.):107–114.

Perrottet, C. (1998). "Don't Hide From Risk—Manage It." *Journal of Business Strategy* 19(5, Sept./Oct.):9–12.

Wallace, J. (1998). "Best Practices in Foreign Exchange Risk Management." *TMA Journal* 18(6, Nov./Dec.):48–55.

Wolk, H., J. Francis, and M. Tearney. (1997). *Accounting Theory: A Conceptual and Institutional Approach*. Boston: PWS KENT.

SOME USEFUL INTERNET WEB SITES

1. *http://www.bajanet.com/currency.html*
   This Web site offers currency conversions. This is helpful, because it details the spot market and exchange rates for currencies.

2. *http://www/imf.external/index.htm*
   This is the IMF's home page. It offers links to IMF news releases, other organizations, and current projects. A good international business link.

3. *http://global-view.com/demo/*
   This Web site offers 24-hour market updates and trades comments about the market. This site is supposed to be for subscribers only, but they have example pages that offer free information on the foreign exchange market.

4. *http://www.goldman.com/about/at-a-glance.html*
   This is Goldman Sachs' home page. It offers links to everything (e.g., treasury, tax, global investment research). This is a great link for any manager or business student.

5. *http://www.risk.ifci.ch*
   This is the Web site of the International Finance and Commodities Institute (IFCI), a nonprofit organization located in Geneva, Switzerland, whose membership includes the world's major derivatives exchanges and financial firms.

6. *http://www.imf.org/*
   This is the Web site of the International Monetary Fund (IMF).

CHAPTER THREE

GLOBAL ORGANIZATION, COORDINATION, AND CONTROL

INTRODUCTION

Decisions about which businesses to be in, where to locate operations, and how to be competitive are all part of a firm's strategy. Strategy is also the firm's response to changes in the global business environment or its attempts to predict, preempt, and exploit future environmental changes for its own benefit.

In this chapter we outline how strategic change is reflected in changes to the firm's organizational structure and control system. The accounting and information systems of a firm, in turn, are presented as an integral part of the firm's control system. These systems are also affected by changes to the firm's organizational structure and will change as structure and strategy change.

ORGANIZATIONAL STRUCTURE

The managerial challenge of the twenty-first century is to coordinate the growing network of interdependent international activities. There are two major classifications of mechanisms for coordinating activities in MNEs:

1. Structural and formal mechanisms
2. Informal and subtle

In practice, control is shifting from the formal to the more informal ways of coordinating activities. To understand the transition from structural to informal and subtle control mechanisms, it is important to better understand the structural issues. As a domestic firm evolves into an MNE, numerous pressures, both internal and external to the firm, put strains on the firm's organizational structure. Some responsibilities are shifted, new ones are created, and occasionally, existing ones are eliminated. As responsibilities change, so do the reporting and communication flows. Furthermore, the degree of control, both exercised and exercisable, changes over time as the firm grows in size, geographic spread, and product lines, and as changes occur in countries' sociopolitical and socioeconomic environments. New opportunities arise, as do new threats. Thus, a firm's organization is constantly evolving. Failure to properly adjust the organizational structure to the changing environments may result in internal conflict and poor performance strains. Internal conflict and poor performance also cause pressure for organizational change.

Domestic Structure

Consider the typical evolution of a multinational firm from its beginning as a purely domestic firm. The first evolutionary stage involves export activities in the form of occasional, unsolicited orders from foreign buyers. Typically, no one in the purely domestic company has much, if any, knowledge about these matters. External experts, such as export management companies and freight forwarders, are used to develop an export strategy.

As exports grow in volume, the use of external experts can become increasingly expensive, and the firm may, and typically does, decide to internalize the export activities by hiring new personnel for what becomes an export department, thereby also gaining greater control over its export activities. As Figure 3.1 shows, this typically begins as a subgroup of the firm's marketing division, with only advisory or clerical capacity and no authority to commit resources.

As foreign market opportunities and sales increase, this export group commensurately grows in size and sophistication. Foreign sales representatives may be added, ultimately leading to the establishment of foreign sales offices to better identify new customers and better serve all customers. By this stage, several internal strains have occurred. The first concerns responsibility for exports. Does the export group merely advise domestic divisions, or is it empowered to make commitments? In the advisory situations, the export group feels constrained and seeks greater authority. In the commitment situation, domestic divisions feel a loss of power. In addition, there are strains related to internal pricing and profit allocations. The export group wants low transfer prices from the domestic division so it can obtain larger profits on its export sales, whereas the domestic division seeks higher transfer prices on goods it sells to the export group so that it can capture more of the profit. Furthermore, the export group may need to rely on the product and technical expertise of the larger domestic divisions, which, if obtained, puts strain on the domestic staff and also leads them to request greater compensation.

International Division Structure

At a later stage, it often becomes advisable to establish foreign production facilities. For example, it may become cheaper to produce abroad, or foreign governments

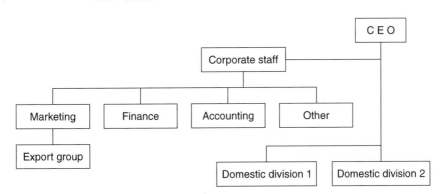

Figure 3.1 Domestic Organization with Initial Export Group

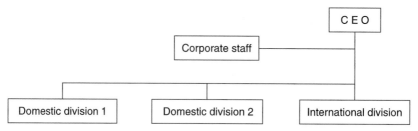

Figure 3.2   International Division

may restrict imports or raise tariffs. Once foreign production is established, be it by a licensing agreement, a joint venture, or a wholly owned subsidiary, some existing organizational pressures abate while others arise. Specifically, many of the previous disputes over production allocation, scheduling, product adaptations, and transfer pricing diminish because previous export markets are now served by foreign rather than domestic production. What arise are new problems of responsibility and control. Someone or some group must take responsibility for the growing foreign operations, and control becomes more difficult because changes occur in at least two operating environments (domestic and foreign). Typically, because of the growing diversity of international operations, an international division replaces the old export division (see Figure 3.2). Further, because foreign activities are still a rather insignificant percentage of total corporate sales, substantial autonomy is given to the new division. As foreign operations expand further, however, the international division itself must exercise tighter control over its numerous operations and activities. To do so, it adds staff and, therefore, complexity. It also begins to fight harder for more corporate resources, which puts it into conflict with domestic divisions that also want greater resources. In essence, the firm can become split into two rival factions, and suboptimization can result.

Global Structure

To minimize conflicts and potential suboptimization, the firm typically undergoes a major reorganization, adopting a global product structure or global geographic structure (see Figures 3.3 and 3.4). In the former, previous distinctions between domestic and international divisions are eliminated, and product division managers are given responsibility and control over the worldwide production and sale of

Figure 3.3   Global Geographically Oriented Organization

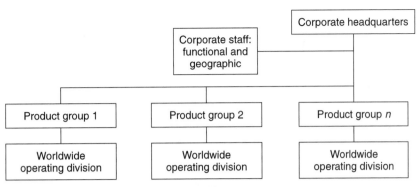

Figure 3.4 Global Product Oriented Organization

their products. In the global geographic structure, existing domestic and international operations become part of one of several geographic divisions.

Firms typically select one of these structures based on a number of criteria related to their products and markets. For example, companies with narrow, relatively simple and stable product lines often choose the global geographic structure, particularly when their products require many local adaptations or expert knowledge of local consumption practices, government policies, and so on. In short, a geographic structure works best when country or regional expertise is more important than product knowledge and expertise.

Conversely, when the product line is wide or when the products are complex and subject to rapid technological change (i.e., product knowledge and expertise is more important), the global product structure is often chosen. PepsiCo, with such diverse product lines as beverages (Pepsi) and restaurants (Pizza Hut, Taco Bell, and KFC), is organized along product lines. Global product structures are also more likely to emerge when there is a greater need for production and logistical coordination, as in vertically integrated firms or firms pursuing international production rationalization. The Procter & Gamble case at the end of the chapter presents an opportunity for you to analyze a recent restructuring decision, its source, and implications.

Yet, as was the case with organizational changes, some old problems and pressures abate while others arise. In the global product structure, old battles between domestic and foreign divisions are reduced, but battles between product divisions are accentuated. As product lines gain worldwide market share, there is a need to develop regional expertise for the product lines. In the geographic structure, new battles emerge between geographic divisions as they fight for the latest in product developments and for resources for expansion.

To better coordinate and control global operations, still another organizational structure emerged—that of the global grid/matrix structure (see Figure 3.5). In this three-dimensional structure, product divisions, geographic areas, and functional areas share power and responsibilities. For example, a proposed expansion of sales of industrial equipment in the Far East involved an MNE's industrial equipment group, its Far East regional group, and finance and marketing groups at headquarters. Through such a combination, the company management hoped there would be better coordination of global activities by taking a more holistic and less suboptimal approach.

In some respects, the global matrix was designed to bring the product line and geographic dimensions of the organization back together. This is illustrated in

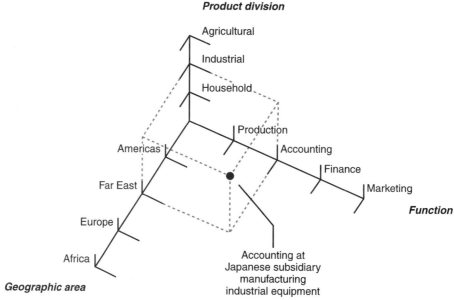

Figure 3.5 Global Grid Organization

the classic Stopford and Wells' stages of international organizations, as adapted by Christopher Bartlett and Sumantra Ghoshal (1989), shown in Figure 3.6. However, the matrix has not turned out to be the solution to organization dilemmas. As Bartlett and Ghoshal (1989:30) note, there are numerous shortcomings to the matrix:

> In practice, however, the matrix proved all but unmanageable especially in an international context. Dual reporting led to conflict and confusion; the prolifer-ation of channels created informational logjams as a proliferation of commit-tees and reports bogged down the organization; and overlapping responsibili-ties produced turf battles and a loss of accountability. Separated by barriers of distance, language, time, and culture, managers found it virtually impossible to clarify the confusion and resolve the conflicts.

The solution to the organizational dilemma is more complex than organiza-tional structure; it involves the attitude toward the role between the parent company and the different affiliates worldwide (the centralization/decentralization dilemma) as well as the frame of mind of top management (the informal and subtle mecha-nisms). These organizational issues strongly influence the managerial accounting system of the firm, from the nature of the information system and the establishment of accounting policies, to the internal controls established to ensure compliance and the evaluation of the performance of foreign operations and their managers.

CENTRALIZATION VERSUS DECENTRALIZATION

As discussed in the previous paragraph, in addition to the base structural issues in designing a global organization, a company must decide to what extent decision making should be held in a few key centers (centralized) or distributed to a large

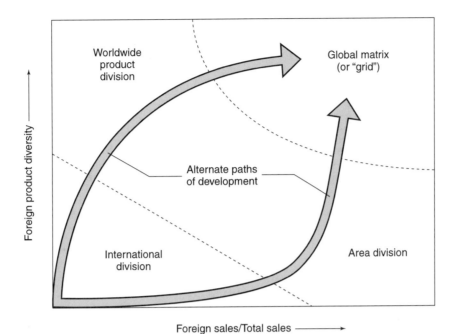

Figure 3.6 Stopford and Wells's International Structural Stages Model

number of business units. The problem with centralization versus decentralization is that the very terms connote a mutually exclusive situation—decision making must be *either* centralized *or* decentralized. However, the global environment is too complex for such a simple dichotomy. Companies can be described as either multidomestic or global in their approach to world markets, with the multidomestic approach allowing individual subsidiaries to compete independently in different domestic markets and the global approach pitting the entire worldwide system of product and market position against the competition.

Hout, Porter, and Rudden (1982) suggest that companies that are more likely to adopt a multidomestic strategy are those that have products that differ greatly from country market to country market. Such companies also have high transportation costs or their industries lack sufficient scale economies to yield the global competitors a significant competitive edge. Economies of scale may be too modest, R&D closely tied to a specific market, transportation costs and government barriers to trade too high, and distribution systems fragmented and too hard to penetrate. A global strategy is more likely when significant benefits gained from worldwide volume—in terms of either reduced unit costs or superior reputation or service—are greater than the additional costs of serving that volume. These volume advantages may come from larger production plants or runs, more efficient logistics networks, higher volume distribution networks, or high levels of investment in R&D. The relationship between the multidomestic/global dichotomy and centralization/decentralization is that as a company becomes more global, the emphasis shifts toward greater centralization. As countries increase in importance, they must be brought within the global manager's reach. However, this is not a given: compare the fairly centralized U.S. firm Procter & Gamble (*www.pg.com*) and the much more decentralized Anglo-Dutch firm Unilever (*www.unilever.com*).

The term *global* can mean different things. Hamel and Prahalad (1992) differentiate between global competition, global businesses, and global companies. Global competition occurs when companies cross-subsidize national market share battles in pursuit of global brand and distribution positions. Rather than focus strictly on the home national market, global competition requires firms to attack competition in markets worldwide, including the home market of the foreign competitor. The first and still ongoing example of this would be the global trade in agricultural products. A more modern example would be the U.S. auto industry, which, placed under threat in the 1980s, had to react by going global. Similar battles have been fought in the airline industry.

Global businesses are those in which the minimum volume required for cost efficiency is not available in the company's home market, forcing those companies to pursue markets overseas, maybe supplying the market from domestic production. A good example might be the steel industry or the international textiles industry. Another example would be the aircraft industry, where Boeing and Airbus attempt to spread their very high R&D costs across global markets to achieve breakeven and above volumes. In the 1990s, one has seen a decline in the number of producers of large commercial aircraft, and cross-industry mergers increased as the cost and risk of designing a single new aircraft became higher and higher.

Global companies have distribution systems in key markets that enable cross-subsidization, international retaliation, and world-scale volume. Again the key players in the airline industry, such as British Airways, KLM, and American, come to mind. More recently, one may need to go beyond the concept of companies to *strategic alliances* such as One World (B.A., American Airlines, Cathay Pacific, and Qantas) or Star Alliance (United Airlines, Lufthansa, SAS, Air Canada, and Thai), where global alliances have distribution systems in key markets that enable cross-subsidization, international retaliation, and world-scale volume.

Bartlett and Ghoshal (1989) identify three global imperatives that influence organizational structure, the degree of centralization of decision making, and the organizational culture of the firm:

1. *Forces for global integration:* The need for efficiency. Companies need to achieve economies of scale in such areas as product lines, parts design, and manufacturing operations. These economies are driven by cost factors as well as by the more harmonized tastes and preferences of consumers.

2. *Forces for local differentiation:* The need for responsiveness. Government interference and different market structures and consumer preferences require closer attention to local differences.

3. *Forces for worldwide innovation:* The need for learning. This imperative involves developing and diffusing worldwide innovations and linking and leveraging knowledge.

The problem for firms is that they need to deal with all three imperatives rather than focus on just one. For example, it is possible for a company to have to focus on integrating some areas while still needing to be responsive to different markets in different countries.

Bartlett and Ghoshal (1989) believe that firms need to move to a transnational strategy rather than a multidomestic or global strategy to deal most effectively with the three imperatives just described. In this approach, corporate assets are dispersed, interdependent, and specialized. This contrasts with multidomestic

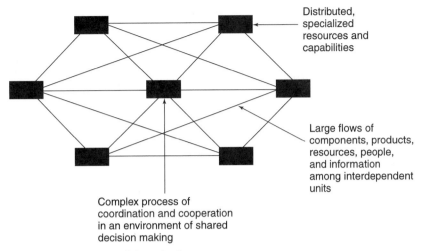

Distributed, specialized resources and capabilities

Large flows of components, products, resources, people, and information among interdependent units

Complex process of coordination and cooperation in an environment of shared decision making

Figure 3.7   Transnational Organization.
Source: Adapted from Bartlett & Ghoshal. *Managing Across Borders p. 102.*

companies, which are decentralized and independent, or global companies, which are highly centralized and globally scaled.

In terms of the role of overseas operations, national units make differentiated contributions to integrated worldwide operations in what is termed a *transnational organizational structure* (see Figure 3.7). In other words, each national unit plays a different role, and these roles vary from country to country. One overseas operation may be a manufacturing facility, while another might define its role on the need to service its local market. On the other hand, multidomestic firms exploit local opportunities, whereas global firms simply implement parent company strategies. Knowledge is developed jointly and shared worldwide. This contrasts with multidomestic firms, which develop and retain knowledge in each local unit, or global firms, which develop and retain knowledge at the center.

In transnational.

FIRM STRUCTURE AND THE ACCOUNTING FUNCTION

Centralization, Strategy, and the Accounting Function

As discussed earlier in the chapter, accounting and control derive their value from what they can provide to the firm's strategy, and are affected by the structure of the firm. For example, the degree of centralization may also affect the nature of the accounting and control function. At its simplest level some types of accounting/record keeping may be fairly easily centralized. Thus many U.S. firms use a central location to process all basic data (e.g., several large insurance companies in the authors' home areas use facilities in Bangalore, India to process the myriad accounting records associated with policy accounting).

There is, however, an argument for the decentralization of control. For example, multidomestic firms face local differences in environmental constraints, which can be cultural, legal, political, and economic. These differences require that they adapt to the way business is done, which is different from the parent country. Sharp and Salter (1997) argue that even the fundamental beliefs about behavior on which control systems are based in the United States and Canada are not valid in Asia. Bartlett and Ghoshal's (1989) transnational organizational philosophy also would influence the accounting function. To be globally competitive and flexible in the multinational arena, management needs to legitimize diverse perspectives and capabilities and develop multiple and flexible coordination processes. Thus, it would appear that the MNE would need to have an information system that provides a significant flow of information from parent to affiliate, from affiliate to parent, and among affiliates. Such a system is very different from either a highly decentralized or a highly centralized operation.

A strong case is made to disaggregate financial accounting as reporting standards vary considerably from country to country, and sometimes governments control the way the books and records of the firm are kept, thus leading to the decentralization of the accounting function. On the other hand, it may be important to centralize the accounting function because of the parent firm's need to consolidate its worldwide operations according to the GAAP of the parent company's country. Local differences may cause a different set of books to be kept, but the parent company will probably still require that a set of books be kept according to parent-company GAAP. Coca-Cola, for example, uses policy manuals to extend a more centralized philosophy to the accounting function. In the mid-1980s, Coca-Cola's management developed a comprehensive, easy-to-reference accounting manual to help maintain strong financial controls over operations. A universal chart of accounts was established so that each account in the balance sheet and income statement would be consistent worldwide. Based on the chart of accounts, definitions of each account were written and policies and procedures governing the use of each account and the flow of information into the financial statements were developed. A separate section was written about translating financial statements from local currencies into U.S. dollars.

The Use of Informal Controls

As noted earlier, the matrix organizational structure was developed to deal with the global complexities involved in product lines and geographic areas. However, it was also noted that the matrix often did not work for a variety of reasons. As one manager pointed out, the challenge is not so much to build a matrix structure, as it is to create a matrix in the minds of our managers. The key is to develop a corporate culture that allows the firm to be competitive globally. The following are three key methods used by successful managers to develop a global orientation:

1. Develop and communicate a clear and consistent corporate vision.
2. Effectively manage human resource tools to broaden individual perspectives and develop identification with corporate goals.
3. Integrate individual thinking and activities into the broad corporate agenda by means of a process called *cooption*, that is, pulling people out of their narrow and isolated areas of responsibility and helping them to develop a broader, more global perspective.

These rules are as true in accounting as they are in marketing or any other function. Accountants need to understand the information needs of the MNE to avoid the narrow parent company perspective so common in globally centralized firms. Several years ago, the authors met with financial managers of several British subsidiaries of U.S. MNEs, who described their frustration with home office accounting personnel. Because of a lack of international experience and expertise, home office personnel had a difficult time relating to the specific problems of the British subsidiaries. This was especially true of any issue related to foreign exchange.

Bartlett and Ghoshal (1989) point out the following with respect to managers (which can be generalized to accountants): "One pervasive problem in companies whose leaders lack this ability [to pull individual managers together] or fail to exercise it, is getting managers to see how their specific responsibilities relate to the broad corporate vision." To involve accountants in this global vision, it is important to recruit, select, and train accountants for the global environment. This involves understanding local accounting issues as well as the global demands of the MNE. In addition, accountants must understand the global vision of the firm. It is not enough to be technically competent; the accountant also must understand the global imperatives of the firm and the ways he or she can contribute to these imperatives through a good information system.

MANAGEMENT INFORMATION SYSTEMS AND THE GLOBAL FIRM

The transfer of data has become a crucial element for global integration. The use of satellite links has dramatically increased the flow of technology. Through satellite hookups, an athletic shoe company in the United States can design a product and demonstrate it through video technology to a manufacturer in South Korea instantaneously. Satellite technology is also used to transmit messages through modems so that computers, virtually anywhere in the world, can transfer electronic mail (e-mail). In addition, with the use of scanners, documents can be transferred through e-mail.

A rapidly emerging field is *electronic data interchange* (EDI). EDI is the movement of business data electronically between or within firms (including their agents or intermediaries) in a structured, computer-processable data format. This permits data to be transferred without rekeying from a computer-supported business application in one location to a computer-supported business application in another. EDI involves the direct transmission of data between firms as well as the exchange of computer tapes. The purpose of EDI is to instantaneously process data rather than waiting for the paper flow to catch up. EDI has been useful in clearing customs internationally, for example. A firm can electronically submit its paperwork, have the item assessed a duty, and be ready to clear customs before the merchandise actually arrives at the border. EDI is used for other business purposes as well, such as purchasing, cash flows, and so on. Banks can use EDI to electronically transfer cash from purchaser to seller without the time delays involved in traditional transactions.

Developments in information technology are dramatically affecting the speed and form in which information is transmitted. *Local area networks* (LANs) connect computers within a building, allowing them to share software and databases, send e-mail, and work simultaneously on documents, schedules, projects, and the like. Through a *private branch exchange* (PBX), computers in a company headquarters can communicate with computers in other sites, including other countries. In addition, companies can communicate with customers, suppliers, and other interested third parties through a *wide area network* (WAN), such as the Internet. The Internet, a worldwide network of computers linked together by telephone lines, is rapidly emerging as a revolutionary way to span companies and time zones quickly.

In addition to communications with the outside world, the Internet is being used for internal corporate communications. Sterling Software® Inc., a U.S.-based software maker, uses the Internet to keep its 3600 employees in seventy-five world-wide offices in touch with headquarters as well as customers. It uses the Internet to distribute e-mail, keep its sales offices connected to its R&D laboratories, and perform interactive demonstrations of software with clients. Management estimates that it saves $10 million a year using the Internet instead of dedicated phone lines for day-to-day business functions. Similarly, PriceWaterhouse Coopers, a global audit firm, uses Lotus Notes® to permit several offices to work on a single set of audit documents. However, the Internet has been slow to penetrate developing countries because telephone lines there are too rare, unreliable, and expensive to support the high-speed communication demanded by Internet applications.

Innovations in information technology are also allowing video conferencing by computer to take place worldwide. This technology allows companies to combine visual communication with telephone communication and computer links to transfer information and images and conduct meetings and interviews around the world.

Theories and Realities of Global Information Processing

Egelhoff (1991) identifies four dimensions or types of information processing that are relevant for MNEs:

1. *Routine*: Inputs are frequent and homogeneous. It is appropriate to have rules and programs, standard operating procedures, and so on.
2. *Nonroutine*: This type of information is relatively unique and infrequent.
3. *Sequential*: Information flows in a predetermined direction across parties to an information-processing event.
4. *Reciprocal*: Information flows back and forth between parties in a kind of give-and-take manner not previously determined.

In general, accounting information for MNEs tends to be relatively routine and sequential. Accounting information tends to be electronically integrated at the parent-company level, and it must have extensive reach within the information technology (IT) platform (i.e., the technology of computers, software telecommunications, and office technology, including the telephone, fax, e-mail, and so on). *Reach* refers to the number of locations that the IT platform can link together. Obviously, reach is much more difficult in the international arena. The key is to figure out how to share information across organizational lines internationally.

MNEs pull together operations in different countries through mergers, acquisitions, and strategic alliances, for example, and it is not uncommon for the various companies to use different software and hardware, resulting in what is known as a *heterogeneous network*. This makes the standardization of the IT platform a nightmare. However, a new category of software designed to solve this problem is called *middleware*. Middleware mediates between the different kinds of hardware and software found on large networks and gives a network the appearance of harmony, even though the individual components change and expand over time.

MNEs and Transborder Data Flows

The free flow of information across national borders is vital to the successful operation of an MNE's management information system (MIS) and, by extension, the operation of the MNE itself. Furthermore, the management of this information flow is as important as the management of company assets and production. The ability of an MNE's computers to communicate with each other in a transnational network allows information to be stored, processed, retrieved, and used in decision making with great efficiency, and it facilitates communications, planning, strategy formulation, and control. However, many countries have enacted legislation that affects transborder (transnational) data flows. For these and a number of other reasons, in the future MNEs will be confronted with increased risks related to transborder flows.

Foremost among the many concerns of nation-states over transborder data flows (TBF) are privacy, economics, and national security. Privacy concerns deal with employee information such as religious and political affiliations, family background, race, sex, and employment history. Economic concerns center on industrial espionage involving corporate data piracy and the impact of TBF on local data processing industries and MNEs' decision-making process. By restricting TBF, some governments have sought to force MNEs to use local processing industries and thereby increase their size and sophistication. Others have hoped that by restricting TBF, more autonomy in decision making would be given to subsidiaries because headquarters would have less information on which to make decisions for subsidiaries. These economic concerns are also related to national security concerns. Countries seek limitations on TBF to protect against political espionage and theft of industrial properties and designs and other economic data that could weaken their security. Satellite communication nets pose a major control problem in this respect.

Governments also affect the flow of information through the infrastructure of the Information Superhighway. It doesn't make sense for companies to invest millions of dollars to establish an internal network that combines data, video, and voice communications when the system grinds to a halt outside the building. Local telephone lines are the primary carriers of information. The transmission speed on these lines often causes data flow to slow dramatically, from 10 million bits per second within the building, to only 56,000 bits per second outside the building. Governments can respond to this challenge by investing huge amounts in building the infrastructure or in deregulating the communication sector so competition will bring in investment, drive service, and drive down costs. However, the deregulation game is not an easy one in that governments worry about the public policy ramifications of any decision.

Management Information Systems and the Strategy of the Firm: Some Final Thoughts

Drawing on the work of Bartlett and Ghoshal (1989), we pointed out that in approaching the global market firms can adopt a transnational or decentralized (multidomestic) approach. Firms that take more of a multidomestic approach tend not to integrate their IT platforms to the same extent as firms that have a more global orientation. MNEs that follow Bartlett and Ghoshal's (1989) transnational model tend to be more interactive. This implies a flow of information that is more

The Evolution of Global Organizational Structure

As leaders of US$7 billion multinational corporations go, Jim Wadia is uncommonly quietly spoken and unassuming. Perhaps it is a form of economy. If you run one of the world's largest management consultancies in the rapidly changing new world order of global commerce, it is wise to conserve your energy. Wadia is the global managing partner of the consultancy Arthur Andersen. He gained a law degree in Britain, became a qualified CPA in 1973, and has been with Andersen for 21 years. The secret of his rise to the top? "Luck," he says.

The Andersen structure is "stateless," or at least geographically challenged, which Wadia believes affords the company an advantage when serving multinational clients. Although an American company in origin, the two divisions, Arthur Andersen (legal and accounting) and Andersen Consulting (information technology), are both based in Geneva. The parent company, which does not practice, is structured as a Swiss cooperative. Andersen's operational headquarters, however, is in Chicago.

Wadia regards this as an exercise of great foresight on the part of the company's progenitors. He says the company has a worldwide voice-messaging system that allows a high level of knowledge sharing, from "Chile to Tokyo to inner Mongolia." Wadia says: "We've been lucky to inherit this structure. Since 1979 we have operated as a global organization: the legal structure has been in place for 20 years."

Wadia says the company is able to operate as a global network, but he emphasizes the need to develop local skills. "We are a virtual management team with no headquarters: to that extent we are stateless. But looking at a particular management position in a particular part of the world, I am not sure you can confuse globalization with loss of national identity."

Source: Business Review Weekly, November 23, 1998.

reciprocal than sequential, a situation especially common in the budgeting process. Arthur Andersen provides us with an interesting example (see International Bulletin 3.1) of its approach to organization as of 1998.

Another alternative is to view this interaction between administrative units of the company using the approach of Gupta and Govindarajan (1991), which is illustrated in Figure 3.8. As this figure shows, knowledge flows can be grouped along two different dimensions: the outflow of knowledge from the subsidiary to the rest

Figure 3.8 Variations in Subsidiary Strategic Contexts: A Knowledge Flows–Based Framework
Source: Anil K. Gupta and Vijay Govindarajan "Knowledge Flows and the Structure of Control Within Multinational Corporations," *Academy of Management Review (1991): p. 774.*

of the corporation and the inflow of knowledge from the rest of the corporation to the subsidiary. These flows of knowledge result in four generic subsidiary roles: global innovator, integrated player, implementer, and local innovator.

1. As a *global innovator*, the subsidiary provides knowledge for other units. Information flows would be sequential, according to the Egelhoff model, but the information would flow from, rather than to, the subsidiary.

2. As an *integrated player*, the subsidiary creates knowledge that is shared with other units in the company, but it also receives knowledge. Information flows would be reciprocal rather than sequential.

3. As an *implementer*, the subsidiary does not generate much knowledge for the rest of the units, but it receives knowledge from other units, principally from the parent company. This is the more traditional MNE, where power and knowledge are centralized.

4. As a *local innovator*, the subsidiary innovates locally, but its innovations are of little value to the rest of the firm. This would be more like a multidomestic firm, where local differences overwhelm common knowledge. Thus, the information flows are kept to a minimum.

CONCLUSIONS

This chapter has covered a lot of territory. The message that we feel is most important is that, for the global as well as the domestic firm, strategy begets structure and strategy and structure affect the role and demands for information and controls systems. For the MNE these fundamental questions become infinitely more complex as different cultures and currency, distance, and time zones intervene. Some amelioration can occur through technology, but this is likely to be only partial. In the next two chapters we will further explore the challenges of MNE control.

SUMMARY

1. The managerial challenge of the twenty-first century is to coordinate the increasing number of dispersed and yet interdependent international activities.

2. There are two ways to coordinate the activities of MNEs: through structural and formal mechanisms and through more informal and subtle mechanisms.

3. There are five major structural and formal mechanisms: departmentalization of organizational units, centralization versus decentralization of decision making, formalization and standardization of policies and procedures, planning, and output and behavior control.

4. When firms first begin exporting, they may rely on external experts or an export department as a unit of the domestic marketing division.

5. When a firm begins to move significantly from exporting to foreign production, an international division is established to deal with foreign transactions, and substantial autonomy is given to the new division.

6. The firm may then move to a global product structure, where product division managers are given responsibility and control over worldwide production and sale of their products.

7. Alternatively, the firm may adopt the global geographic structure, where existing domestic and international operations become part of one of several geographic divisions.

8. In a global grid or matrix structure, an attempt is made to coordinate the activities of product, geographic, and functional organizations.

9. An alternative approach, the transnational organizational form attempts to deal with the complexities of the international environment by dealing with the forces of global integration, differentiation, and worldwide innovation in a relatively flexible manner.

10. The finance and accounting functions tend to be more centralized than the personnel and marketing functions. Many companies standardize their accounting function in order to get more comparable information worldwide.

11. A sound management information system is required to provide the information that is needed in the more formal reporting structure and to provide information that makes the informal and subtle control systems work.

DISCUSSION QUESTIONS

1. The implication from the discussion in this chapter is that as a company becomes more global, it concentrates more on the informal and subtle mechanisms for controlling global operations than it does the structural and formal mechanisms. Why is this so? Do you think structural and formal mechanisms are becoming obsolete? Discuss your reasons.

2. What impact does the organizational structure of a firm have on the control system?

3. Look at the annual report of an MNE. As you read about the product lines and geographical operations, what kind of organizational structure would you guess the company has?

4. What challenges would your chosen MNE face in designing an effective management control system?

5. Why is the accounting function of a firm likely to be centralized? What aspects of the accounting function should be centralized?

6. What role does MIS play? Do they have a chief information officer? Do they have a Web site? How in-depth do you consider it to be? You may wish to compare it with other sites.

7. What are some of the major ways that information technology is helping MNEs overcome the problems of time and space?

8. What is electronic data interchange, and what is its contribution to the control system in an MNE?

9. Why is it so difficult for MNEs to transfer data from one country to another?

EXERCISES

1. United Airlines entered into a strategic alliance with Thai Airways to develop and market airline services. Would you characterize this strategic alliance as a global innovator, an integrated player, a local innovator, or an implementer from the standpoint of United? What is your logic for your choice? What are some of the problems that United might face in establishing appropriate informal and subtle control mechanisms for the strategic alliance?

2. Hoechst is a German chemical company operating in different product lines and different geographic areas. Its major business areas are chemicals (23% of sales), fibers (15%), polymers (17%), health (24%), engineering and technology (15%), and agriculture (6%). Across these product lines, Hoechst produces products as diverse as phos-

phorus and phosphates used in detergents, textile dyes, polyester auto tire cords, cellulose acetate fibers for cigarette filters, polyvinyl chloride (PVC), automotive paints, pharmaceuticals, cosmetics, offset printing plates, engineering ceramics, herbicides, and animal vaccines. Most of Hoechst's product lines face significant global competition. On the geographic side, Hoechst sells products in the European Union (51% of total sales); other European countries (7%); North America (21%); Latin America (7%); and Africa, Asia, and Australasia (14%). What type of an organizational structure makes the most sense for Hoechst, and what would be some of the major international accounting problems Hoechst might face?

CASE

Procter & Gamble 2005

Organization 2005 Drive for Accelerated Growth Enters Next Phase

June 9, 1999: Changes will lead to greater stretch, innovation, and speed.

CINCINNATI, June 9, 1999—The Procter & Gamble Company today announced details of the next phase of Organization 2005, P&G's far-reaching, strategic initiative to accelerate the company's growth. Overall, P&G expects Organization 2005 to increase long-term annual sales growth to 6–8 percent and accelerate earnings per share growth (excluding program costs) to 13–15 percent in each of the next five years, through fiscal 2004.

The Organization 2005 program will cost $1.9 billion after tax and affect 15,000 jobs worldwide over this time period, beginning this fiscal year. The program is anticipated to generate annual after-tax savings of approximately $900 million by fiscal 2004.

Program elements include: standardizing production lines and aligning manufacturing capacity with the new global business units to increase speed to market; implementing P&G's new Global Business Services organization to standardize systems, reduce internal transactions and better serve global customers; and simplifying P&G's organization structure to reduce hierarchy and speed decision making.

"The cost of Organization 2005 is well-justified by both the ongoing operational benefits of our new structure and the substantial financial benefits it will generate for our shareholders," said P&G's Chief Executive Durk I. Jager. "The redesign of our organizational structure, work processes and culture will pay off in bigger innovation, faster speed to market and greater growth."

Organization 2005

Under Organization 2005, P&G is moving from four business units based on geographic regions to seven Global Business Units (GBU) based on product lines—a change that will drive greater innovation and speed by centering strategy and profit responsibility globally on brands, rather than geographies. It also involves new Market Development Organizations (MDO), which will tailor the global programs for local markets and develop market strategies to build P&G's entire business based on superior local consumer and customer knowledge.

With Organization 2005, P&G also has created Global Business Services (GBS). This new organization brings together business activities such as accounting, human resource systems, order management and information technology into a single global organization to provide these services to all P&G business units at best-in-class quality, cost and speed. Lastly, P&G has redefined the role of corporate staff. Most corporate staff have moved into the new business units, with the remaining staff refocused on developing cutting-edge new knowledge and serving corporate needs.

The company has been transitioning to the new organization design over the past nine months and will officially begin managing and reporting the business on the new basis effective July 1, 1999. "Organization 2005 marks the most dramatic change to P&G's structure, work processes and culture in the company's history," said Jager. "The design efforts undertaken around the world since our announcement last September have identified more opportunities than we originally imagined to simplify work processes and streamline our operations. The result will be bigger innovation, faster speed to market and greater growth."

Organization 2005 Impacts

Of the approximately $1.9 billion after tax in costs associated with the Organization 2005 program, approximately $400 million after tax will be incurred in the current year, and approximately $1.0 billion after tax over the next two fiscal years. The remaining costs are expected to be incurred in fiscal years 2002–2004; however, these costs are expected to be more than offset by savings from the program.

The program is anticipated to begin generating significant savings by fiscal 2001, reaching annual going savings of approximately $900 million after tax by fiscal 2004. The company anticipates that of the 15,000 jobs affected over the next six years beginning this year (approximately 13 percent of P&G's work force worldwide), 10,000 positions will be eliminated through fiscal 2001 with a further 5,000 after 2001.

"We have always said that Organization 2005 is about accelerating growth, not cutting jobs. These job reductions are principally an outgrowth of changes, such as standardizing global manufacturing platforms, to drive innovation and faster speed to market," said Jager. "As always, we have considered these decisions very carefully with deep concern for the impact on our people."

"We will carry out the changes with maximum respect and attention to the welfare and future of our employees," Jager continued. "To that end we will make maximum use of normal attrition and retirements, hiring reductions, re-locations, job retraining, and voluntary separations to help reduce the number of potential involuntary separations." "In cases of involuntary separations, we will work with our people and offer them financial assistance to help them bridge to new careers. We will continue to set a high standard in supporting and respecting our employees' futures at this time of major change."

Program Details

Key elements of the program include:

Product Supply: P&G's Organization 2005 initiative has provided the opportunity to look at the company's product supply organization from a truly global perspective. Of the program costs associated with the changes to product supply, the majority relate to global simplification and standardization of production lines to deliver greater flexibility and reduce the time required to convert production equipment to support new initiatives. The remaining costs involve aligning the company's manufacturing operations with the needs of the new global business units. These changes will translate to faster speed to market and lower costs.

The program involves the intent to close about 10 plants, as well as a number of individual production modules, resulting in the elimination of 6,700 positions globally over the next six years. While P&G has specific plans for standardization and realignment projects, there is still more detailed sourcing work to be completed to validate the current direction. Impacted organizations will be given information regarding closures with adequate time to allow for a smooth transition and shorten any period of uncertainty.

Global Business Services (GBS): The implementation of GBS involves the move of currently dispersed business activities to regionally based centers to leverage scale and standardize work processes to simplify transactions, provide better service and reduce costs. The GBS service centers will be in the following locations:

- North America and Latin America: Cincinnati (USA), San Jose (Costa Rica)
- Europe, Middle East, Africa: Newcastle (UK), Brussels (Belgium), Prague (Czechoslovakia)
- Asia: Kobe (Japan), Manila (Philippines), Guangzhou (China), Singapore

The implementation of this new organization is expected to result in the elimination of 3,900 current positions globally with the majority of these impacts occurring three to five years from now.

Other 2005 Costs: The remaining costs and work force reductions relate to aligning the organization with the new global structure. This includes reducing hierarchy to speed decision making, streamlining organizations to reflect external changes such as global trade customer consolidation, and other organization simplification to deliver the Organization 2005 design. In total, this part of the program will result in the elimination of 4,400 positions over the next six years.

This element also includes the costs for relocation to the new regional GBU center in Geneva, the co-location of the regional management of all Latin American GBU operations in Caracas, Venezuela.

Regional Impact

Of the total work force reduction anticipated, approximately 42 percent will occur in Europe, Middle East and Africa; 29 percent will occur in North America; 16 percent in Latin America; and 13 percent in Asia. Specific facilities and businesses will not be identified publicly until specific plans have been validated and affected employees have been notified.

Focus on Growth

"Organization 2005 is focused on one thing: leveraging P&G's innovative capability. Because the single best way to accelerate our growth—our sales, our volume, our earning growth—is to innovate bigger and move faster consistently and across the entire company," said Jager. "The cultural changes we are making will also create an environment that produces bolder, more stretching goals and plans, bigger innovations and greater speed. For example, we have redesigned our reward system to better link executive compensation with stretch business goals and results. This will help encourage more breakthrough results and stronger growth."

Procter & Gamble markets approximately 300 brands to nearly five billion consumers in over 140 countries. They include Tide, Ariel, Crest, Pantene Pro-V, Always, Whisper, Pringles, Pampers, Oil of Olay, Vicks and Didronel. Based in Cincinnati, Ohio, USA, P&G has on the ground operations in over 70 countries and employs more than 110,000 employees worldwide.

Questions

Review related material at P&G's Web site (www.pg.com) and answer the following questions:

1. Review the nature and history of P&G's business activities.
2. How has P&G's interaction with the global business environment changed over time?
3. Who are P&G's major competitors? (*Hint:* you may wish to visit Unilever's Web site: *www.unilever.com.*)

4. What caused P&G to change their strategy?

5. How did the strategy change P&G's organizational structure?

6. Does the structure match any of the organizational models proposed in the chapter?

7. What were the costs and benefits of the proposed change?

8. How does the organizational structure compare with P&G's competitors such as Unilever?

9. What implications does this proposed organization have on the control system of P&G?

10. What was the stock market's reaction to the announcement?

REFERENCES AND FURTHER READING

Allen, T.J. and M.S. Scott-Morton, Eds. (1994). *Information Technology and the Corporation of the 1990s: Research Studies.* New York: Oxford University Press.

Baden-Fuller, C. and M. Pitt. (1977). *Strategic Innovation: An International Casebook on Corporations for Value Creation.* San Francisco: Jossey-Bass.

Bartlett, C.K. and S. Ghoshal. (1998) *Managing Across Borders.* Boston, MA: Harvard Business School Press.

Crainer, S., Ed. (1995). *The Financial Times Handbook of Management.* London: FT/Pitman Publishing.

Egelhoff, W.G. (1991). "Information-Processing Theory and the Multinational Enterprise." *Journal of International Business Studies:* Vol. 22, 341–368.

Ghoshal, S. (1996). *Fast Forward: The Best Ideas on Managing Business.* Boston, MA: Harvard Business School Press.

Gupta, A.K. and V. Govindarajan. (1991). "Knowledge Flows and the Structure of Control Within Multinational Corporations." *Academy of Management Review:* Vol. 16, No. 4, 768–792.

Hamel, G. and C.J. Prahalad. (1992). "Do You Really Have a Global Strategy?" In *Transnational Management,* C. Bartlett and S. Ghoshal, Eds. Homewood, IL: Richard D. Irwin.

Hout, T., M.E. Porter, and E. Rudden. (1982). "How Global Companies Win Out." *Harvard Business Review* (Sept.–Oct.), 98–108.

Mintzberg, H. and J.B. Quinn. (1996). *The Strategy Process: Concepts, Contexts, Cases.* Upper Saddle River, NJ: Prentice Hall.

Nohria, N. and S. Ghoshal. (1997). *The Differentiated Network: Organizing Multinational Corporations for Value Creation.* San Francisco: Jossey-Bass.

Sharp, D. and S. Salter. (1997). "Project Escalation and Sunk Costs: A Test of the International Generalizability of Agency and Prospect Theories." *Journal of International Business Studies:* Vol. 28, No. 1, 101–121.

SOME USEFUL INTERNET WEB SITES

1. **Global Business Strategies:** *http://www.g7e.com/index.html*
   This is a commercial site that discusses the pros/cons and possible implications of a global strategy.

2. **British Gas:** *http://www.bg-group.com/*
   This site discusses BG's strategy for a global world.

3. **Global Business Web:** *http://www.GlobalBusinessWeb.com*
   A comprehensive and free online trade resource, to assist organizations in doing business internationally. Comprised of more than 5,000 information resources, articles, discussions, and services from every corner of the world.

4. **Virtual International Business Academy (VIBA):** *http://www.viba.msu.edu/*
   This is an Internet-mediated virtual community of business practitioners, educators, and students engaged in active learning of global business strategies, decisions, and transactions. VIBA has been developed and is maintained by the Center for International Business Education and Research (CIBER) at Michigan State University's Eli Broad College of Business.

5. *www.pg.com/about/news/structure.htm*
   Proctor & Gamble's Structure for Future Growth. The Organization 2005 structural changes are designed to drive greater leverage, innovation, and speed through the creation of new organization units and the redesign of work to take a global approach to building leadership brands.

CHAPTER FOUR

COMPARATIVE INTERNATIONAL MANAGEMENT ACCOUNTING

INTRODUCTION

In this chapter we begin by presenting an introduction to management control as it applies across borders. Particular emphasis is placed on the objectives, form, and role of management control in different countries. Cross-national differences in setting overall corporate objectives and budgeting are examined in some detail. This approach essentially uses the national corporation as the unit of analysis, although it is possible or even likely that what happens to an MNE in its home country will be extended to its subsidiaries outside that country.

This approach to cross-national analysis is quite different from the multinational level of analysis. The latter is covered in Chapter 5 and examines how multinational enterprises (MNEs) resolve problems that are unique to companies that operate across borders. These problems include the treatment of foreign currencies, selecting an appropriate control tool for each unit, the issue of transfer pricing, and, finally, the issue of strategy and control.

What Is Management Accounting?

The field of managerial accounting in a global business environment has the interesting property of being a mixture of two disciplines. The first is the relatively soft approach of management, which, at least as far as *international* is concerned, finds its origins in anthropology and pyschology and attempts to provide a perspective on the unique behavioral problems of controlling a business entity. The second element, *accounting*, deals with the technical side of recording and manipulating information to provide what may be described as an optimal package or set of information. This chapter attempts to look at both areas as they relate to doing business in various countries.

As Horngren and Foster (1991) have shown, management accounting should provide information for the following purposes:

- Routine internal reporting to provide information and influence behavior regarding cost management and the planning and controlling of operations.

- Nonroutine or special internal reporting to managers for strategic and tactical decisions on such matters as pricing products or services, choosing which products to emphasize or deemphasize, investing in equipment, and formulating overall policies and long-range plans

Management accounting started as a method to calculate accurate costs for inventory and sales pricing in the industrial midlands of the United Kingdom. While it was certainly used to assist in pricing goods, its role was that of an information source that was not seen as impacting the behavior of individuals or moving the organization in a particular direction. Management accounting, or cost accounting as it is sometimes referred to, includes the skill of understanding how costs are made up and how they change. It also concentrates on how certain costs are allocated or computed. In addition, as mathematical modeling techniques developed, management accounting became a science of computing how and why costs changed, using regression analysis and similar techniques. Recently, management accounting has begun to focus on how costs can be reduced to match market possibilities. In summary, management accounting involves a highly quantitative science that incorporates many techniques familiar to mathematicians and engineers.

Management Control

The basic challenges of the management control process can be formalized as follows:

1. What is the strategic objective of the firm?
2. What types of resources does the firm need and where does it anticipate getting them in the short term (operating budgets) and longer term (capital budgets)?
3. Is there a system in place that tells the firm it is going off track and needs to make corrections? How does the firm know that it has arrived at where it wants to go?
4. How does the firm evaluate and reward the performance of the manager?

In the cross-border setting, the following questions are added:

5. How do the external and internal environments affect information needs and questions?
6. Are there different views in different countries on answers to questions 1 through 4, and why?

Another view of the complete management control value chain or process that proceeds it is contained in Figure 4.1.

Does Management Accounting Mean Management Control?

We begin our understanding of differences in the role of management accounting and management control in an international framework by briefly reviewing and explaining the subtle differences between management accounting and management control.

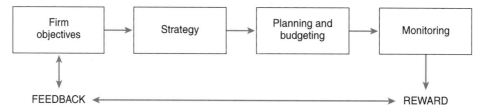

Figure 4.1   The Management Control Value Chain

Management control has very different roots and a different emphasis. Management control, although often described in terms of systems and procedures, is very much about the people side of organization management. The objectives of management control and the management control system can be stated in terms of effectiveness and efficiency of operations and analysis of risk and opportunity. People throughout the organization, including the board of directors, management, and all other staff, effect management control. Management control is, in turn, carried out through organizational influences on people's motivations and behaviors. In order to effectively carry out management control there must be an understanding of individual behavior and how individuals interact within an organization.

While organizations are constantly adapting in response to changes in the external environment, they should have a fairly clear objective. The element of control in an organization must fit with the organization's objective, be consistent with each other, and change and adapt. An assessment of management control is necessarily an assessment, albeit partial, of how the organization is managed. Management control does not constitute everything involved in managing an organization. While management control supports the reliable achievement of objective it does not tell people what objectives to set. Thus management control cannot prevent the taking of strategic and operational decisions that are, in retrospect, incorrect decisions based on a failure to understand objectives or how a particular decision or course of action is likely to affect achieving those objectives.

CULTURE, MARKETS, AND CONTROL

An Introduction to Culture

A firm's social and business environment appears to affect the strategy and control dimensions. These environmental dimensions can often be distilled into two words, *culture* and *markets*. Let us then briefly examine the role of culture and markets as they affect accounting systems. This theoretical concern aside, there is considerable evidence that the core objective of the corporation can differ from country to country or culture to culture. While one can cite many reasons for cross-national differences in choice of objective (e.g., history, economic conditions, etc.), the long-term effects of all these conditions can be distilled into a system of beliefs broadly referred to as culture. Many authors have attempted to define what culture is and classify countries by culture. Few have been more successful or accepted than Hofstede (1980, 1984, and 1991).

Hofstede (1980) developed a model of culture as "the collective programming of the mind which distinguishes the members of one human group from another" (Hofstede, 1980:26). Hofstede identified a series of dimensions of human values that affect every decision that a society or individual makes with special reference to the work situation.

The four basic Hofstede dimensions are *individualism, uncertainty avoidance, power distance,* and *masculinity.* These dimensions may be defined as follows:

1. *Individualism versus Collectivism:* The fundamental issue addressed by this dimension is the degree of interdependence a society maintains among individuals. It relates to people's self-concept: "I" or "we."

2. *Large versus Small Power Distance:* Power distance is the extent to which the members of a society accept the fact that power in institutions and organizations is unequally distributed. This affects the behavior of the less powerful as well as the more powerful members of society. People in *large power distance* societies accept a hierarchical order in which everybody has a place that needs no further justification.

3. *Strong versus Weak Uncertainty Avoidance:* Uncertainty avoidance is the degree to which members of a society feel uncomfortable with uncertainty and ambiguity.

4. *Masculinity versus Femininity (Achievement Orientation):* Masculinity stands for the preference in society for achievement, heroism, assertiveness, and material success. Its opposite, *femininity*, stands for the preference for relationships, modesty, caring for the weak, and the quality of life.

In a later study, Hofstede and Bond (1988) added another dimension to Hofstede's initial four dimensions. This is called *Confucian dynamism,* otherwise referred to as *long-term orientation* (LTO), which distinguishes societies with a long-term view of problems (high-LTO Asian societies) from those with a relatively short-term view (primarily European and Anglo-Saxon countries). China is a country with a more long-term perspective compared to western countries (see International Bulletin 4.1 and Table 4.1).

Culture has been shown by empirical analysis and case study to affect many dimensions of human activity. Some areas of human activity that have been shown to be affected are:

- Organizational structure of society
- Organizational behavior and theory
- Appropriate models of organizational development
- Existing patterns of economic wealth
- National economic growth rates

Culture and Control

The impact of each individual cultural variable on management accounting is not always clear. The studies that have been done suggest that the key values that affect the management control value chain are the degree of individualism, power distance, and possibly long-term orientation. It is interesting to note that the Asian nations, which are less individualistic and by and large more long-term oriented, tend to pick objectives that less directly reflect immediate returns, choosing those objectives that fit a longer-term market dominance profile. This reflects prior work in the field of financial accounting, which links cultural background and financial reporting practice (see, for example, Salter and Niswander, 1995, and Gray, 1988).

Business Culture - Chinese Style

Although China seems to be quick at adapting to the Western style of capitalism, there may be much deeper differences between Chinese and Western perceptions of business. One observer says China has a different concept of time. "Whereas we (Westerners) tend to be always in a hurry, the Chinese take a very long-term perspective. The whole notion of time and how one treats return on investment is very different. Asian people generally take a multi-generational view."

This distinction will not bear too much scrutiny: many European countries have adopted a multi-generational view of wealth creation, and Asia is still relatively new to the industrialisation process. However, there may be some fundamental differences of orientation. Post-industrial, developed countries are exhibiting a tendency to emphasize the short-term aspects of capital. China, which is still making the transition from an agrarian to an industrial economy—which requires heavy spending on infrastructure—is yet to fully asimilate the Western dynamic of money.

More subtle may be different notions of history: China does not necessarily share the belief in progress that is taken for granted in the West (industrialisation and the underlying concepts of money contain implied assumptions about time). Author G. J. Whitrow, in his book *Time in History*, says the Chinese have had a different concept of history, which affected the country's long-term industry formation. For example, the Chinese developed sophisticated clocks in the 11th century, well before Europe, yet when Western missionaries arrived in the sixteenth century, there was no trace of the invention.

Whitrow says the Chinese tend to view time as circular, emphasizing flux and the rise and fall of dynasties. "Despite acquiring a mass of archival material stretching over a very long period, the Chinese never developed anything corresponding to the Western concept of history."

As "globalisation" gathers pace, it is likely that these cultural differences will lead to significant tensions. Jussuf Wanandi, chairman of the Centre for Strategic and International Studies in Indonesia, says: "Globalization is so fast and so deep we cannot yet anticipate how to overcome it. It can only be compared with the Reformation and the Industrial Revolution, and we don't know how to deal with it."

Source: Excerpt from *Business Review Weekly*, November 9, 1998.

As with objective setting, budgeting process and practice is likely to vary across nations. Collectivist societies, for example, are likely to plan and reward at the group level, whereas individualist cultures might set up a series of budgets that, when linked together, become a contract linking reward and performance for each employee. The budget process in a collectivist society should be less formal in the absence of a need for documentary evidence establishing individual budget contracts.

Participation levels in budgeting and other facets of management control may also be determined by the power distance dimension. As outlined above, power distance is the extent to which the members of a society accept that power in institutions and organizations is unequally distributed. A high power distance society is thus one where those ruled tolerate and expect power to come from above. This would seem to preclude the consultative participative budgeting more common in societies where power is more evenly distributed. One might also expect less feedback.

Table 4.1   A Selection of Hofstede's Scores

Countries	Individualism	LTO	Masculinity	Power Distance	Uncertainty Avoidance
United States	91	29	62	40	46
Australia	90	31	61	36	51
United Kingdom	89	25	66	35	35
Canada	80	23	52	39	48
New Zealand	79	30	58	22	49
Germany	67	31	66	35	65
S. Africa	65	N/A	63	49	49
Japan	46	80	95	54	92
Mexico	30	N/A	69	81	82
Hong Kong	25	96	57	68	29
Singapore	20	48	48	74	8
Taiwan	17	87	45	58	69
Median score	38	33	49	60	68
Range	6–91	0–118	5–95	11–104	8–112

Notes:
1. N/A = not available.
2. Data abstracted from Hofstede (1991).
3. Hofstede's scores are not perfectly scaled. Medians and ranges are indicated above. Scores above the median are considered to be high.

Looking at performance measurement, group rewards that would be more common in collectivist societies often take longer to emerge, so planning may well be longer term. Finally, if there is less need to assign blame or reward to a particular individual within a group or company, there is a proportionally lower need to define which part of the budget plan is controllable by a particular office or office holder. In fact, it is not unreasonable to say that the western concept of management accounting's checks and balances is based on the assumption that the individual is responsible and that the individual is culpable, and therefore the individualist culture is the basis of the system. In this vein, certain recent works question whether basic western theories of behavior that underlie management accounting and control, such as agency theory, are internationally relevant on the grounds of cultural relativity (Sharp and Salter, 1997; Chow et al., 1997).

Of the remaining dimensions that Hofstede (1991) describes, the masculinity/femininity (need for achievement) dimension seems to have little relevance in the field of management accounting. Uncertainty avoidance also appears to be of limited relevance. While it is perhaps not unreasonable to expect that societies which fear uncertainty will prepare long-term detailed plans, the point can equally be made that in certain situations, society might abandon planning altogether, leaving a few key persons to deal with and protect lesser individuals. In addition, there has been some criticism (see Harrison, 1995) that uncertainty avoidance measures are less effective in eastern cultures.

In a theoretical sense, therefore, what Hofstede (1991) tells us is that there is a considerable probability that certain aspects of culture will affect business, and in turn, management accounting. While this is to some extent supposition, the next section examines some of the studies that have attempted to test the relevance of culture in general and Hofstede's work in the real world in particular.

EMPIRICAL STUDIES OF DIFFERENCES IN MANAGEMENT ACCOUNTING AND CONTROL PRACTICES ACROSS NATIONS

Setting Objectives: A Global Overview

A great deal has been written on strategy for the corporation. As it relates to multinationals, the setting of strategic objectives usually requires managers to focus on choosing a suitable numeric target. Objectives can be quantified in terms of a particular budget number or financial ratio and seem to vary considerably from country to country. Possible targets include:

- Return on investment
- Sales
- Cost reduction
- Quality targets
- Market share
- Profitability
- Budget to actual

Each of these methods has its value. The most appropriate method to be used in a multinational is, in theory, best defined by the focus of the unit for which the target is being set. Sales or market share is particularly relevant for a unit that has no control over its input costs and whose primary purpose is to sell the goods of some other unit. Profitability, measured as a ratio or some other measure, is most appropriate for a fully fledged strategic business unit (i.e., a unit of a group of companies that makes its own business decisions at all levels, e.g., a major division or subsidiary). In addition, targets for a unit may be linked not only to its objective, but also to that part of its operations that it controls. This theoretical concern aside there is considerable evidence that the core objective of the corporation differs from country to country or culture to culture. The studies that follow illustrate this point.

Studies of U.S. Multinationals   In one of the first important studies of the objectives of MNEs, Robbins and Stobaugh (1973) studied nearly 200 U.S.-based MNEs, representing almost all major U.S. industries with investments abroad and ranging in size of annual foreign sales from $20 million upward. With regard to measures of financial performance, five conclusions from their research were as follows:

1. The many tangible and intangible items that entered into the original investment calculations were rarely taken into account in evaluating the foreign subsidiaries' performance—for example, the value or cost of a parent company's loan guarantee for a subsidiary, cost of safety stocks of inventory for foreign and U.S. operations, or the potential cost of being excluded from a market by a competitor who moves first.

2. Foreign subsidiaries were judged on the same basis as domestic subsidiaries.

3. The most utilized measure of performance for all subsidiaries was return on investment (ROI).

4. Because of the inherent limitation and problems of calculating ROI equitably for all subsidiaries, nearly all the multinationals used some supplementary device to gauge foreign subsidiaries' performance.

5. The most widely used supplementary measure was comparison to budget.

Additional support for the findings of this study continues even though some twenty-seven years have passed since the original study. In a sample of seventy U.S. chemical multinationals (see Morsicato, 1980) it was found that multiple measures were used, including, in descending order of use, profit, ROI, and budgeted versus actuals for profit and sales. Abdallah and Keller (1985), in a survey of sixty-four U.S. MNEs, identified four key factors (see Table 4.2). As with other studies, budgets, profits, and ROI dominate the list.

After the initial studies of U.S. corporate performance objectives, a variety of studies have examined practices in other countries. Some of the countries are culturally quite similar to the United States.

Studies of U.K. Multinationals   Appleyard, Strong, and Walton (1990) studied the performance objectives of eleven British MNEs and found that the British companies preferred to use budget/actual comparisons, closely followed by some form of ROI. In the ROI measure, the profit measure used was either profit before interest and tax or profit after interest but before tax, even though tax rates vary significantly from country to country. In addition, they found that British firms tended to use the same ROI measure for foreign subsidiaries that they do for domestic subsidiaries.

Studies of Japanese Multinationals   Studies in countries that are culturally significantly different from the United States often produce very different results. Shields et al. (1991) reviewed the objectives used by Japanese and U.S. MNEs as found in the literatures of the two countries and identified several important performance objectives used to evaluate divisional managers. As Table 4.3 shows, there are some major differences between the two countries. The Japanese tend to rely on sales as by far their most important criterion, whereas U.S. firms prefer ROI.

Similarly, Bailes and Assada (1991) studied and compared the objectives of 256 Japanese and 80 U.S. MNEs. The respondents were asked to identify the first,

Table 4.2   Evaluating Foreign Subsidiaries and Foreign Subsidiary Managers

	Percent of the Total 64 MNEs	
Financial Measures	Foreign Subsidiary (%)	Foreign Subsidiary Manager (%)
Return-on-Investment (ROI)	74	67
Profits	78	66
Budgeted ROI compared to actual ROI	66	64
Budgeted profit compared to actual profit	86	87
Other measures	36	36

Source: W. Abdallah and D. Keller, "Measuring the Multinational's Performance," *Management Accounting* (1985) Vol. 67(4)28.

Table 4.3   Criteria Used for Evaluating Divisional Managers

Sources	Japan A (%)	United States A(%)
Sales	69	19
Sales growth	28	28
Market share	12	19
Asset turnover	7	13
Return-on-sales	30	26
ROI	7	75
Controllable profit	28	49
Residual income	20	13
Profit minus corporate costs	44	38
Manufacturing costs	28	13
Other	8	17

Source: Michael Shields, Chee W. Chow, Yutaka Kato, and Yu Nakagawa, "Management Accounting Practices in the U.S. and Japan: Comparative Survey Findings and Research Implications, *Journal of International Financial Management and Accounting* 3, no. 2 (Spring 1991):68.

second, and third goals for division managers; their answers are summarized in Table 4.4. Bailes and Assada (1991) found that most Japanese firms (86.3%) preferred to use sales volume as their overall objective, with net profit after corporate profit being a poor second (44.7%). American companies by contrast tend to use ROI most often as the divisional budget goal (68.4%) followed by controllable profit (51.8%). A full analysis of the results is contained in Table 4.4. It is important to note how unimportant ROI appears to be to the Japanese firms. Demirag (1994) found that Japanese companies in the United Kingdom tended to use sales and market share targets over the longer term.

Studies of APEC Multinationals   Looking at East Asia, Merchant, Chow, and Wu (1995) found little evidence suggesting a link between national culture and firms' goals in Taiwan. However, the sample consisted of only four firms. Comparing the

Table 4.4   Top Budget Goals for Division Managers

	Japan (%)	United States (%)
Sales volume	86.3	27.9
Net profit after corporate overhead	44.7	35.0
Controllable profit	28.2	51.8
Profit margin on sales	30.7	30.5
Sales growth	19.4	22.4
Return on investment (ROI)	3.1	68.4
Production cost	40.7	12.4

Source: Jack C. Bailes and Takayuki Assada, "Empirical Differences Between Japanese and American Budget and Performance Evaluation Systems," *International Journal of Accounting* 26, no. 2 (1991):137.

perspectives of over 400 managers in Australia, the United States, Singapore, and Hong Kong, Harrison and Harrell (1994) simply concluded that Anglo-Saxon managers prefer shorter-term but more quantitative objectives.

Taken together these studies find that the objectives of companies from various nation states vary considerably. Asian nations clearly are less individualistic and by and large more long-term oriented. They focus less directly on immediate returns and choose objectives consistent with a longer-term market dominance profile.

The Budget Process Across Countries: Basics

The budget process involves taking the firm's objectives and setting them out in a series of formal plans, both short and long term. The issues that generally need to be resolved are:

- Is there a formal budget-setting process?
- Who participates in the budget process and how?
- What style of communication (formal versus informal) should be used?
- How are the budget objectives set?

Other more general issues of concern are, for example:

- What time period should be covered (short versus long term)?
- Should there be a specific monetary objective for the plan or would a non-quantitative objective be more appropriate?

Cross-National Studies of Participation in Budgeting

How culture may impact

Much of the Anglo-American practice in budgeting assumes that the budget process is improved through the participation of the persons involved in carrying out the budget. If managers are permitted to participate in setting their own budget targets, they not only feel better about them (satisfaction) but also tend to perform better. This type of behavior was documented in a series of experiments by Brownell (1982), who suggests that for participation to fully work, managers must feel like insiders (i.e., feel that their participation will actually influence decisions and have some impact on the outcome). This concept of insider/outsider is described as *locus of control.*

This concept of the value of participation in budgeting may be uniquely Anglo-American. It implies first that managers at all levels care that their opinions are sought and feel that they can make a contribution without retribution. Frucot and Shearon (1991), for example, conducted a study using Mexican managers to test this proposition. As can be noted from Table 4.1, Mexico is a high power distance/low individualism culture. Frucot and Shearon (1991) anticipated that, given this cultural profile, Mexican managers might not favor participation even given insider status (i.e., they would rather be dictated to).

Studies of Mexican Companies   Frucot and Shearon (1991) tested their hypotheses on a sample of 83 Mexican managers in both indigenous firms and subsidiaries of U.S. multinationals. The results were initially surprising. Overall, the *performance* of the Mexican managers in indigenous firms was related to participation and locus of control. Therefore, it initially appeared there was no difference between the behavior of Mexican managers and typical U.S. managers.

However, unlike U.S. managers, the insider/outsider dimension did not affect the *satisfaction* levels of Mexican managers (in indigenous firms). The managers of the firms studied initially appeared to be happier and motivated by a higher level of participation regardless of whether they saw themselves as running the show. However, when the sample of Mexican managers was divided by company rank, lower-level managers seemed to prefer a less participative style. This is, as one would expect, given Mexico's culture.

What is of greatest concern to MNEs is that Mexican managers of entirely foreign-owned subsidiaries showed almost no desire to participate in the budgeting process. Unlike their American counterparts, they regarded themselves as powerless and the process as alien. An American, or for that matter, British firm, would receive a rude shock when it realized that its employees in Mexico had little commitment to the budget process and that they might well tell their managers merely what they expected to hear.

Studies of APEC Multinationals A similar series of experiments was conducted, comparing Australia (low power distance/high individualism) and Singapore (high power distance/low individualism). Harrison (1992) anticipated that there would be a significant international difference in the ability of budget participation to explain levels of satisfaction among managers. Coming from a relatively authoritarian culture, the Singaporeans were expected to dislike or perhaps feel uncomfortable with budget participation. Harrison (1992) hypothesized that Singaporeans, therefore, would prefer a lower level of participation than their Australian counterparts. In fact, there was no significant relationship between national origin and participation, interaction, and satisfaction. Overall, both groups seemed to prefer a participative style of budgeting. Harrison therefore argues that budgetary participation universally enhances job satisfaction regardless of culture. It should be noted that Harrison makes no comments about performance, which after all is the objective of participation. Harrison does not attempt to stratify his sample as Frucot and Shearon (1991) did. We therefore do not know if Asian senior managers take a different perspective from those in the junior ranks, a key concept when one is trying to argue that the power structure affects the desire to participate. Overall, the research to date appears to indicate that some of the western participative budgetary techniques are transferable, but one must be very careful at what level they are transferred.

Other Issues in the Budgeting Process

The previous section discussed the role of participation in the budget process. While this is certainly important, it is only one facet of the process. This section goes on to look at other key variables, such as how communication takes place (formal versus informal), the time frame for budgets (long versus short), and the objectives.

Research into the budget process as it unfolds in different countries has primarily focused on differences between Anglo-Saxon and Asian cultural groups. More recently, research in this area, while continuing to focus on Asia, has switched to the ASEAN region in what has colloquially been referred to as the *Five Dragon* or *Mini Dragon* area. This includes Hong Kong, Singapore, Taiwan, Malaysia, and possibly Thailand and Indonesia. While this group is not monolithic in culture structure, it is generally seen as sharing common Confucian values, which include long-term orientation and an unwillingness to *lose face*. This Asian culture tends to be collectivist in that citizens of most countries in the group tend to subjugate individual rights to group needs and are moderate to high on the power distance scale.

US/Japan comparisons   Some of the implications of these cultural differences appear in studies of the budgeting process that compare Asian and Anglo-Saxon countries. Bailes and Assada (1991) compared the budgetary behavior of 80 U.S. and 256 Japanese listed companies. Their results indicated that over 90 percent of companies in both countries prepared master budgets. However, they found that the process of arriving at this master budget varied. Among the points that are statistically significant are the following:

- The average length of time spent preparing annual budgets was nearly twelve days longer for the American companies (69.72 days) than for the Japanese companies.

- As previously discussed, the primary budget objective arising from the Japanese process was increased sales volume or market share. From the U.S. companies, the primary budget objective was, overwhelmingly, ROI.

- Division managers in American firms are more likely to participate in budget committee discussions and influence the budget committee than are their counterparts in Japan.

- Japanese companies also tended to follow a bottom-up approach, where all levels participated in the planning though much of the contribution was informal. Formal meetings tended to be infrequent, and whereas managers' wishes were considered, they were less important in the process than group consensus.

- Japanese managers are more likely to use budget variances to recognize problems on a timely basis and to use budgets to improve the next period's budget.

- American managers are more likely to be evaluated by the budgets.

- The bonus and salary of an American manager are much more likely to be influenced by budget performance than are those of Japanese managers.

These differences are very interesting. American managers tend to be more involved in the budgeting process, are evaluated by budgets, and are rewarded or penalized by budgets. Japanese managers tend to look at budget variances as a way to improve performance. Between the Americans and the Japanese, there is clearly a national difference in budgeting.

Ueno and Sekaran (1992) also compared U.S. and Japanese budgeting practices, framing their discussion more formally within Hofstede's cultural paradigm. Using a sample of controllers and other senior managers at manufacturing companies, they found several culturally predictable phenomena. As found in Bailes and Assada (1991), U.S. managers used more formal meetings, communication, and coordination in budget planning. Put in its cultural context, Ueno and Sekaran (1992) interpret this as control of the natural outcropping of individualism. Thus the process of budgeting becomes one of drawing together the diverse and often conflicting interests that manifest themselves in an individualist society.

Some of the other budgetary trends found in Ueno and Sekaran (1992) also appear to have cultural roots. U.S. budget makers tended to create more slack, which was ascribed to individuals trying to enhance their own power bases and self-esteem. This calculating behavior of creating slack, which in turn created comfortable goals and more easily achievable targets, was linked to the individualism dimension and the individual reward structure of most U.S. companies. Finally, as would be expected from a country high on the Confucian dimension, Japanese managers tended to care less about identifying controllability of items and tended to measure performance over a longer time horizon than U.S. managers. A few of the findings of Ueno and Sekaran (1992) run contrary to the view of Bailes and Assada (1991). Despite having a longer performance reward period, Japanese managers did not have an appreciably longer planning horizon than U.S. managers did. One must remember, however, that much very-long-term planning takes place outside of the formal numeric atmosphere of a budget.

Studies of APEC Multinationals   Harrison et al. (1994) examined the budgetary and planning systems of Australia and the United States and then Singapore and Hong Kong. They draw on the national dimensions of power distance, individualism, and Confucian dynamism to predict and explain differences in philosophies and approaches to organizational design, management planning, and control systems in Asian and Anglo-Saxon countries. Data were gathered by survey questionnaires mailed to senior accounting and finance executives in 800 organizations.

Harrison et al.'s (1994) results were largely as predicted and, in general, provide support for the importance of national culture in influencing organizational design and management planning and control systems. In particular, the cultural values of Anglo-American society relative to East Asian society are associated with a greater emphasis on decentralization, and responsibility centers in organizational design and quantitative and analytical techniques in planning and control. By contrast, the cultural values of East Asian society are associated with a greater emphasis on long-term planning and on group-centered decision making.

CONCLUSIONS

We have now covered the first three dimensions of the management control value chain. The results of the studies available thus far indicate that nations separated by cultures have different objectives, planning processes, and preferred outcomes. The results of all the studies detailed above are important to present and future managers in global organizations. The reader needs to understand the cultural basis of observed differences in organizational and management planning and control practices in Anglo-American and Asian nations. Asia and the growing nations of Latin America represent the largest potential areas for expansion of business and trade globally and are likely to see ongoing investments by Anglo-American countries. As the CEO of Procter & Gamble observed in the 1998 annual report, describing P&Gs goals:

> Expanding P&G's leadership in emerging markets. Today, in North America and Western Europe, for example, Procter & Gamble sells $40 worth of our brands annually for every man, woman and child. This compares to $2 in the remainder of the world. Clearly, the opportunity to grow in these (emerging) markets is extraordinary. (Chairman's Statement, Procter & Gamble *Annual Report,* 1998)

Further, in the case of Japan, many Westerners are experiencing the joys and frustrations of dealing with a control system based on Japanese rather than U.S. values. The large Japanese investments in Europe and North America are only likely to enhance this position. Therefore, while our studies indicate that national culture may impact on the management of national companies, as these national companies become multinational there is a strong possibility that persons in other nations will need to understand the cultural underpinnings of their employer's management control system in order to function adequately.

SUMMARY

1. The role of the management accountant in the strategic planning process is to identify the criteria of performance and to monitor achievements against these criteria.

2. There are a number of benefits to having a well-developed strategic planning process, but the firm needs to be careful not to allow the process to become too rigid.

3. Differences in national environmental and cultural characteristics make it difficult and complicated to establish and implement a strategic control system.

4. Several studies have been conducted on the performance evaluation measures of global companies. They tend to conclude that MNEs use multiple measures to evaluate performance, but budgets and ROI are especially popular forms of evaluation. Major differences exist from one country to another. Japanese managers tend to rely more on sales data and relatively little on ROI in contrast to U.S. managers.

DISCUSSION QUESTIONS

1. How can management accounting play a role in the strategic planning process?

2. Discuss some of the major dimensions of the international business environment that make it difficult to establish a strategic control system.

3. MNEs often transfer their domestic performance evaluation systems into the international environment. Why is that the case? What problems could they run into by using the same system?

4. Based on some of the studies of performance evaluation, what are the most widely used techniques? What are some of the strengths and weaknesses of these techniques?

CASE

The Ameripill Company

Located in Bartow, Alabama, the Pharmaceutical Division of Ameripill Company ranks among the top fifteen drug companies in the world. The Pharmaceutical Division is divided into three worldwide operating units with a vice president in charge of each: North America, Europe, and the rest of the world including South America, Africa, and Asia. The European Vice President, Gene Roget, views Europe as one strategic unit with many markets. He thinks

Source: this case was prepared by Susan F. Haka, Barbara A. Lamberton, and Harold M. Sollenberger of Michigan State University as a basis for class discussion rather than to illustrate either effective or ineffective handling of a situation. All rights reserved to the authors. Reprinted from *Issues in Accounting Education,* vol 9, no. 1, Spring 1994, pp. 168–190. Permission to use this case was obtained from the authors and the American Accounting Association.

strategically about market share, product innovation, acquisitions, and financial success. Organizationally, he works closely with Collen Stein, Pharmaceutical Vice President of Finance. Stein has recently combined the international and U.S. domestic finance groups. The international subsidiary financial analysis activities are concentrated in one unit under Stein called International and Domestic Financial Services. An abbreviated organization chart for the company is shown in Exhibit 1. Except for the international country general managers and the Puerto Rico and The Hague manufacturing managers, all executives are based in Bartow.

Important and explicit responsibilities of Stein are to develop financial policies, make measurement decisions, and monitor results to optimize Ameripill's pharmaceutical profit levels. On an international level this becomes an extraordinarily complex task. Included are direct and indirect responsibilities to:

- Design a financial performance evaluation system to encourage general managers in specific countries to maximize their contribution to corporate earnings.

- Help maximize company-wide gross margin from pharmaceutical sales through effective marketing, product strategies, and increased market shares.

- Minimize the company-wide tax liability through international transfer pricing.

- Coordinate country-by-country pricing strategies to maximize total sales dollars and global gross margin. This includes decisions to market or not market a specific drug in a specific country.

- Obtain approvals for marketing drugs and for prices in each country since most non-U.S. countries control pharmaceutical prices, as well as access to their markets.

- Minimize production costs by selecting optimal manufacturing locations, while balancing in-country requirements and production loading.

- Maximize cash flows back to Bartow and minimize non-transferable cash balances, exposure risk due to currency exchange fluctuations, and transfer penalties.

- Develop financing strategies to help acquire other companies and to create intercorporate relationships that will contribute to Company sales, to market share, and directly to profits.

- Create capital and legal structures to optimize financial, operating, legal, and political needs and avoid operating losses and protect Company investments in non-U.S. countries.

The staffs to accomplish these responsibilities are divided among Stein, the corporate CFO's office, and certain other units reporting to Stein. Coordination occurs through a working group called the International Profitability Group (IPG) chaired by Olivia Cassells, Director of International and Domestic Financial Services. Group membership includes Cassells; the Corporate Directors of Taxes, Treasury, and Financial Reporting; the Pharmaceuticals Division Managers for International Pricing and Manufacturing Accounting; and representatives from the Vice President of Business Development and the General Counsel offices. This group meets regularly to review problem areas, to recommend courses of action within the finance area, and to communicate possible financial impacts to the executive group.

Stein believes many of the goals and responsibilities listed above are inevitably linked to the international incentive evaluation system created and operated by the staff of International and Domestic Financial Services. Over the past two or three years, several complaints have been lodged with Roget and Stein by the international subsidiaries' general managers (GMs) regarding their incentive scheme. Stein has decided to use the coming year's results to evaluate the effectiveness of the international incentive scheme.

Exhibit 1 Ameripill Company and Pharmaceutical Division Organization

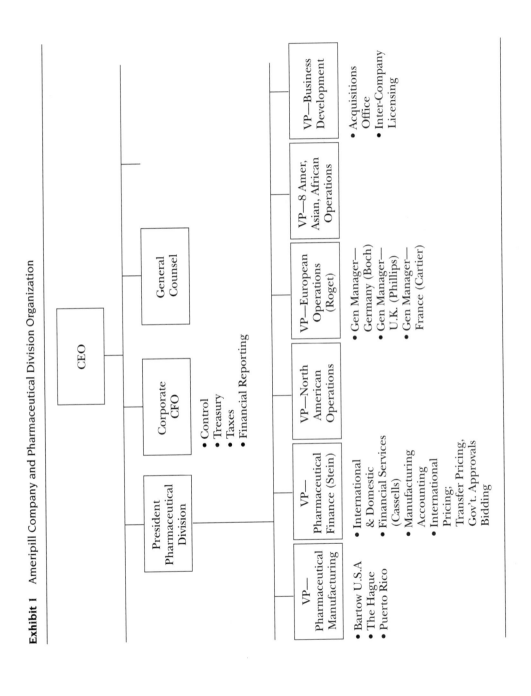

The Profit Measurement System

Ameripill domestic units are evaluated on growth in market share, sales volume, and revenue. Because of the complexities of international markets, the international profit measurement system has three reporting levels—legal entity earnings, responsibility earnings, and global earnings. Legal entity earnings are used for required reporting needs such as for tax and regulatory purposes within each country. Responsibility earnings include import and export sales that country managers can influence, given what is known to them about prices, costs and transfer prices. Global earnings is a broader corporate view of sales and costs and represents an economic earnings view of each subunit. The global earnings figure is calculated by and only known to the Bartow financial and operations executives. For international subsidiaries, the country general managers are evaluated in two ways:

1. Actual results compared to budgeted, focusing on gross margin, ROA, cash flow, and inventory and receivables levels. The evaluation looks at the entire operation using "responsibility earnings" and "earnings before taxes" and is the basis for evaluating and comparing the performances of all international general managers.

2. A management incentive system administered through the International Financial Performance System (IFPS). The IFPS is the bonus sytem and focuses on a subsidiary's contribution to "global earnings," "earnings before taxes," "responsibility earnings" growth over last year, return on managed assets, inventory levels, and market share performance. IFPS bonuses are based 60 percent on the local unit's results and 40 percent on the region's contribution to "global earnings."

Exhibits 2, 3, and 4 present preliminary results for 1992 and a forecast for 1993 for the United Kingdom, France, and Germany in the format sent to Bartow for early analysis of 1992 performance.

Exhibit 2   Financial Results—United Kingdom
International Pharmaceutical Subsidiaries Financial Summary (000 Omitted)

	Budget, 1993	**Actual, 1992**
Sales	$49,960	$48,080
Cost of sales	$(21,982)	$(21,155)
Direct expenses	(14,658)	(14,512)
Other income (expense)	(1,499)	(1,155)
Responsibility earnings	$11,821	$11,258
Interest income (expense)*	(358)	(241)
Exchange gain (loss)†	(142)	(338)
Division charges‡	(1,629)	(1,640)
Earnings before tax	$9,692	$9,039
Managed assets	$84,500	$88,860
IFPS goals		
Earnings before tax (EBT) = 18%	19.4%	18.8%
Return on assets (ROA) = 15%	11.5%	10.2%
Responsibility earnings growth = 5%	5.0%	4.8%
Inventory (months supply) = 1.0 mo.	2.5 mo.	3.2 mo.

*Based on locally incurred debt.
†Based on average 1992 exchange rate ($1.4 per U.K. pound).
‡Fixed charge negotiated annually between Bartow and the subsidiary.

Exhibit 3 Financial Results—Germany
   International Pharmaceutical Subsidiaries Financial Summary (000 Omitted)

	Budget, 1993	Actual, 1992
Sales	$156,840	$137,440
Cost of sales	$(65,872)	$(57,995)
Direct expenses	(50,286)	(46,603)
Other income (expense)	(300)	(210)
Responsibility earnings	$40,382	$32,632
Interest income (expense)*	(1,312)	(939)
Exchange gain (loss)†	(150)	(210)
Division charges‡	(4,700)	(4,123)
Earnings before tax	$34,220	$27,360
Managed assets	$73,760	$72,900
IFPS goals		
EBT = 18%	21.8%	19.9%
ROA = 15%	46.4%	37.5%
Responsibility earnings growth = 5%	23.7%	15.6%
Inventory (months supply) = 1.0 mo.	1.2 mo.	1.5 mo.

*Based on locally incurred debt.
†Based on average 1992 exchange rate ($0.62 per German DM).
‡Fixed charge negotiated annually between Bartow and the subsidiary.

Exhibit 4 Financial Results—France
   International Pharmaceutical Subsidiaries Financial Summary (000 Omitted)

	Budget, 1993	Actual, 1992
Sales	$108,720	$102,560
Cost of sales	$(53,414)	$(50,254)
Direct expenses	(31,529)	(29,742)
Other income (expense)	(946)	(1,026)
Responsibility earnings	$22,831	$21,538
Interest income (expense)*	(1,033)	(1,047)
Exchange gain (loss)†	(272)	(286)
Division charges‡	(3,262)	(3,077)
Earnings before tax	$18,264	$17,128
Managed assets	$74,220	$73,460
IFPS goals		
EBT = 18%	16.8%	16.7%
ROA = 15%	24.6%	23.3%
Responsibility earnings growth = 5%	6.0%	5.2%
Inventory (months supply) = 1.0 mo.	0.9 mo.	1.1 mo.

*Based on locally incurred debt.
†Based on average 1992 exchange rate ($0.16 per French franc).
‡Fixed charge negotiated annually between Bartow and the subsidiary.

Comments from the Wednesday Meeting

A meeting of the International Profitability Group is planned for Friday, December 11, 1992. It is Wednesday, and Olivia Cassells and Collen Stein are meeting in Bartow to review the agenda and supporting discussion documents that will be sent to each attending member. Cassells has materials from Vice President Roget's office, the directors in the Pharmaceutical Division, and the corporate offices. Cassells is sure that several controversial issues will be raised. Selected items from the agenda include:

A. Final financial staff approval of the acquisition of Koblenz Chemie Company.

B. Problems using cash balances in the U.K. and possible production changes at the U.K. subsidiary.

C. Problems with the IFPS.

D. Price increase for a product in the French market.

After a quick review of the tentative 1992 international subsidiary results, attention turns to the agenda.

Acquisition of Koblenz Chemie Company

Olivia Cassells begins the Wednesday meeting by discussing a recommendation from the Business Development office and Roget that the Board of Directors acquire Koblenz Chemie Company for 25,000,000 DM ($15.5 million), about 8 times earnings. The Koblenz Chemie Co. management has forecasted 1993 sales to be 12,000,000 DM ($7.4 million).[1] Cassells notes that the acquisition has several advantages. First, it gives Ameripill access to a key German generic drug market. Koblenz has an eight percent market share in Germany in its product lines. Second, it provides Ameripill with the opportunity to have a stronger market position in Germany, particularly in the newly opened former East German market. In recent years, Ameripill's German market share has remained at about two percent of the total pharmaceutical market. Third, Ameripill can offer Koblenz access to international markets.

Stein inquires about inputs from Hans Drossel, controller of the German subsidiary, about the acquisition. Cassells replies: "I'm not sure Drossel knows about it. Our acquisition guys researched this one. They think that the integration of Koblenz into our German organization shouldn't be a problem since they're both located within 50 kilometers of each other." Both Stein and Cassells agree that even though the price seems high given Koblenz's earnings since 1989, Koblenz appears to be a quality operation in all respects. Stein notes: "The Koblenz acquisition seems to be a sure thing. I hear the accounting records are a mess. That's not surprising given that it was a privately owned firm. We'll have some work to do to get it into Ameripill's reporting and cash management systems." Cassells agrees that system compatibility problems exist but goes on to suggest that no problems with final financial approval of the deal are likely to occur.

Cassells reminds Stein that another German issue might be affected by this acquisition. Due to the rapid changes in the former eastern bloc, Business Development has been studying the situation. They recommended that we begin to expand our sales force and enter the former East German market. Business Development projects this potential market to be $300 million and conservatively estimates that Ameripill could capture 10 percent of this market by the year 2000. Preliminary contacts have been made with former government officials with whom Ameripill has had previous business relationships. Ameripill sales in the entire eastern bloc have been very low.

A request from the German GM to create a sales force in eastern Germany, now nearly eight months old, has been reviewed by Business Development. Cassells says, "Business Devel-

---

[1]Assume that the acquisition of the Koblenz business in 1993 will cause the German subsidiary's Sales, Cost of Sales, and Direct Expenses to increase by the same percentage. Other subsidiary income and expenses are not expected to change.

opment thinks the near-term financial feasibility looks dim but the question of having an Ameripill presence must be discussed. Roget is pressing all of us for a positive response. I hear he has given the okay to the German GM and controller to create a temporary eastern Germany sales force. Roget says it's now or never." Cassells believes these unilateral steps may be premature and have adverse effects on the German subsidiary's bottom line for 1992 and 1993.

Cash Balances in the U.K. and Production Changes at the U.K. Subsidiary

Item B on the agenda generates more concern. Stein begins by discussing the historical tax problems associated with moving cash between international locations and the U.S. Stein notes that the U.K. subsidiary has generated a sizable cash position. Stein points out that strategies must be created to move cash back to the U.S. or other locations where it can be invested profitably. Cassells suggests expanding manufacturing in the U.K. as a way to move the cash surplus without incurring costly penalties. Stein comments "I thought that the tax law limited our options about transferring cash from the U.K. to the States." Cassells agrees, but suggests that "we could expand manufacturing and export to other countries, such as Germany, at cost. We may need the cash in Germany to pay for other acquisitions and expansion we see in eastern Germany. Also, we may have more flexibility in transferring cash back to the United States."

Cassells and Stein then have a long discussion about implementing the export strategy of moving cash from the U.K. to Germany. Cassells suggests that Smoothkare, a product currently manufactured at The Hague for export to Germany, could be manufactured in the U.K. Cassells remarks "I'm sure we could easily replace the lost Smoothkare manufacturing volume at The Hague with an equally profitable product." However, a sizable investment would be required to expand manufacturing capacity in the U.K.

Stein reminds Cassells that the cash problem was becoming worse each day, and a two to three year wait would only compound the problem. Stein suggests that perhaps current manufacturing capacity could be converted to produce Smoothkare, which could be transferred to Germany at cost. Stein asks Cassells if she had considered these options.

Cassells responds "Yes, the U.K. general manager won't be too keen on this idea. He has written a detailed memo to Roget outlining the problems associated with expanding manufacturing in the U.K. (see Exhibit 5). First, producing Smoothkare will require us to increase the U.K.'s managed assets to approximately $90 million. Also the U.K. GM complained that at the current volume, nearly half of his time is spent on production problems. Yet, his performance is measured by responsibility earnings and ROA numbers—all sales based. Also, the pressure to keep working capital low backfires in two ways. Low inventories mean that short, frequent, and expensive batches cause per-unit costs to be well above The Hague's and Puerto Rico's manufacturing unit costs. And since cash can't be moved out without significant tax penalties, large near-cash balances cause total working capital to balloon. I'll bet the U.K. GM will think that expanding manufacturing will divert attention away from marketing and that U.K. profits will tumble. The U.K. GM will see both of these as bad news for evaluating the U.K. subsidiary's responsibility earnings results and for his IFPS evaluation."

Problems with the International Financial Performance System (IFPS)

Stein notes the problems associated with moving cash out of the U.K. are related to the incentive scheme—an item next on the agenda. Cassells and Stein begin discussing the IFPS and its impact on international decisions. Cassells points out that several previous complaints had been forwarded from the U.K. GM. The regional Vice President (under Roget) and one of the financial analysts visit each subsidiary three times a year. During the last visit to the U.K., the GM raised several questions about the IFPS and the annual performance review. Cassells relays the essence of these complaints to Stein: "The GM is not clear how the IFPS measurements are calculated. He only sees reports that show his U.K. responsibility earnings in pounds sterling as they come from the U.K. accounting records. He says the ratios used in the budget and the IFPS are seriously distorted by manufacturing operations in the U.K."

Exhibit 5   Memo to Roget: U.K. Problems with IFPS

Date: March 20, 1992
To: Gene Roget
        Vice President, European Operations
From: John Phillips
        General Manager, United Kingdom
Subject: Difficulties with the IFPS in the U.K.

As you and I have discussed on several occasions, the performance evaluation system for international subsidiaries has a number of negative impacts on our operations here in the U.K. The heavy emphasis on sales, profit margins, and rates of return overlook the significant management effort put into our manufacturing operations here. Comparing us with a pure sales subsidiary is like comparing Yorkshire pudding and apple strudel. The changes made in the IFPS in 1991 have made the problem all the more severe for us since it focuses more on U.K.'s results.

Manufacturing means a large investment in plant and equipment, managing production planning and operations, maintaining inventories of materials, and often billing out product at a price just above—certainly not below—normal markups. We are also a satellite plant and therefore often produce overflow from The Hague plant. To keep our inventories down for working capital purposes, we are forced to make frequent runs that inflate our per unit costs.

While we are working in a very competitive sales market in the U.K., I estimate that my managers and I spend nearly half our time on production issues. I strongly urge a quick review of the performance evaluation system and the IFPS.

If I might, I would like to offer the following suggestions:

- Vice president Stein could be asked to separate the evaluation of U.K. production and sales operations—particularly the investment base and the prices of U.K.-manufactured products.

- If no separate evaluation is possible, U.K.-manufactured products could be priced out of our plant at a world-wide wholesale price—either as a real transfer price or as a pseudo-transfer price set in Bartow.

- A revision of the working capital and investment base definitions for country sales subsidiaries to give consideration to non-sales activities they might have.

I am very willing to discuss these and other operating, evaluation, and reporting issues to improve Ameripill's results and the U.K. performance—both real and as reported.

Collen Stein asks, "Is the U.K. GM the only subsidiary that is concerned?" Cassells says, "Not really. None of them seem to understand the incentive system or how their bonus is determined. The U.K. GM's complaint is one that we have heard over and over again from other GMs. They want to know what 'global earnings' is and how it's calculated."

Stein recalls, "Yes, now that I think about it, Roget has complained to me about the IFPS scheme and even threatened to send each GM the details of how each subsidiary compares to one another. I assumed that the changes we made in '91 which shifted the scheme away from company-wide uniformity to more emphasis on individual subsidiary goals solved these concerns. Maybe the IPG needs to look at this issue and suggest some improvements.

Product Pricing in the French Market

Cassells and Stein move to the last item on the agenda, the price increase for Saincoeur in France. Saincoeur is a highly successful treatment for heart attack victims sold under other names in all of Ameripill's markets. Stein begins by telling Cassells that he understands that the International Pricing office will recommend raising the price of Saincoeur in France. Its low price in France is causing problems for the rest of the European markets. Cassells suggests two options. First, Ameripill could push hard to get approval for a price increase; second, we could withdraw Saincoeur from the French market to protect prices of the same product in other countries. Roget had reported pricing inquiries and pressure from Italy, Switzerland, and even Germany to reduce the price for the equivalent drug in their markets. The International Pricing office also suggested that, without a quick resolution of the pricing issue, Saincoeur should be withdrawn from the French market.

Stein asks, "Olivia, what kind of price concession would that mean for the other European markets? What's the financial impact?" Cassells notes that Saincoeur is barely profitable at the French price. "If Ameripill isn't careful, our margins for the equivalent products will decline all over the European market." Cassells and Stein decide to review the financial summaries for the product at a later date. However, Cassells concludes by stating, "Clearly, withdrawing from the French market is better than cutting our margin for the rest of Europe. Based on our preliminary reading of the data, the potential damage to Ameripill's total global earnings is as much as ten times the French's Saincoeur earnings loss."

Meanwhile in the International Subsidiaries

Managers in each subsidiary meet on a weekly basis to assess operations, problem shoot, and review operating plans. During these weekly meetings information is exchanged among each subsidiary's management group members. In particular, communications from the parent are typically announced and discussed in these weekly meetings. The following meetings took place within ten days of Cassells' and Stein's Wednesday meeting.

France

In France, the General Manager, Jacques Cartier, his Director of Marketing, and his Controller are discussing operations and strategies in their weekly meeting. The Controller mentions a rumor she heard from the Bartow Financial Analyst who had just been in France for his quarterly visit. The Controller comments, "I heard a rumor that the Bartow pricing group is recommending withdrawing Saincoeur from our market. Italy and the Swiss are pressuring Ameripill to match the French price. Bartow is concerned that their margins will suffer all over Europe."

Cartier expresses immediate concern since Saincoeur is 10 percent of France's 1993 sales forecast. Cartier commented, "the French subsidiary currently has problems attaining the corporate goal of 18 percent earnings before tax (EBT). Loss of Saincoeur will make meeting that goal more difficult and reduce our return on assets (ROA) since we lose sales volume without any impact on our investment base. Sales and cost of sales will decrease proportionately, but direct expenses will decrease by only 10 million francs. Other financial accounts will be unaffected. As a result, French bonuses from the IFPS scheme will be reduced." The Director of Marketing comments, "Americans! I bet that the real financial impact is not that big. What do they care as long as the company overall is making a little more money?"

The Controller replies, "I've heard that they are looking at the impact on global earnings. I wish I knew how that was calculated. I have no idea how that is going to impact our bonuses."

United Kingdom

It's Monday in the United Kingdom subsidiary headquarters in Maidenhead near London, and the weekly meeting between the General Manager, John Phillips, and the Controller, Lee Grant, is about to start. Phillips brings in a FAX received late Friday from corporate about expanding manufacturing in Great Britain. The memo requested input from the U.K. General Manager about the possibility of producing Smoothkare and then shipping Smoothkare at a little above cost to Germany. Smoothkare is a prescription drug used to treat skin problems in elderly persons and has been produced solely at The Hague plant for world-wide distribution. He points out that corporate is thinking about expanding the U.K. subsidiary's manufacturing capacity.

Phillips wants to persuade corporate to adopt the desired U.K. strategy, whether it is to expand and produce Smoothkare or not. He wonders whether the person that wrote the memo has read any of his reports and memos about IFPS. Grant points out that the U.K. subsidiary already produces several products transferred at close to cost and that those products provide no positive weight in the evaluation process. Phillips wondered if expanding the manufacturing operation would improve the IFPS bonus numbers.

Phillips says, "I don't know, corporate hasn't said too much about timing, but they could implement the expansion fairly quickly. For example, Ameripill could buy that old Worsley manufacturing facility next door and have it operational in less than a year." He adds, still thinking about his communications with Bartow, "You know, I've never seen a report on what our combined sales and manufacturing efforts contribute to Ameripill's profits. There is a basic conflict between its emphasis on sales and our need to sell and manage this factory too." Grant adds, "I've had a number of conversations with Cassells about the incentive scheme. I am not sure that they realize the significance of the problems created by the incentive scheme. For example, the pressure to keep our inventories down and improve our ROA causes us to schedule many short manfacturing runs. As a result, we'll never get our unit costs close to The Hague numbers."

Phillips, now more agitated, states, "One thing I know, expanding manufacturing to include Smoothkare will not help our earnings, will create more manufacturing problems, and will increase our operating costs—all bad news for us, particularly for our IFPS results. Our asset base will increase, inventories will grow, and we'll need more people to handle the manufacturing. I heard that Germany paid The Hague about 8,500,000 pounds for Smoothkare this year. They use cost plus 20 percent for a transfer price, I think. We would have to use the same transfer price that The Hague used because Bartow guaranteed that price to the German subsidiary for a five-year period. Our manufacturing costs would be at least 15 percent higher than The Hague's if past comparisons hold."

Germany

Hans Drossel, Controller of the German subsidiary, schedules lunch with Dr. Jochim Boch, the general manager. Both have been active in building a sales force in the former East German portion of the new Germany. This effort has fortunately begun to at least cover the out-of-pocket costs of building this new staff. Now near the end of 1992, the tentative financial results show strong potential. Boch says, "I didn't think our Eastern sector strategy would pay off as fast as it has. It was risky, with only Roget's informal okay, but I think it's working." Drossell looks at the numbers and adds, "You know, it's the only way to get the growth we need to meet the financial goals we have in our 1993 budget. Right now the eastern German sales forecast is 2,000,000 marks, and the potential is two or three times that if we had a strong generic drug product line. We just don't have the product lines to get a bigger market share. I think we'll have some explaining to do in our annual financial review when Cassells' people arrive from Bartow."

After looking at the product line sales data, Drossel comments, "Our ability to price Smoothkare just under our main competitor really helped sales and our responsibility earnings. I hope we can get another cost reduction from The Hague plant in 1993." Boch shakes his head affirmatively.

Boch then asks Drossel about rumors that Bartow had made a formal decision to enter the former eastern block markets. "You know I think our proposal about the Eastern markets must have gotten lost in the mail. Roget says it's being studied by the financial guys, but eight months is ridiculous. Not only that, but several really profitable small pharmaceutical firms have been gobbled up by the big Swiss drug companies. Where are our people?" Drossel responds, "We seem to be preoccupied with bottom line results while the Swiss seem to be looking for market share and let the profits develop later."

Questions

1. Estimate the impact on in-country International Financial Performance System (IFPS) goals of:

   a. United Kingdom: Expanding current manufacturing capacity by acquiring the Worsley plant.

   b. Germany: Acquisition of Koblenz Chemie Co.

   c. France: Withdrawing Saincoeur from the French market.

2. Discuss potential strategic reactions of the General Managers in the United Kingdom, Germany, and France to parts (a), (b), and (c), respectively, of question 1.

3. Discuss the strengths and weaknesses of Ameripill's IFPS plan.

4. Make specific recommendations for changing the IFPS plan. Support your recommendations by citing specific case examples.

REFERENCES AND FURTHER READING

Abdallah, W. and D. Keller. (1985). "Measuring the Multinational's Performance." *Management Accounting:* Vol. 67(4): 26–30.

Appleyard, A., N. Strong, and P. Walton. (1990). "Budgetary Control of Foreign Subsidiaries." *Management Accounting (U.K.)* (September): 44–45.

Bailes J. and T. Assada. (1991). "Empirical Differences Between Japanese and American Budget and Performance Evaluation Systems." *International Journal of Accounting* 26(2): 131–142.

Brownell, P. (1982). "A Field Study Examination of Budgetary Participation and Locus of Control." *Accounting Review* 57 (4): 766–777.

Chow, C.W., P. Harrison, T. Lindquist, and A. Wu. (1997). "Escalating Commitment to Unprofitable Projects: Replication and Cross-cultural Extension." *Management Accounting Research* 8; 347–361.

Frucot, V. and W. Shearon. (1991). "Budgetary Participation, Locus of Control, and Mexican Managerial Performance and Job Satisfaction." *Accounting Review* 66(1): 80–99.

Gray, S. J. (1988). "Towards a Theory of Cultural Influence on the Development of Accounting Systems Internationally." *Abacus* 24(1): 1–15.

Gray, S. J. (1995). "Cultural Perspectives on the Measurement of Corporate Success." *European Management Journal* 13 (3, Sept.): 269–275.

Harrison, G. (1992). "The Cross-Cultural Generalizability of the Relation Between Participation, Budget Emphasis and Job Related Attitudes." *Accounting Organizations and Society* (17)1. 1–15.

Harrison, G. (1995). "Satisfaction, Tension and Interpersonal Relations: Across-Cultural Comparison of Managers in Singapore and Australia." *Journal of Managerial Psychology* (10)8: 13–19.

Harrison, G. J., L. McKinnon, P. Sarala, and M. Leung. (1994). "The Influence of Culture on Organizational Design and Planning and Control in Australia and the United States Compared with Singapore and Hong Kong." *Journal of International Financial Management & Accounting.* 3: 242–261.

Harrison, P. and A. Harrell. (1994). "An Incentive to Shirk, Privately Held Information and Managers' Project Evaluation Decisions." *Accounting Organizations and Society* 19(7): 569–577.

Hofstede, G. (1980). *Culture's Consequences: International Differences in Work-Related Values.* Beverly Hills: Sage.

Hofstede, G. (1984). "Cultural Dimensions in Management and Planning." *Asia Pacific Journal of Management.* Vol.(2): 81–99.

Hofstede, G. (1991). *Cultures and Organizations: Software of the Mind.* London: McGraw-Hill.

Hofstede, G. and M. Bond. (1988). "The Confucius Connection: From Cultural Roots to Economic Growth." *Organizational Dynamics* (Spring) Vol. 16: 5–21.

Horngren, C.T. and G. Foster. (1991). *Cost Accounting: A Managerial Emphasis,* 7th ed. Englewood Cliffs, NJ: Prentice Hall.

Merchant, K., C. Chow, and A. Wu. (1995). "Measurement, Evaluation, and Reward of Profit-Center Managers: A Cross-Cultural Field Study." *Accounting Organizations and Society* 20: (7–8):619–638.

Morsicato, H. (1980). *Currency Translation and Performance Evaluation in Multinationals.* Ann Arbor, MI: UMI Research Press.

Robbins, S.M. and R. Stobaugh. (1973). *Money in the Multinational Enterprise: A Study in Financial Policy.* New York: Basic Books.

Salter, S. and F. Niswander. (1995). "Cultural Influence on the Development of Accounting Systems Internationally: A Test of Gray's (1988) Theory." *Journal of International Business Studies,* Vol. 26(2): 379–397.

Sharp, D. and S. Salter. (1997). "Project Escalation and Sunk Costs: A Test of the International Generalizability of Agency and Prospect Theories." *Journal of International Business Studies,* Vol. 28 (1): 101–121.

Shields, M., C. Chow, Y. Kato, and Y. Nakagawa. (1991). "Management Accounting Practices in the U.S. and Japan: Comparative Survey Findings and Research Implications." *Journal of International Financial Management and Accounting* 3(1): 61–77.

Ueno, S. and U. Sekaran (1992). "The Influence of Culture on Budget Control Practices in the USA and Japan: An Empirical Study." *Journal of International Business Studies* 23(4): 659–674.

SOME USEFUL INTERNET WEB SITES

A number of company Web sites provide useful information about their financial objectives and performance measures. See for example:

1. *http://www.nestle.com*

2. *http://www.pg.com*

3. *http://www.philips.com*

4. *http://www.hoechst.com*

5. *http://www.nokia.com*

6. *http://www.glgc.com/g500.html*

This site has links to Web sites for most of the Fortune Global 500 companies.

CHAPTER FIVE

PLANNING AND PERFORMANCE EVALUATION IN MULTINATIONAL ENTERPRISES

INTRODUCTION

In this chapter we look at some of the special problems faced by management in controlling the multinational enterprise. As with control in a domestic environment, control in the global environment begins with a strategic objective and includes all elements of planning and monitoring the success of a global strategy to meet those objectives. The focus of the planning process is to give strategic direction to the firm and then an operational plan to get the firm to achieve the strategic direction. The role of the management accountant in this planning process is to work with top management to identify the necessary performance criteria and then to monitor achievements against these criteria.

THE STRATEGIC CONTROL PROCESS

In a study of European MNEs by Professors Gupta and Govindarajan (1991), the following four stages in a formal strategic control system were identified:

1. Periodic strategy reviews for each business, typically on an annual or less frequent basis
2. Annual operating plans, which increasingly include nonfinancial measures along with the traditional financial ones
3. Formal monitoring of strategic results, which may be combined with the budget monitoring process
4. Personal rewards and central intervention

Having too rigid a strategic control system can be difficult for a company that is in a rapidly changing industry, but there are some distinct benefits from a formal process:

- Greater clarity and realism in planning
- More "stretching" of performance standards
- More motivation for business unit managers
- More timely intervention by central management
- Clearer responsibilities

For such a system to work, it is necessary to select the right strategic objectives based on an analysis of the competition and the strengths of the firm. Then suitable targets need to be set according to the strategy of the firm. However, most articles on setting strategic objectives focus on choosing a suitable numeric target including ROI, sales, and so on, as discussed in Chapter 4.

Profitability, measured as a ratio or by some other measure, is most appropriate for a fully fledged strategic business unit (i.e., a unit of a group of companies that makes its own business decisions at all levels, e.g., a major division or subsidiary). In addition, targets for a unit may be linked not only to its objectives, but also to that part of its operations that it controls. Many firms attempt to benchmark their performance based on key competitors, but it is often difficult to get good data on global competitors. The system needs to be tight enough and demanding enough to put pressure on management to perform. It is common to find strategic plans that are too general, so there is a real challenge to take the plans and targets and use them to push management. Finally, it is important not to let the process get so big, complicated, and bureaucratized that it gets in the way of creative thinking and solid performance.

Trying to implement this concept in a global environment is not easy. Different operating environments make it difficult and complicated to establish and implement a strategic control system. Such operating environments include culture; legal systems (which may limit a strategic objective to increase market share or become the market leader); political differences that could influence the role the firm is allowed to play in the country; and economic systems, including inflation and market size and growth. An example of strategic objectives is shown in Figure 5.1.

CHALLENGES OF CONTROL IN THE GLOBAL FIRM

Planning and Budgeting Issues

Multinational corporations contend with an array of external factors, internal considerations, and other forces that influence budget policies, composition, and control. Budgeting in a global business environment calls for an enhanced level of coordination and communication through the company because of the variety of powerful components that affect organizational performance. While multinationals need to be concerned about cultural differences and their impact on national budgeting practices, there are additional considerations in the budgeting process of these companies. Of particular importance is the impact of foreign exchange differences on cross-border operations as outlined in Chapter 2.

Indeed, the major international issue surrounding the establishment of a budget for an MNE is to determine the currency in which the budget should be prepared: the local currency or the parent currency. For a Swiss MNE, for example, is it better to evaluate all its foreign operations in terms of the local currency results or the results translated into francs? This choice can be highly significant if major

Faster, Bigger Innovation

These results are good, yet we can and must do better. In particular, we are not satisfied with our rate of volume and sales growth. We must significantly accelerate our progress if we are to achieve the goals we've reported here in previous years:

- To double our business in ten years,
- To grow shares in categories representing the majority of our volume, and
- To remain consistently among the top third of our peer companies in TSR performance.

We know the key is faster, bigger innovation in every part of our business. And we've made important strides in the past year to strengthen our pipeline of innovations on established brands and on new brands entering test market. But there is much more we intend to do. We must bring even better products to more markets with greater speed than ever before. And we must release the untapped power of our organization.

Important Changes to Accelerate Growth

For some time, we've been examining how our organization should evolve, and in the coming weeks, we will announce details of a comprehensive plan to simplify the way we're structured and to strengthen how we operate. The changes, while consistent with the direction in which we've been growing, are significant and will improve our ability to create and build even more profitable leadership brands around the world.

Four changes, in particular, are worth noting here:

- We will move from our current regional business units to product-based, global business units—a direction we've been heading since the late 1980s with the start of Global Category Management.
- We will strengthen our already-strong, country-based organizations to provide even deeper knowledge of local consumers and stronger partnerships with our customers. These local market organizations will be essential to bringing our product initiatives to consumers with the highest impact possible.
- We will create a new Global Business Services organization to support the global business units and the local market organizations. This move will bring together business services that are currently dispersed throughout the organization. It will also help us achieve significant economies of scale, while improving the overall quality and speed of these services.
- And finally, we will streamline our corporate staff. We will align many corporate resources with the business units and refocus others on developing the cutting-edge, functional knowledge and innovation important to our future growth and success.

To support these new structural advantages, we are also making important changes in our culture and in our reward system—all to encourage greater speed, innovation and flexibility in the organization.

Taken together, we believe these improvements will enable us to build stronger global brands; achieve faster, bigger innovation; produce accelerated business growth; and result in greater satisfaction for our people. These are the kinds of changes we've made throughout P&G's 161-year history—changes always designed to get us closer to consumers and to keep our business growing at a level we—and you—have every right to expect, given the extraordinary caliber of the men and women of Procter and Gamble.

Figure 5.1   Procter & Gamble *Annual Report 1998*: Extract from Management Letter to Shareholders on Future Strategy

what about our shareholders?

changes occur in the exchange rates. It is possible for a profit in local currency to become a loss in the parent company's currency, and vice versa. If a Swiss company's Mexican subsidiary earned a profit in pesos but a loss when translated into francs, should the subsidiary's performance be evaluated favorably or unfavorably? Most firms resolve this dilemma by considering the main purpose of the foreign operations. If it is to provide a return to parent company shareholders that maximizes their domestic purchasing power, then typically an "after-translation" basis is used. A "before-translation" basis is more likely to be used by a firm that truly considers itself a multinational firm seeking global optimization or one that leaves considerable autonomy to each foreign operation.

The foreign currency issue also raises the issue of controllability. Whether a currency rises or falls in value and by how much is clearly beyond the control of a single MNE or any one of its parts. Therefore, because proper performance evaluation should exclude the impact on results of events over which the unit or person had no control, one can argue that the before-translation basis is better than the after-translation basis. In the case of the Swiss-Mexican situation, if the peso profits become translated into franc losses, the Mexican manager should not be penalized for a result out of his or her control. On the other hand, if the Mexican manager is given the authority and responsibility to hedge against potential foreign exchange losses, then he or she could be evaluated in terms of translated profitability.

The value of establishing the budget in the local currency is that management operates in that currency, and the local currency is more indicative of the overall operating environment than the present currency would be. In addition, the exchange rate is something over which local management has no control, so it would be unwise to have a key uncontrollable item as part of the budgeting and evaluation process.

On the other hand, it is often difficult for top management in the parent country to understand budgets generated in different currencies. This is especially true for a geographically diverse firm like Coca-Cola, which might have budgets generated in a hundred or more different currencies. Translating the budgets into the parent currency allows top management to consolidate the budgets into a firmwide view of the coming year. Also, because top management has to report to shareholders in the parent currency, they might want the strategic business unit (SBU) or subsidiary management to think in terms of parent country profitability as well.

There are three possible approaches for dealing with foreign exchange in the budgeting process as it relates to performance evaluation of managers:

1. Allow operating managers to enter into hedge contracts with corporate treasury so they can "contract away" their exposures.

2. Adjust the actual performance of the unit for variations in the real exchange rate after the end of the period.

3. Adjust performance plans in line with variations in the real exchange rate.

Ways to Bring Foreign Exchange into the Budgeting Process

Donald Lessard and Peter Lorange (Table 5.1) identify the different ways that firms can translate the budget from the local currency into the parent currency and then monitor actual performance. Three different exchange rates are used in Table 5.1. The first is the actual exchange rate in effect when the budget was

Table 5.1   Possible Combinations of Exchange Rates in the Control Process

Rate Used for Determining Budget \ Rate Used to Track Performance Relative to Budget	Actual at Time of Budget	Projected at Time of Budget	Actual at End of Period
Actual at time of budget	A-1	A-2	A-3
Projected at time of budget	P-1	P-2	P-3
Actual at end of period (through updating)	E-1	E-2	E-3

Source: Donald R. Lessard and Peter Lorange, "Currency Changes and Management Control: Resolving the Centralization/Decentralization Dilemma." *Accounting Review* 52 (July 1977):630.

established, the second is the rate that was projected at the time the budget was established in the local currency, and the third is the actual exchange rate in effect when the budgeted period actually takes place. The attractiveness of the first exchange rate is that it is an objective spot rate that actually exists on a given day. It is a reasonable rate to use in a stable environment, but it may be meaningless in an unstable foreign exchange environment. The projected rate is an attempt on the part of management to forecast what it thinks the exchange rate will be for the budgeted time period. For example, management might project in June 2000 that the exchange rate between the U.S. dollar and the British pound will be $1.6500 during December 2000, so that would be the projected exchange rate used in the budgeting process. The actual exchange rate found in cell E-3 is an update of the exchange rate that was in effect when the budget was established. It provides the actual exchange rate in effect at the end of the budgeted time period.

These three exchange rates need to be considered both for establishment of the budget and for the monitoring of performance. In cells A-1, P-2, and E-3, the exchange rate used to establish the budget and monitor performance is the same, so any variances will be due to price and volume, not the exchange rate. The value of P-2 over A-1 and E-3 is that it forces management to think initially of what its performance will be if the forecast is reasonably accurate. A-1 never takes into account what the exchange rate will be, and it does not attempt to reconcile the budget from the original rate with that of the actual rate. Given the instability in exchange rates, however, some would argue that a forecast exchange rate is no more accurate than any other exchange rate. E-3 does take into consideration what performance is at the actual exchange rate, but it does not force management to be forward thinking during the budget process.

A-3 and P-3 result in a variance that is a function of operating results and exchange rate changes. Under A-3, the budget is established at the initial exchange rate, but actual performance is translated at the actual exchange rate. Thus, there is an exchange rate variance that is the difference between the original and the actual rate. P-3 results in a variance that is the difference between what management thought the exchange rate would be and what it actually was at the end of the operating period. If management's forecast was reasonably accurate, P-3 should result in a very small foreign exchange variance. If the exchange rate between the parent and local currency is relatively stable, A-3 should also result in a relatively small foreign exchange variance. However, it is important to realize that the use of A-3 and

Table 5.2 The Flexible Budget—a Foreign Currency Analysis

The Flexible Budget in British Pounds

	(1) Actual Results	(2) (1)–(3) Exchange Rate Variance	(3) Actual Results at Budget Rate	(4) (1)–(5) Flexible Budget Variances	(5) Flexible Budget	(6) (5)–(7) Sales Volume Variances	(7) Static (Master) Budget
Units Sold	5,500			0	5,500	(500)	6,000
Sales Revenues	852,500			27,500	825,000	(75,000)	900,000
Variable Costs	605,200			(55,000)	550,000	50,000	600,000
Contribution Margin	247,500			(27,500)	275,000	(25,000)	300,000
Fixed Costs	200,000			0	200,000	0	200,000
Operating Income	47,500			(27,500)	75,000	(25,000)	100,000

Total Sales Volume Variance (7–5) 25,000 Unfavorable
Total Flexible-Budget Variances (5–1) 27,500 Unfavorable
Total Static-Budget Variances (7–1) 52,500 Unfavorable

The Budget Translated into Dollars at A-1

	(1) Actual Results	(2) (1)–(3) Exchange Rate Variance	(3) Actual Results at Budget Rate	(4) (1)–(5) Flexible Budget Variances	(5) Flexible Budget	(6) (5)–(7) Sales Volume Variances	(7) Static (Master) Budget
Units Sold	5,500			0	5,500	(500)	6,000
Sales Revenues	1,449,250			46,750	1,402,500	(127,500)	1,530,000
Variable Costs	1,028,500			(93,500)	935,000	85,000	1,020,000
Contribution Margin	420,750			(46,750)	467,500	(42,500)	510,000
Fixed Costs	340,000			0	340,000	0	340,000
Operating Income	80,750			(46,750)	127,500	(42,500)	170,000

Total Sales Volume Variance (7–5) $42,500 Unfavorable
Total Flexible-Budget Variances (5–1) $46,750 Unfavorable
Total Static-Budget Variances (7–1) $89,250 Unfavorable

Table 5.2 The Flexible Budget—a Foreign Currency Analysis (*continued*)

The Flexible Budget in British Pounds

	(1) Actual Results	(2) (1)–(3) Exchange Rate Variance	(3) Actual Results at Budget Rate	(4) (1)–(5) Flexible Budget Variances	(5) Flexible Budget	(6) (5)–(7) Sales Volume Variances	(7) Static(Master) Budget
The Budget Translated into Dollars at P-2							
Units Sold	5,500			0	5,500	(500)	6,000
Sales Revenues	1,364,000			44,000	1,320,000	(120,000)	1,440,000
Variable Costs	968,000			(88,000)	880,000	80,000	960,000
Contribution Margin	396,000			(44,000)	440,000	(40,000)	480,000
Fixed Costs	320,000			0	320,000	0	320,000
Operating Income	76,000			(44,000)	120,000	(40,000)	160,000
Total Sales Volume Variance (7–5)				$40,000 Unfavorable			
Total Flexible-Budget Variances (5–1)				$44,000 Unfavorable			
Total Static-Budget Variances (7–1)				$84,000 Unfavorable			
The Budget Translated into Dollars at E-3							
Units Sold	5,500			0	5,500	(500)	6,000
Sales Revenues	1,389,575			44,825	1,344,750	(122,250)	1,467,000
Variable Costs	986,150			(89,650)	896,500	81,500	978,000
Contribution Margin	403,425			(44,825)	448,250	(40,750)	489,000
Fixed Costs	326,000			0	326,000	0	326,000
Operating Income	77,425			(44,825)	122,250	(40,750)	163,000
Total Sales Volume Variance (7–5)				$40,750 Unfavorable			
Total Flexible-Budget Variances (5–1)				$44,825 Unfavorable			
Total Static-Budget Variances (7–1)				$85,575 Unfavorable			

(*continued on the next page*)

Table 5.2 The Flexible Budget—a Foreign Currency Analysis (*continued*)

The Flexible Budget in British Pounds

	(1) Actual Results	(2) (1)–(3) Exchange Rate Variance	(3) Actual Results at Budget Rate	(4) (1)–(5) Flexible Budget Variances	(5) Flexible Budget	(6) (5)–(7) Sales Volume Variances	(7) Static(Master) Budget
The Budget Translated into Dollars at A-3							
Units Sold	5,500		5,500		5,500	(500)	6,000
Sales Revenues	1,389,575	(59,675)	1,449,250	46,750	1,402,500	(127,500)	1,530,000
Variable Costs	986,150	42,350	1,028,500	(93,500)	935,000	85,000	1,020,000
Contribution Margin	403,425	(17,325)	420,750	(46,750)	467,500	(42,500)	510,000
Fixed Costs	326,000	(14,000)	340,000	0	340,000	0	340,000
Operating Income	77,425	(3,325)	80,750	(46,750)	127,500	(42,500)	170,000
Total Sales Volume Variance (7–5)							
Total Flexible-Budget Variances (3–5)							
Exchange Rate Variances (1–3)							
Total Static-Budget Variances (7–1)							

Total Sales Volume Variance (7–5) $42,500 Unfavorable
Total Flexible-Budget Variances (3–5) $46,750 Unfavorable
Exchange Rate Variances (1–3) $3,325 Unfavorable
Total Static-Budget Variances (7–1) $92,575 Unfavorable

	(1) Actual Results	(2) (1)–(3) Exchange Rate Variance	(3) Actual Results at Budget Rate	(4) (1)–(5) Flexible Budget Variances	(5) Flexible Budget	(6) (5)–(7) Sales Volume Variances	(7) Static(Master) Budget
The Budget Translated into Dollars at P-3							
Units Sold	5,500		5,500		5,500	(500)	6,000
Sales Revenues	1,389,575	25,575	1,364,000	44,000	1,320,000	(120,000)	1,440,000
Variable Costs	986,150	(18,150)	968,000	(88,000)	880,000	80,000	960,000
Contribution Margin	403,425	7,425	396,000	(44,000)	440,000	(40,000)	480,000
Fixed Costs	326,000	6,000	320,000	0	320,000	0	320,000
Operating Income	77,425	1,425	76,000	(44,000)	120,000	(40,000)	160,000

Total Sales Volume Variance (7–5) $40,000 Unfavorable
Total Flexible-Budget Variances (3–5) $44,000 Unfavorable
Exchange Rate Variances (1–3) $1,425 Favorable
Total Static-Budget Variances (7–1) $82,575 Unfavorable

P-3 means that someone, usually local management, will be held accountable for exchange rate variances.

Table 5.2 provides a complex example of a flexible budget that involves foreign exchange. Assume that this budget is established in British pounds for the British subsidiary of a U.S. firm. The budget is established in pounds, but U.S. management wants the budget and actual performance translated into dollars for evaluative purposes. The budget for April 2000 is established at a sale price of £150 per unit and a variable cost of £100 per unit. The actual selling price is £155 per unit, and the actual variable cost is £110 per unit. The budgeted volume is 6,000 units, and the actual number of units sold is 5,500.

There are three important (hypothetical) exchange rates for this example:

1. $1.7000—the actual exchange rate on October 1, 1999, when the budget was established
2. $1.6000—the projected exchange rate for April 2000
3. $1.6300—the actual average exchange rate for April 2000

Following the budget and actual results in British pounds are the translated versions of the financial statement and variance analysis according to the following approaches outlined in Table 5.1: A-1, P-2, E-3, A-3, P-3.

For approaches A-1, P-2, and E-3, there is no exchange rate variance because the same exchange rate is used to translate the budget and actual results from British pounds into U.S. dollars. Column 3 is the same as column 1 because the exchange rate for budget and actual results is the same. Thus, there are no exchange rate variances in column 2.

Under approach A-3, columns 3 through 7 are translated at the exchange rate in effect on October 1, 1999, and column 1 is translated at the actual average rate for April 2000. Under approach P-3, columns 3 through 7 are translated at the projected exchange rate, and column 1 is translated at the actual average exchange rate for April 2000. The important point to emphasize is that under the latter two approaches, there is an exchange rate variance that arises because the budget and the actual results are translated at different exchange rates. Thus the difference between flexible budget and actual performance is a function of an exchange rate variance and operating budget variance.

Budget and Currency Practices

What do MNEs actually do? In the Robbins and Stobaugh study (1973), fewer than half the firms surveyed judged subsidiary performance in terms of translated dollar amounts, and only 12 percent used both standards. Morsicato (1978) found that a significant number of firms in her sample used both dollar and local currency budgets compared with actual profits and actual sales.

In his study of British subsidiaries of Japanese firms, Demirag (1994) noted that the "companies indicated that financial statements presented in sterling (local currency) provided them with better understanding of the performance of their companies' operations and their management . . . . None of the companies translated their profit budgets into yen for performance evaluation purposes . . . [and] none of the parent companies sent a copy of the translated yen statements." The parent currency financial statements were sent to Japan for translation into yen at a company fixed standard exchange rate. In essence, subsidiary managers were unaware of their performance in parent currency terms.

Capital Budgeting

Capital budgeting is the longer-term relation of the operational budgeting discussed above. However, many of the considerations discussed, particularly as they relate to economic exposure, continue to apply. As in short-term planning or budgeting, long-range planning or capital budgeting must take into consideration anticipated exchange rate movements for discounting cash flows. This becomes part of the risk factor involved in discounting future cash flows, along with any environmental uncertainty. Environmental uncertainty can be mild, such as the risk of unexpected heavier taxation, or severe, such as the risk of expropriation. In general, the risk effect is greater in less-developed countries than in wealthier countries, but even in the latter, there are many adverse events that are unpredictable.

Whether or not standardized reporting practices are used in a multinational company, there is a real issue as to whether foreign operations and their managers can be evaluated on a global basis or merely on a national basis. It was noted in Chapter 4 that comparing ROIs is a primary method used to evaluate both individual operations and individual managers on a standardized or global basis. But can effective decisions be arrived at in this manner? Sometimes, when environmental factors are used in long-term strategic decisions, the outcome may appear to be at odds with the quest for strong ROIs on a year-to-year basis. Therefore, capital budgeting may require even more judgment than operational budgeting.

INTRACORPORATE TRANSFER PRICING

One of the additional elements of management of the multinational is intracorporate transfer pricing. This refers to the pricing of goods and services that are transferred (bought and sold) between members of a corporate family—for example, parent to subsidiaries, between subsidiaries, from subsidiaries to parent, and so on. As such, internal transfers include raw materials, semifinished and finished goods, allocation of fixed costs, loans, fees, royalties for use of trademarks, copyrights, and other factors. In theory, such prices should be based on production costs, but in reality they often are not.

One of the important reasons for arbitrarily establishing prices is taxation. However, taxation is only one of a number of reasons why internal transfers may be priced with little consideration for market prices or production costs. Companies may underprice goods sold to foreign affiliates, and the affiliates can then sell them at prices that their local competitors cannot match. If tough antidumping laws exist on final products, a company could underprice components and semifinished products to its affiliates. The affiliates could then assemble or finish the final product at prices that would have been classified as dumping prices had they been directly imported into the country rather than domestically produced.

High transfer prices might be used to circumvent or significantly lessen the impact of national controls. A government prohibition on dividend remittances could restrict the ability of a firm to maneuver income out of a country. However, overpricing the goods shipped to a subsidiary in such a country would make it possible for funds to be taken out. High transfer prices would also be of considerable value to a firm when it is paid a subsidy or earns a tax credit on the value of goods it exports. The higher the transfer prices on exported goods, the greater the subsidies earned or tax credit received.

High transfer prices on goods shipped to subsidiaries might be desirable when a parent wishes to lower the apparent profitability of its subsidiary. This might be desirable because of the demands of the subsidiary's workers for higher wages or greater participation in company profits; because of political pressures to expropriate high-profit, foreign-owned operations; or because of the possibility that new competitors might be lured into the industry by high profits. There might also be inducements for having high-priced transfers go to the subsidiary when a local partner is involved, the inducement being that the increase in the parent company profits will not have to be split with the local partner. High transfer prices may also be desired when increases from existing price controls in the subsidiary's country are based on product costs (including high transfer prices for purchases).

Matching Price to Market Conditions

Table 5.3 summarizes the particular conditions that firms use to utilize a particular level of transfer price. The maximum advantage would be gained when all these conditions line up on a country basis. For example, the parent operates from a country whose characteristics call for high transfer prices coming in and low transfer prices going out, while the conditions of the subsidiary's country call for the opposite.

Consider the left column of Table 5.3. If the parent sells at low prices to the subsidiary and buys from it at high prices, income is shifted to the subsidiary, lessening the overall tax burden. At the same time, the impact of a high ad valorem tariff in the other country is lessened. In addition, the impact of foreign exchange rationing on imports from the parent and dividend payments to the parent are lessened, the subsidiary's ability to penetrate its local market is enhanced, the parent is less affected by its government's restrictions on capital outflows, and so on.

Table 5.3   Conditions in Subsidiary's Country Inducing High and Low Transfer Prices on Flows Between Affiliates and Parent

Conditions in Subsidiary's Country Inducing *Low Transfer Prices* on Flows from Parent and *High Transfer Prices* on Flows to Parent	Conditions in Subsidiary's Country Inducing *High Transfer Prices* from Parent and *Low Transfer Prices* on Flows to Parent
High ad valorem tariffs	Local partners
Corporate income tax rate lower than in parent's country	Pressure from workers to obtain greater share of company profit
Significant competition	Political pressure to nationalize or expropriate high-profit foreign firms
Local loans based on financial appearance of subsidiary	Restrictions on profit or dividend remittances
Export subsidy or tax credit on value of exports	Political instability
Lower inflation rate than in parent's country	Substantial tie-in sales agreements
Restrictions (ceilings) in subsidiary's country on the *value* of products that can be imported	Price of final product controlled by government but based on production cost
	Desire to mask profitability of subsidiary operations to keep competitors out

Source: Jeffrey S. Arpan, *Intracorporate Pricing: Non-American Systems and Views* (New York: Praeger, 1972).

Under this set of conditions, the subsidiary country gains somewhat more than the parent country: more funds, more taxable income, greater economic growth of the subsidiary, and more export revenues. It loses somewhat in other areas, however, as local competitors may suffer adversely, have lower profits, pay less taxes, and lay off workers if the foreign subsidiary actively pursues a market penetration strategy. The government pays greater subsidies or gives more tax credits because of the subsidiary's artificially high value of exports and, like the government of the other country, its national control is lessened.

Unfortunately for firms, conditions seldom line up as nicely from their standpoint as either column of Table 5.3 depicts. It is far more likely that a country will simultaneously experience conditions from both sides of the table. Thus, it is difficult to determine whether the firm will receive a net benefit from high or low transfer prices. For example, a country experiencing balance-of-payments difficulties typically would be restricting dividend outflows and the amount or value of imports. A company using high transfer prices on sales to its subsidiary in such a country would gain with respect to taking out more money than it might otherwise have been able to get out but would lose by having to decrease the quantity of imported materials its affiliate needs to compete. Alternatively, a country may have high ad valorem tariffs and high income tax rates. Underpricing goods shipped to an affiliate in such a country lessens the duties and increases subsidiary profits as a result of lower input costs, resulting in higher taxes for the subsidiary. Therefore, in situations in which conditions in a country resemble those from both columns of Table 5.3, the company must weigh the gains and losses from utilizing a particular level of transfer prices.

Allocation of Overhead

As with transfer pricing of goods, the allocation of overhead has national and cross-national implications. On the cross-national side, firms must determine what to do with corporate overhead. For example, IBM's world headquarters is located in New York, but its operations are located worldwide. How does IBM allocate those costs to its operations in different countries, and what are the tax implications of this issue? This becomes a real issue for performance evaluation, because the allocation of corporate overhead directly reduces operating profit, which reduces return on invested capital, potentially pushing that return below the company's cost of capital. On the purely national side, companies struggle with the general concept of allocating overhead and the ways this affects product costs.

Cross-National Allocation of Expenses

If it were not for differences in tax rates worldwide, companies could allocate corporate overhead based on sales revenues in each subsidiary or on some other basis. However, different tax rates complicate the situation. For companies headquartered in high-tax countries, there is an incentive to charge as many expenses as possible against parent company income. However, this practice tends to overstate expenses, understate income, and understate taxes in the parent company.

In the United States, for example, the Internal Revenue Service (IRS) allocates and apportions all of a firm's expenses, losses, and other deductions to specific sources of income (sales, royalties, dividends) and then apportions the expenses between domestic and foreign source income. The IRS provides specific guidelines on how to allocate expenses between domestic and foreign source income.

The problem with using tax law to allocate overhead is that it likely eliminates any possibility for the firm to select an allocation basis that is consistent with its manufacturing strategy. When tax implications are ignored, overhead is allocated differently. The Japanese, for example, have established a direct link between allocating overhead and corporate goals.

As Hiromoto (1988) shows, Japanese managers are less concerned about how allocation techniques measure costs than they are about how the allocation techniques motivate employees to drive down costs. An example involves Hitachi, the Japanese electronics firm. In one highly automated plant, the Hitachi cost accounting system allocates overhead based on direct labor hours, which does not seem to make sense in a highly automated environment. However, Hitachi management is trying to reduce direct labor as a way to reduce cost, so allocating overhead based on direct labor encourages management to automate faster.

Another important aspect of overhead we have learned from the Japanese is that overhead cannot be reduced over the long run by simply cutting costs; the entire manufacturing process needs to be redesigned. Mark Blaxill and Thomas Hout (1991) point out that as automation and organizational complexity increase—a real problem for MNEs—so too does overhead. However, MNEs find that they really have to struggle to pick up or maintain market share against global competitors. In addition, the high-tech companies have to devote more and more of their scarce resources to R&D, so there is pressure on management to react. The reaction usually comes in one of two ways: prices are dropped and costs are cut, or the firm gets out of certain product lines and develops a niche. What we have learned from the Japanese is that companies can permanently lower overhead and remain competitive only if they design controllable and highly integrated manufacturing processes. For example, through redesigning its manufacturing process, Toyota has been able to maintain a 90 percent machine uptime in one of its leading-edge forging cells, compared with the 50 percent uptime for U. S. competitors. In addition, Toyota's overhead cost averages one person per $1 million in sales, compared with five people per $1 million in sales for its U.S. competitors. Thus, the amount of overhead that is allocated can be dramatically affected by changes in the production process.

COSTING

Traditionally, prices are a function of costs and market conditions. As barriers to trade have come down in most of the industrialized markets, there is strong competition for sales, causing firms to price very aggressively. In many cases, price competition has made it difficult to generate large profit margins. Many multiproduct firms, such as General Electric (GE) in the United States, have determined that they do not want to be in any business that has a profit margin below a certain level. That is one of the reasons why GE sold its household products division. If it is not possible to drive down costs or keep market share and prices high enough to earn a good margin, it may not be possible to stay in a particular line of business.

Thus, the relationship between pricing and cost is very important. One of the ways that MNEs have been able to drive down costs is to source production offshore. Such outsourcing can be achieved by another firm producing parts and components or by setting up one's own production facilities abroad.

Offshore production is often attractive because of lower labor costs. For example, the hourly wages in manufacturing in the United States were $11.74 in

1995, compared to those in Mexico, which were slightly more than $1.00 in the Mexican *maquiladora* industry along the border with the United States.

However, offshore production can also create a number of problems. If a British company were to purchase components manufactured in China and pay for the parts and components in Chinese currency, the company would face a foreign exchange risk. This makes it very difficult to determine a standard cost. Moreover, transportation costs and distance can create problems not only in direct cost but also in the necessity of holding a larger inventory as a safety stock.

One approach that firms use to attempt to control costs of production is *standard costing*. Quantity and cost standards are established as benchmarks for performance. They are typically based on engineering estimates, forecasted demand, worker input, time and motion studies, and the type and quality of direct materials. Standards can be used to prepare budgets and to evaluate the performance of firms and individuals. They can also be used to help establish appropriate selling prices. To be useful, standard costs need to be realistic and practical. The standards need to be tight but attainable, allowing for normal inefficiencies. Variances established by comparing actual performance with standards can be used to identify problems that occur outside of normal inefficiencies and that need to be corrected.

Although standard costs can be very helpful in determining inventory values and the like, MNEs need to determine if the standard cost of a product should be the same in different production sites around the world. Given that standards are based on such factors as the quality of available materials, the degree of capital intensity used in the production process, and the skill level of workers and managers, it is difficult to imagine that a cost standard developed for a product in the United States would be the same as that used in Brazil. However, identifying standard costs in a consistent manner using a consistent philosophy would be possible.

Caterpillar, the large, U.S.-based heavy equipment manufacturer, uses standard costing for inventory valuation. Caterpillar has developed a managerial product costing system that is separate from its standard cost system, and it uses the same system worldwide. The objective of Caterpillar's cost system, which is an activity-based costing system, is to "identify the activities consumed by products and through a logical, reliable and consistent process assign the related costs properly to each [product]." Thus, product costs are based more on cost rates for different activities that the product must pass through than on standard costs for materials, labor and overhead. This does not mean that the cost rates are exactly the same from country to country, just that all subsidiaries use the process of establishing cost rates and assigning them to products.

Target Costing

Another approach to developing costs is a market-driven system, often called target costing. Target costing, which was developed by the Japanese, differs from engineering-driven costing in that it determines the product cost by establishing a competitive market price and then subtracting a profit margin that is consistent with the company's long-range strategy. Target costing more broadly refers to the process of reducing the time for developing products, defining quality for a new product, and generally containing costs.

Once the cost is determined, the departments that contribute to the production of the product determine their standard cost, assuming no innovation. Somewhere between these two estimates is the target cost the firm shoots for. As production begins, each department tries to ratchet down its costs so that the target cost moves closer to the ideal. Thus, production processes need to be altered and adjusted to move down the target cost. This is very different from the typical standard costing system. Daihatsu, the auto company that learned this process from Toyota, tightens its monthly costs by using a cost-reduction rate based on short-term profit objectives.

Target costing is very similar to an ideal-standard cost system, where the standard can be attained only in ideal conditions. Variances include both normal inefficiencies and abnormal inefficiencies, which are usually the target of control. There is a difference of opinion as to whether these ideal standards motivate workers and managers. The target costing described here is more a function of prices than of ideal standards, but the target cost established for production managers is very similar to an ideal standard.

In 1992, Toyota Motor Company (TMC) installed the target costing system it developed in Japan at its factory in the United Kingdom. The target cost for the autos manufactured in the U.K. facility (TMUK) is determined by TMC with significant input from TMUK. The target price for the autos is determined by consulting Toyota's marketing and engineering division in Europe. The target cost cannot be the same in the United Kingdom as it would be in Japan because there are trade rules in the European Union that determine the local content of autos, requiring TMUK to get 60 to 70 percent of its parts from Europe. TMC implements the following steps in its target costing system: (1) set the target cost for each vehicle; (2) set the target cost for each component; (3) implement value engineering; (4) check achievement of targets; and (5) provide continual feedback to design engineers. The purchasing department of TMUK identifies European producers of subcomponents that meet TMC's strict product specifications. Then TMUK expects the suppliers to reduce costs and improve operations as part of TMUK's efforts to achieve its target costs. TMUK's purchasing department and technical support team visit suppliers to examine the layout of their plant and facilities to help them drive down costs.

QUALITY

Another way to drive down costs is to improve quality. There have been some significant changes in recent years in the attitude of management toward defects. The assumption had always been that production processes needed to be designed to keep the amount of defects at a tolerable level, known as the *acceptable quality level* (AQL). The prevailing wisdom was that if you try too hard to eliminate all defects, you will end up with a more costly manufacturing process.

The Japanese once again shattered that myth with the concept of *total quality management* (TQM). TQM is the process a firm follows to achieve quality. It does not mean "cheap," because some things that a firm must do to achieve high quality might be expensive. The goal under TQM is to eliminate all defects.

The difference between the Japanese and others can be found in the attitude toward quality, which is what TQM is trying to achieve. In a western setting, quality occurs when a product meets or exceeds engineering standards. In Japan, quality is defined in the following way: "The product is so good that the customer wouldn't think of buying from anyone else." The goal of TQM is to simplify and establish a strong focus on everything the firm does. TQM also implies a proactive strategy. Firms that benchmark the industry leaders and attempt to emulate what they do will always be in second place. TQM implies that you try to be the best at whatever you do.

There are four main costs identified with TQM: prevention costs, appraisal costs, internal failure costs, and external failure costs. U.S.-based Texas Instruments, one of the largest electronics firms in the world, identified several dimensions to their cost of quality. Prevention costs include quality engineering, receiving inspection, design engineering, and quality training. Appraisal costs include design analysis and product acceptance. Internal failure costs include scrap and rework costs. External failure costs include the net cost of returned products, repairs, travel costs related to quality problems, and liability claims. The easiest to identify are the prevention costs, the appraisal costs, and the internal failure costs. The most difficult to identify are the external failure costs, but they might be the most important.

Kaplan (1983) points out that executives who have adopted the philosophy of zero defects claim that long-run production costs decrease as defects decrease. He also describes three important aspects of the discussion of TQM. The first is determining what percentage of production makes it all the way through the production process without rework. Many firms do not even keep that statistic, but it is a crucial one for the Japanese, who are trying to eliminate all defects. A second key is determining what the impact is of an increase in quality and a decrease in defects on the cost of manufacturing. Finally, it is important to include in the capital equipment purchase decision the savings in manufacturing cost that lead to the improvement in quality and the decrease in defects that will occur if the equipment is purchased.

PERFORMANCE EVALUATION ISSUES

Budgets both long and short term are, in essence, plans. Transfer prices and target costing can affect prices. In the end these plans must be implemented. With the help of these techniques, whether singly or as a combined plan, managers must perform if the firm is to survive. The performance of those carrying out the plan thus needs to be measured and rewarded. Properly measuring the performance of an individual, a division, or even a company as a whole is never simple or easy. One reason for this is that different bases of measurement result in different measures of performance. Moreover, the individual or unit being evaluated does not control many events affecting performance. Strategic differences in subsidiaries may also result in different performance evaluation measures.

For example, Gupta and Govindarajan (1991) identify several issues surrounding performance evaluation that are complex in the global environment. Subsidiaries can be global innovators, integrated players, implementers, or local innovators. Global innovators and integrated players tend to be high transferors of knowledge to other units. Gupta and Govindarajan propose that units that are global innovators and integrated players need performance evaluation systems that are relatively flexible compared with the other two groups. They tend to rely more on behavioral controls, that is, those involving surveillance of the manger's decisions and actions, and less on output controls, that is, end results of performance, than do the other two groups. Global innovators also tend to need more autonomy than do implementers, with integrated players and local innovators somewhere in between. In addition, Gupta and Govindarajan propose that global innovators tend to rely more on internal control of their performance than on external control—the control of powerful others, luck, and so on. These major differences in the strategic objectives of subsidiaries can obviously influence performance evaluation dramatically.

There are a variety of events that affect performance evaluation that are out of the control of managers and subsidiaries. First, let us consider the basis of measurement. There are many possible criteria against which to judge performance. Furthermore, no single basis is equally appropriate for all units of an MNE. For example, a production unit is more appropriately evaluated on cost reduction, quality control, meeting shipment targets (dates and quantities), and other measures of efficiency. For a sales subsidiary, however, these measures are less appropriate (if appropriate at all) than such measures as market share, number of new customers, or other measures of effectiveness. Similarly, profitability may be appropriate for a subsidiary that is a true profit center but inappropriate for a subsidiary in a high-tax-rate country that, for global tax minimization purposes, is instructed to minimize profits or even maximize losses. These situations suggest the desirability and advisability of using multiple bases for performance measurement—that is, different ones for different kinds of operations in different countries. Yet even multiple measures have their problems. First, it is more difficult to compare the performance of different units measured under different criteria. Second, it is more expensive to set up and operate a multiple-criteria system. Thus, the decision must be based on a cost-benefit analysis.

Making matters even more complicated are the interdependencies of an MNE's operations. For example, a multinational automobile company may produce its steel in Japan, have it stamped in the United States, have its tires made in Canada, its axles in Mexico, its engines in Germany, and its radios in Taiwan, all for final assembly in the United States. If any one part of its far-flung operations experiences performance problems, that operation's problems will spread to the other operations. Thus, a dock strike in Germany could affect the performance of the German subsidiary, the U.S. assembly plant, and all sales subsidiaries worldwide. Proper performance evaluation would have to eliminate these uncontrollable impacts for the interdependent subsidiaries as well as for the German subsidiary. Furthermore, if other than arm's-length transfer prices were used on any of the intercorporate sales, the reported results would not be within the control of either the selling or buying subsidiary (unless they both agreed to the transfer price), and in any case, would not reflect real performance.

Separating Managerial and Subsidiary Performance

It is also difficult but important to separate managerial performance from subsidiary performance. It is possible to have good management performance despite poor subsidiary performance, and vice versa, again largely as a result of noncontrollables. In other words, a manager may have done a superb job in the face of real adversities largely beyond his or her control even though the subsidiary's performance did not measure up to expectations. Similarly, a subsidiary's good performance may have been due to considerable luck or occurred despite poor managerial performance. Thus, in order to properly reward and keep good managers and not inadvertently reward poor managers, the evaluation system must be able to separate subsidiary and managerial performance.

Gupta and Govindarajan point out that some subsidiary managers are better able to cope with the uncertainty inherent in the foreign environment than are others. In particular, they propose that managers in charge of companies that are global innovators and integrated players are better able to deal with ambiguity than are managers of companies that are implementers and local innovators.

Properly Relating Evaluation to Performance

One of the more curious aspects of empirical studies discussed in the previous chapter was the finding that multinationals from western countries especially rely on ROI as the major or one of the most important measures of performance. Where intercorporate transfers are significant and are not at arm's-length prices, the ROI income numerator is highly arbitrary and, in one sense, fictitious. Also, a subsidiary manager whose evaluation is based on ROI may choose to borrow heavily in the local currency. This in turn affects the borrowing capacity of the entire firm and potentially the price of its stock, possibly subjecting the parent's consolidated financial statements to significant foreign current losses if the borrowings are in hard currencies. Perhaps most important, ROI is not appropriate for some foreign operations, such as subsidiaries producing only for other subsidiaries, sales subsidiaries buying all their products from other subsidiaries, or subsidiaries striving to break into highly competitive, low margin markets. The problems related to using ROI as a standard measure of performance apply to other measures as well.

The need for standardization brings us back to the one method of performance evaluation that can meet most criteria without undue limitations: the comparison of performance with plan. This method permits each affiliate to be judged on its own, according to the plan it was given, and can be used to compare subsidiary performances. However, it is a reasonable basis of performance measurement only if the original plans were logical and reasonable. Therein lies one danger of the comparison to plan technique. The other danger is that subsidiary managers' inputs to the plan may be tempered by their desire to surpass the plan's expectations. For example, they might deliberately project a bleak picture. However, if the planning and budget process is sufficiently deliberative, participative, iterative, and honest, both of these dangers can be minimized.

Emerging Trends in Performance Evaluation

The restructuring of companies in the 1980s and 1990s has resulted in a focus on more specific strategies, such as quality, global efficiency, productivity improvement, and the building of critical mass.

One important change is the movement from subsidiaries as a major focus of evaluation to strategic business units (SBUs). Using the SBU as the key profit center for the firm allows it to concentrate on global competitors in that same line of business.

The shift to an SBU focus has resulted in the use of the following three major trends in indicators: more use of ratios, more use of cash flows, and more use of nonfinancial criteria. Although profits are identified as the most important indicator of performance for U.S.-based MNEs, ratios such as return on sales (ROS), return on assets (ROA), return on equity (ROE), and return on investment (ROI) are being heavily utilized again. This may not be true of Japanese firms, but it is true of U.S. firms.

Cash flows are important because they are the basis for the calculation of shareholder value (i.e., the value of the firm's equity stock, an important characteristic that raiders monitor). The focus is on long-term cash flows, discounted in the same way as with capital budgeting.

Reengineering the Budgeting Process

How many companies have attempted to reengineer their budgeting? And how many find that budgeting still eats up week after dismal week of managerial time? Instead of reforming the budgetary beast, Jeremy Hope and Robin Fraser argue that companies should kill it, and learn to operate without budgets. What good are budgets anyway, when the market can render them obsolete so quickly?

Hope and Fraser are research directors of the Beyond Budgeting Round Table, a British-based consortium of 20 large companies investigating life without budgets. When companies get rid of budgeting, they say, good things happen. The politics, gaming, and sandbagging endemic to the process vanish overnight. As much as 20% of management time is freed up for greater productivity, and companies learn to develop management methods more appropriate to today's mercurial world. They learn to allocate resources on the fly, in response to current market opportunities, rather than at an annual marathon session. They monitor performance by tracking trends and forecasts on a few critical indicators, rather than by tracking variances against a months-old budget.
A few pioneering companies are already harvesting these benefits. Svenska Handelsbanken, in Sweden, has been budgetless for decades, and now has the lowest cost structure of any bank in Europe. Volvo Cars gave up budgets about five years ago, replacing the process with rolling forecasts from a close monitoring of key indicators.

Source: Business Review Weekly, July 16, 1999.

Some companies have also experimented with a reengineered approach to budgeting (see International Bulletin 5.1).

Nonfinancial criteria are also increasing in importance. Some of the important measures that are being used are market share, volume, productivity, and quality.

ECONOMIC VALUE ADDED

A relatively recent tool that companies are using to measure performance is *economic value added* (EVA®), something economists call *economic profit.* Basically, EVA is after-tax operating profit minus the total annual cost of capital. It is a measure of the value added or depleted from shareholder value in one period. A positive EVA requires that a company earn a return on its assets that exceeds the cost of debt *and* equity, thus adding to shareholder value. EVA is an actual monetary amount of value added, and it measures changes in value for a period. EVA is also used primarily for performance evaluation and compensation rather than for capital budgeting purposes. EVA is calculated as follows:

ROIC   Return on invested capital: same as operating profit minus cash taxes paid divided by average invested capital

CofC   Weighted average cost of capital: (net cost of debt × % debt used) + (net cost of equity × % equity used)

AIC   Average invested capital: average stockholders equity + average debt

$$EVA = [ROIC - CofC] \times AIC$$

As an example of EVA, assume the following data:

Total revenues	$6,500 (million)
Total costs	4,000
Total operating expenses	1,800
Cash taxes paid	230
Stockholders equity (average)	1,500
Debt (average)	2,370
After-tax cost of debt	5.5%
% debt used	40%
Cost of equity	13%
% equity used	60%

$$\text{Operating profit} = 6500 - 4000 - 1800 - 230 = 470$$
$$\text{AIC} = 1{,}500 + 2{,}370$$
$$\text{ROIC} = 470/3870 = 12.1\%$$
$$\text{CofC} = (5.5\% \times .40) + (15\% \times .60) = 11.2\%$$
$$\text{EVA} = (12.1\% - 11.2\%) \times 3870 = 34.83$$

Although EVA is not a large number in this example, ROIC is greater than cost of capital, so the company is adding to shareholder value. As former Coca-Cola CEO Roberto Goizueta noted, "we raise capital to make concentrate, and sell it at an operating profit. Then we pay the cost of that capital. Shareholders pocket the difference."

CONCLUSIONS

The strategic control of the multinational requires a clear objective and a well-crafted plan coupled with relevant performance evaluation measures. Since the world of the multinational is made far more complex by foreign exchange, tax regimes, and cultural differences, the making and carrying out of such plans is often time consuming. The plans need to be flexible to reflect the volatility of the markets the firm is involved in but in the end they come down to rewarding the behavior that is best suited to achieving the firm's objectives. A multinational needs to bear in mind that the behavior of the manager may be affected by his or her cultural norms and that performance and success can be measured only in terms of those elements that the manager has control over and has a reasonable chance of achieving.

SUMMARY

1. A major aspect of establishing a good management control system is to have a thorough understanding of the purpose of a strategic business unit or overseas subsidiary.

2. It is important to determine whether performance evaluation measures should be developed in the local currency or the parent currency. The local currency is fairer to the local manager, but the parent currency is important because top management needs to answer to shareholders based on parent currency performance.

3. Highly integrated MNE operations create problems for foreign subsidiaries because of transfer pricing problems and the different purposes underlying the existence of the subsidiaries.

4. It is important to separate managerial performance evaluation from that of the subsidiary because a profitable subsidiary can exist independent of good management and a good manager can work in a tough, unprofitable environment.

5. In establishing the budget and monitoring performance, management can use the exchange rate in effect when the budget was established, a projected exchange rate, and the exchange rate in effect when actual performance has occurred.

6. Transfer pricing of goods and the allocation of expenses can affect the measurement of success of the firm and its managers.

7. Capital budgeting in a global context is complicated by environmental factors that make it difficult to estimate cash flows and to determine the proper rate of return needed.

DISCUSSION QUESTIONS

1. Should the local currency or the parent currency be used for performance evaluation? Explain your answer.

2. Which of the methods for setting the budget and monitoring performance as discussed by Lessard and Lorange eliminate the impact of foreign exchange variances? Which of those approaches would you prefer to use and why?

3. Most companies use the same reports to evaluate the performance of the subsidiary and of subsidiary management. What are some of the dangers in doing this?

4. What are some of the national similarities and differences in performance evaluation techniques?

5. What are SBUs beginning to use as major indicators of performance in the global setting, and why are they being used?

6. What is EVA, and how can it be used in a global context?

7. Identify several aspects of the international environment and the global strategy of the MNE that influence the budgeting process.

EXERCISES

1. MultiCorp is a French-based company with operations in the United Kingdom. In determining the budget for 2001, MultiCorp looks at its historical performance in the United Kingdom and notes that for March 2000, its operations were as follows:

Number of units sold	5,000
Direct cost of materials and labor	£400,000
Fixed manufacturing costs	£350,000
Selling price	£100 per unit

In trying to establish the budget in British pounds for March 2001, MultiCorp does not anticipate a change in fixed costs, but its direct cost of materials and labor are expected to rise 10 percent, and its selling price is expected to rise by 15 percent.

At the time the budget is established, the spot rate (hypothetically) is FF7.6 per pound, and the projected average exchange rate for March 2001 is FF7.5 per pound.

At the end of March 2001, MultiCorp's management looked at actual results and discovered the following: the actual average exchange rate was FF7.7, the selling price £112, and the cost per unit of direct materials and labor was £90 per unit. A total of 4,800 units were sold.

Determine the sales volume variances, the flexible budget variances, the foreign exchange variances, and the total static budget variances in British pounds for the following budget translation techniques according to the Lessard and Lorange model:

    a.   A-1
    b.   A-3
    c.   P-2
    d.   P-3
    e.   E-3

2. Use the data and questions in Exercise 1, but change the exchange rate as follows:

FF7.6	Exchange rate when the budget was established
FF7.8	Projected exchange rate
FF7.5	Actual exchange rate during March 2001
	5,200 units actually sold

CASE

Niessen Apparel

Juan Valencia was upset. As General Manager of the Niessen Apparel Peruvian assembly plant, he believed that his performance over the past two years was not being evaluated fairly. He had recently sent a memo to parent company headquarters itemizing his complaints and asking for an immediate response. Charles Niessen, president of the company, asked his son Chuck to review the matter and report back to him immediately because he did not want to risk losing Valencia (who had threatened to quit).

Background

Niessen Apparel was a medium-size U.S. manufacturer of women's and children's clothing. Because of rising domestic production costs, Niessen had investigated the possibilities of sewing the garments outside the United States, after which they would be shipped back and sold in the United States. In this manner, they could lower overall production costs and be in a better position to compete with both domestic and imported products. This could be achieved by utilizing cheaper labor in a developing country for the most labor-intensive part of the production process—assembly—and taking advantage of a favorable section of the U.S. tariff code. This section allowed U.S. companies to export components to a foreign operation, then import the finished products, paying duty only on the value added outside the United States rather than on the full value of the product. Thus, a product imported from a Peruvian operation would have a smaller tariff than one imported from a strictly Peruvian company. This, of course, would give a U.S. company an advantage over a foreign company not owned by a U.S. corporation. For example, a product costing $100 imported from Peru might have a tariff of $20 levied against it (20 percent of its value). However, if the product had $50 worth of U.S. components in its value, then under the code the U.S. tariff would be $10 (20 percent of the value added outside the United States). Thus, the full import price would be $110, compared with the $120 import price of the nonqualifying imports.

The Method of Performance Evaluation

To justify the Peruvian sewing plant, Niessen believed that it should be evaluated as a profit center. This would allow the operation's profitability to be compared to the next best alternative use of funds. Valencia was to be responsible for the profitability of the Peruvian operations and was to be evaluated and rewarded on that basis. In addition, Niessen believed that the subsidiary's performance should be evaluated in terms of U. S. dollars rather than local Peruvian currency because its value to him and his company was its contribution to U.S. earning power.

Problems with the Operations and Systems

Initially, a transfer pricing system was established on an arm's-length basis for all intercompany shipments. This was consistent with the profit center concept in that any other method would result in artificial profits. However, over the past two years the transfer prices on components shipped to Peru had been increased, and the transfer prices on finished goods shipped back to the United States had been decreased. These changes were made to take better advantage of the special tariff provisions (i.e., to pay less import duty) by increasing the U.S. content and decreasing the foreign value added to the finished product. This change in strategy was considered desirable by the U.S. marketing people, who wanted to sell more competitively in the United States, and by the treasurer, who wanted to save on import duties. In order to avoid problems with U.S. and Peruvian government agencies, the transfer prices had been adjusted gradually but steadily each month. Helping to conceal this procedure was the continued decline of the Peruvian currency relative to the U.S. dollar. This, in itself, increased Peruvian import (purchasing) costs while lowering U.S. import prices (costs).

Although the effects of the new transfer prices and currency values worked out very well for the U.S. marketing manager (whose profits increased significantly), just the opposite occurred for Valencia. The performance evaluation of its subsidiary's operations deteriorated to the point were one member of the U.S. staff who was unaware of what had been going on suggested that Valencia be fired or the Peruvian operation be terminated. In addition, Valencia's annual salary bonus had virtually disappeared because it was based largely on his subsidiary's profit performance. To make matters worse, slower than anticipated U.S. sales growth had caused a cutback in shipments to and from Peru, idling much of the Peruvian capacity. And because the Peruvian subsidiary sold only to the U.S. parent, it could not use its surplus production capacity, causing its costs to rise further and its profits to decrease further.

Questions

1. What were the strengths and weaknesses of Niessen Apparel's original method of performance evaluation?

2. What factors should Niessen consider in deciding whether to change the company's method of performance evaluation?

3. Should the old evaluation method be changed for the Peruvian operation? If so, why and how?

REFERENCES AND FURTHER READING

Arpan, J. (1972). *Intracorporate Pricing: Non-American Systems and Views*. New York: Praeger.

Blaxill, M. and T. Hout. (1991). "The Fallacy of the Overhead Quick Fix." *Harvard Business Review* (July/August): 93–101.

Demirag, I. (1994). "Management Control Systems and Performance Evaluations in Japanese Companies: A British Perspective." *Management Accounting*, 72 (7, July/August): 18–20,45.

Demirag, I. and A. Tylecote. (1996). "Short-term Performance Pressures on British and Scandinavian Firms: Case Studies." *European Management Journal*, 14(2, April): 201–206.

Gupta, A. and V. Govindarajan. (1991). "Knowledge Flows and the Structure of Control Within Multinational Corporations." *Academy of Management Review*, 16(4, Oct.): 768–792.

Hiromoto, T. (1988). "Another Hidden Edge—Japanese Management Accounting." *Harvard Business Review* (July/Aug.): 22–26.

Kaplan, R. (1983). "Measuring Manufacturing Performance: A New Challenge for Managerial Accounting Research." *Accounting Review* 58(4): 686–705.

Lessard, D. (1996). "International Financial Markets and the Firm." *Journal of Finance* 51(2, June): 765–767.

Lessard, D. and S. Zaheer. (1996). "Breaking the Silos: Distributed Knowledge and Strategic Responses to Volatile Exchange Rates." *Strategic Management Journal* 17(7, July): 513–533.

Lessard, D. and P. Lorange. (1977). "Currency Changes and Management Control: Resolving the Centralization/Decentralization Dilemma." *Accounting Review* (July) Vol. 53(3): 628–637.

Morsicato, H. (1978). "An Investigation of the Interaction of Financial Statement Translation and Multinational Enterprise Performance Evaluation," unpublished Ph.D. diss., Pennsylvania State Unversity, 1978; and *Currency Translation and Performance Evaluation in Multinationals* (Ann Arbor, MI: UMI Research Press, 1980).

Robbins, S. and R. Stobaugh. (1973). "The Bent Measuring Stick for Foreign Subsidiaries." *Harvard Business Review* (Sept.–Oct.): 80–88.

SOME USEFUL INTERNET WEB SITES

1. PeopleSoft/performance management: *http://www.disruptive.com/en/think_tank/performance_en.html*
   Industry experts and PeopleSoft visionaries discuss the trends and best practices on performance measurement. There are links to PeopleSoft's operations in most regions of the world. Some local links include:
   - PeopleSoft Australia: *http://www.peoplesoft.com/en/worldwide/australia/*
   - PeopleSoft Singapore and Malaysia: *http://www.peoplesoft.com/en/worldwide/singapore/*

2. Management Internet sources: *http://library.adelaide.edu.au/guide/eco/man/mannet1.html*
   A guide to various online management and performance resources and journals.

3. National professional organizations: These are the Web sites of some professional organizations for management accountants. They typically have back-issue e-copies of their magazines that contain interesting global topics from time to time. There are also links to global topics and where appropriate local chapters outside their country.
   - The Certified Management Accountants of Canada: *http://www.cma-canada.org/*
   - CIMA (UK): *http://www.cima.org.uk/*
   - The Institute of Management Accountants (USA): *http://www.imanet.org/*
   - IFAC (Financial and Management Accounting Committee): *http://www.ifac.org/Committees/FMAC/index.html*
     The FMAC publishes guidance, sponsors research programs and facilitates the international exchange of ideas to develop and support financial and management accounting professionals.

CHAPTER SIX

TAXATION AND THE MULTINATIONAL ENTERPRISE

INTRODUCTION

The MNE faces two challenges when it reviews taxation of its global operations. First, it must deal with a variety of taxes and types of taxable income on a global basis. Second, it must increasingly deal with home governments seeking to tax its global income. The key taxes as far as corporations and MNEs are concerned are direct taxes such as the corporate income taxes and indirect taxes such as the value-added tax or goods and services tax.

DIRECT TAXES

Corporate Income Tax

The two approaches to taxing corporate income are the classic and the integrated systems. The classic system used in the United States, Belgium, the Netherlands, and Luxembourg, for example, taxes income when it is received by each taxable entity. Thus, the earnings of a corporation are taxed twice—when the corporation earns them and when they are received as dividends by shareholders.

The integrated system tries to take taxation of both the corporation and the shareholder into consideration in order to eliminate double taxation. In most cases, there is only partial rather than full integration, so double taxation is not completely eliminated. There are two ways to integrate a system:

1. Through a split rate, e.g., Germany, in which the normal tax rate for most companies is 45 percent; the rate is reduced, however, to 30 percent for profits that are distributed.

2. The second and dominant approach to integration is imputation, which involves taxing earnings at the same rate whether remitted as a dividend or not, but allowing a partial or full tax credit for the shareholders. This is the approach followed by most of the remaining countries in the European Union, as well as such non-EU countries such as Canada, Australia, New Zealand, and Japan—but with different results. Most of the European

countries using the integrated approach have adopted a system of giving partial credits to shareholders on tax paid by the corporation when income is distributed to the shareholder. This is the approach followed in the United Kingdom where the corporate tax rate is a flat 31 percent. When shareholders are taxed on their dividends, a portion of the corporate income tax paid by the corporation is imputed to the shareholders so the income is not double taxed. Other countries, like Italy and France, have a full imputation system in which shareholders get a tax credit that eliminates their tax burden.

It is interesting to note that in general, corporate tax rates have been coming down in recent years, notably in the OECD and EU (see Table 6.1).

What Income Is Taxable?

Even without leaving home a corporation may begin to interact with the nuances of different tax systems: income derived from the export of goods and services as well as from a foreign branch or foreign corporation. Worldwide foreign source income from the export of goods and services is taxable when earned. Tax incentives, such as the Foreign Sales Corporation in the United States, may be used to encourage exports, however, and these incentives have the effect of taxing foreign source income differently from domestic income.

Taxing the earnings of foreign branches and foreign corporations is more complex. Two different approaches to the taxation of foreign source income are the territorial approach and the worldwide approach. The territorial approach as used in Hong Kong, for example, and asserts that only income earned in Hong Kong should be taxed there; foreign source income should be taxed in the country where it is generated, not in Hong Kong.

Table 6.1   OECD and EU Average Corporate Tax Rates—1995–1999

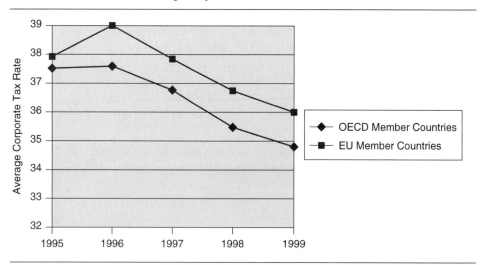

Source: www.tax.kpmg.net.

The worldwide approach, as used in the United States, taxes both domestic and foreign source income. This has the potential to lead to double taxation because that income may be taxed in two different countries. The two major ways to minimize double taxation where foreign source income is taxed is through the tax credit (allowing the company a direct credit against domestic taxes for the foreign income taxes already paid) and tax treaties. In addition, some countries that use the worldwide approach do not tax earnings of foreign subsidiaries until the parent receives a dividend. This is known as the deferral of taxation of foreign source income.

Within a given country, the tax authorities normally tax income on earnings of all corporations, even when foreign investors own them. For example, the German subsidiary of General Motors is taxed like all corporations in Germany. The domestic branch of a foreign corporation is normally taxed at the same rate as domestic corporations.

Determination of Expenses

Another factor that causes differences in the amount of taxes paid is the way countries treat certain expenses for tax purposes. Expenses are usually a matter of timing. If R&D expenses are capitalized, for example, their impact on taxable income will be spread over the period in which they are written off. If they are treated as expenses in the period in which they are incurred, the impact will be immediate.

Opinions also differ from country to country as to the useful life of an asset. If one government allows a company to write off an asset in five years, whereas in another country the same asset has a taxable useful life of ten years, the tax burdens in the two countries will be quite different.

In addition, there may be a big difference between a country's statutory and effective tax rate. A high statutory tax rate with a liberal determination of expenses may result in a relatively low taxable income and thus low effective tax rate, and this is the rate that is of concern to the investor. A good example of this is that when the United States passed the Tax Reform Act (TRA) of 1986, the U.S. government lowered tax rates, but it broadened the base of taxable income so it would continue to collect roughly the same amount of revenue. Thus, the effective tax rate did not change as much as the statutory tax rate did. This same effect spread throughout most of the other OECD countries during the late 1980s where rates were reduced and the tax base broadened. A few exceptions are France, Germany, and Italy, where tax rates were reduced but the base was not broadened.

Withholding Tax

The income earned by the foreign subsidiary or affiliate of a multinational is taxable in the foreign country, and the tax is levied against the foreign corporation, not against the parent. However, the actual cash returns to the parent in the form of dividends, royalties (payments made by the foreign corporation to the parent for the use of patents, trademarks, processes, and so on), and interest on intracompany debt are taxable to the parent. Normally a country levies a withholding tax on payments to the nonresident investor. This tax varies in size from country to country and depends on whether the country has a tax treaty with other countries.

INDIRECT TAXES

Value-Added or Goods and Services Taxes

In some countries, such as the United States, the individual direct income tax is the most important source of revenue for the government. In other countries, like France, indirect taxes are very important. Examples of indirect taxes are consumption taxes (such as the sales tax in the United States), the value-added tax (VAT) or goods and services tax (GST), excise taxes, estate and gift taxes, employment taxes, and different kinds of user fees.

In Europe, the VAT, sometimes referred to as the TVA, is a source of considerable government income and is also the major source of revenue for funding the operations of the European Union. The basic concept behind the VAT is that a tax is applied at each stage of the production process for the value added by the firm to goods purchased from the outside, which have been subject to the VAT. The tax is charged by businesses on the value of their sales, but the tax burden eventually falls on the consumer because a company that pays VAT on its own expenses can reclaim that tax already paid. The major method for computing the VAT and the one required in the European Union is the subtractive method. Table 6.2 demonstrates how to compute the VAT in the United Kingdom, where the VAT rate is 17.5 percent. The VAT differs from a sales tax in that the entire sales tax appears at the retail level rather than at each stage of the process. In addition, the VAT is not listed separately to the consumer. For example, the consumer would not pay the retailer £23.5 plus a VAT of £4.11. The £23.5 that the consumer pays the retailer includes the VAT.

THE AVOIDANCE OF DOUBLE TAXATION OF FOREIGN SOURCE INCOME

Credits and Deductions

The foreign branches and subsidiaries of MNEs are subject to a variety of taxes, both direct and indirect, in the countries where they operate. The problem is that

Table 6.2   The Value-Added Tax

Calculation	Manufacturer	Wholesaler	Retailer	Consumer
Net cost of goods	£0.00	£10.00	£14.00	£23.50
Markup		£4.00	£6.00	
Net selling price	£10.00	£14.00	£20.00	
VAT chargeable (17.5% × net (selling price)	£1.75	£2.45	£3.50	
Gross selling price	£11.75	£16.45	£23.50	
Accounting for VAT				
Due to customs and excise	£1.75	£2.45	£3.50	
Recoverable from customs and excise	£0.00	£1.75	£2.45	
Net VAT paid	£1.75	£0.70	£1.05	

the income earned in the foreign country may be subject to income taxes twice: when the earnings are realized in the foreign location and when they are realized in the parent country.

For example, in the United States, income from foreign corporations is usually taxed when a dividend is remitted to the parent company. The company may choose to treat the taxes paid as a credit that can be applied against their tax liability, or it can deduct the tax from income to reduce taxable income.

The simple illustration in Table 6.3 demonstrates the difference in U.S. tax liability that arises from double taxation, a tax deduction, and a tax credit. In the double taxation column, the foreign source income is taxed at 30 percent in the foreign country and at 35 percent in the United States (using the U.S. federal rate). Thus, the total tax paid is $65, the net income after all taxes is only $35, and the effective tax rate is thus 65 percent. In the deduction column, the U.S. tax rate of 35 percent is levied on the income that results from deducting the foreign income tax from the gross income of the foreign corporation. Thus, the U.S. tax is only $24.50, the total tax paid is $54.50, and the net income after tax in both countries is $45.50, definitely better than in the double taxation situation. Notice that under the tax credit column, U.S. income tax of $5.00 is assessed against the foreign source income because the tax rate in the foreign country (30%) is lower than it is in the United States (35%). In U.S. tax law, an excess credit (if the foreign tax rate exceeds the U.S. tax rate) can be carried back and applied against foreign source income of prior years or carried forward to be applied against foreign source income in future years.

A key point is that a tax must be considered an income tax to be creditable; the VAT described earlier would be eligible for deduction but not for the credit. In determining the tax credit in the United States, for example, the predominant nature of the foreign tax must be that of an income tax as defined in the United States. Thus, a tax might be considered an income tax in one country but still not be eligible for the credit if that tax is deemed something else from the perspective of the IRS in the United States.

It should be noted that in the United States the tax credit is available only for taxes on income paid directly by the U.S. corporation (e. g., the withholding tax on dividends) or deemed to have been paid by it. The deemed direct tax is the corporate income tax actually paid by the foreign corporation to the foreign government and deemed to have been paid by the U.S. parent.

Table 6.3 Treatment of Foreign Corporate Income Tax

	Double Taxation	**Deduction**	**Credit**
Income earned by the foreign corporation	$100.00	$100.00	$100.00
Foreign tax at 30% on $100	30.00	30.00	30.00
Net income after tax	$70.00	$70.00	$70.00
U.S. tax at 35% on $100	35.00		
U.S. tax at 35% on $70		24.50	
U.S. tax at 35% on $100 less foreign tax at 30% on $100			5.00
Net income after taxes in U. S.	$35.00	$45.50	$65.00
Effective tax rate	65%	54.5%	35%

Tax Treaties

As we have noted, with the spread of business worldwide, income earned in one country may be subject to taxation in other countries. Differences in philosophy about how income should be taxed have given rise to treaties between countries to minimize the effect of double taxation on the taxpayer, protect each country's right to collect taxes, and provide ways to resolve jurisdictional issues. In the area of double taxation, treaties can specify that certain classes of income would not be subject to tax, can reduce the rate on income and/or withholding taxes, and can specifically deal with the issue of tax credits. Although the latter point could be considered a duplication of the Internal Revenue Code, its specification in a tax treaty would simply strengthen the tax credit concept. It could also deal with specific types of taxes that could be considered creditable, and so on. Among other things, tax treaties tend to reduce or eliminate the taxes on dividends, interest, and royalty payments.

A pattern of tax treaties was developed by the OECD in 1963, and subsequently amended and reissued. That pattern, initially resisted by the U.S. government, was accepted in principle in the model tax treaty approved by the United States in 1977. The treaty contains twenty-nine articles dealing with such issues as the taxes covered, the persons and organizations covered, relief from double taxation, the exchange of information between competent authorities on contracting nations, and the conditions under which a treaty may be terminated. The model treaty also deals with issues such as who is allowed to tax income, how income is to be characterized, how expenses are to be allocated, what rights exist to certain types of deductions, and how rates of tax on foreign investors can be reduced.

Sometimes treaties are comprehensive, other times they amend existing treaties or deal with specific issues. In 1994, for example, the United States and Canada signed an agreement resulting in significant reductions in tax rates on cross-border payments of dividends, interest, and royalties. The rate on direct investment dividends would be reduced to 5 percent from 10 percent; the rate on interest would fall to 10 percent from 15 percent; and the rate on most royalties would drop to zero from 10 percent.

MINIMIZING GLOBAL TAX

Tax Haven Concept

A phenomenon that has emerged from a philosophy that foreign source income should not be taxed at all or should be taxed only when declared a dividend is the tax haven. A tax haven may be defined as a place where foreigners may receive income or own assets without paying high rates of tax. Tax havens offer a variety of benefits, including low taxes or no taxes on certain classes of income. Because of these benefits, thousands of *mailbox companies* have sprung up in such exotic places as Liechtenstein, Vanuatu (formerly New Hebrides), and the Netherlands Antilles.

Some examples of types of tax haven countries are as follows:

- Countries with no income taxes, such as the Bahamas, Bermuda, and the Cayman Islands.
- Countries with taxes at low rates, such as the British Virgin Islands.
- Countries that tax income from domestic sources but exempt income from foreign sources, such as Hong Kong, Liberia, and Panama.

- Countries that allow special privileges; generally their suitability as tax havens is limited.

To take advantage of a tax haven, a corporation would ordinarily set up a subsidiary in the tax haven country through which different forms of income would pass. The goal is to shift income from high-tax to tax haven countries. This is normally accomplished by using the tax haven subsidiary as an intermediary. For example, a British manufacturer could sell goods directly to a dealer in Germany and concentrate the profits in Britain. It could equally well sell the goods to a tax haven subsidiary at cost and then sell the goods to the German dealer at a profit, thus concentrating the profits in the tax haven corporation.

Many countries are naturally concerned to minimize the opportunities for using tax havens where they are likely to be disadvantaged. The OECD, for example, plans to impose sanctions on countries offering "harmful" tax competition (see International Bulletin 6.1).

Tax Incentives

For the purposes of this chapter, tax incentives are of two major types: incentives by countries to attract foreign investors and incentives by countries to encourage exports of goods and services.

Tax incentives to invest usually involve tax holidays of one form or another. The Brazilian government provides a ten-year tax holiday for companies that invest in the impoverished northeast and Amazon regions of the country. Mexico does

---

International Bulletin 6.1

Globalisation and Tax Competition

As globalisation ebbed and flowed, the taxman's share of economic output went relentlessly up, despite warnings from politicians that globalisation would make it harder for government to collect taxes and thus to provide public services. But now a new factor has entered the equation: the Internet. It epitomises borderlessness, and the irrelevance of being in a particular physical location. By being everywhere and nowhere at once, it seems certain to speed up globalisation. And in doing so, according to the Organisation for Economic Cooperation and Development, it might damage tax systems so badly that it could "lead to governments being unable to meet the legitimate demands of their citizens for public services."

SHOPPING AROUND

The Internet has dawned just as tax collectors are getting worried about another aspect of globalisation: tax competition. Both the European Union and the OECD have declared war on "harmful" low-tax policies used by some countries to attract international businesses and capital. The OECD says that tax competition is often a "beggar-thy-neighbour policy" which is already reducing government tax revenues, and will start to be reflected in the data during the next couple of years. The Internet has the potential to increase tax competition, not least by making it much easier for multinationals to shift their activities to low-tax regimes, such as Caribbean tax havens, that are physically a long way from their customers, but virtually are only a mouse-click away. Many more companies may be able to emulate Rupert Murdoch's News Corporation, which has earned profits of £1.4 billion ($2.3 billion) in Britain since 1987 but paid no corporation tax there.

Source: The Economist, January 29, 2000.

not offer a tax holiday for foreign investors, but it provides tax credits for companies that invest in counties located outside the metropolitan areas, such as in Baja and along the border with the United States.

Another popular form of incentive involves exports. In the European Union, many export products are zero-rated, which means that exports are not assessed to VAT. This allows firms to offer their products at a lower price than they otherwise could. Both Japan and Mexico also have an internal VAT but do not apply the VAT against exports.

Within the United States and United Kingdom many local authorities can and do offer reductions in or the elimination of local property taxes. U.S. cities and states can often be persuaded for a major investment to waive state and city income taxes. At the U. S. federal level there are de facto reductions of earnings from export income through the Foreign Sales Corporation (FSC).

The Controlled Foreign Corporation

As noted earlier, a U. S. corporation may choose to produce and sell in the foreign country through a branch or foreign corporation. The tax implications of these situations are interesting. The income or loss of a foreign branch must be combined with parent income for tax as well as book purposes in the period in which the income or loss occurs. In the case of a foreign corporation, however, a U.S. parent does not declare income from a foreign corporation for tax purposes until it actually receives a dividend. This is the principle of deferral—the income is deferred from U. S. taxation until it is received as a dividend.

The deferral principle works most of the time, but an exception is made for a certain class of income, basically the passive (in contrast to active) income of a controlled foreign corporation (CFC). A CFC is a foreign corporation in which "U.S. shareholders" hold more than 50 percent of the voting stock. If a foreign company owned by U.S. citizens is deemed to be a CFC, its passive income is immediately taxable in the U.S., regardless of whether a dividend has been paid.

TAX DIMENSIONS OF EXPATRIATES

Most countries tax the earnings of their residents. However, the United States goes further than many industrialized countries by taxing the worldwide income of its citizens. A survey by *Business International* revealed that of eight major Western countries, the United States is the only one that taxes its expatriates on worldwide income. The United States does, however, provide some relief for citizens who have been a resident outside of the United States for an uninterrupted period that includes an entire taxable year.

INTRACORPORATE TRANSFER PRICING

Internal pricing, also known as intracorporate transfer pricing or transfer pricing, refers to the pricing of goods and services that are transferred (bought and sold) between members of a corporate family—for example, parent to subsidiaries, between subsidiaries, from subsidiaries to parent, and so on. As such, internal transfers include raw materials, semifinished and finished goods, allocation of fixed costs, loans, fees, royalties for use of trademarks, copyrights, and other factors. In theory, such prices should be based on production costs, but in reality they often are not. As discussed in Chapter 5, transfer pricing is also a management control tool and tax minimization may clash with management's best practice. An example of this is given in the Niessen Apparel case at the end of Chapter 5.

Although industrial countries such as the United States have been concerned about the transfer pricing policies of their own domestic firms, they are now becoming concerned about the transfer pricing policies of foreign investors. In 1992, there was significant discussion in the United States over possible transfer pricing violations by Japanese auto firms. The concern was that the Japanese were underinvoicing the import of parts and components used in U. S. assembly operations, thus minimizing customs duties and giving the firms a competitive advantage over U. S. manufacturers. Table 6.4 shows the results of a survey by Tang (1992) of factors influencing the transfer pricing decisions of Fortune 500 companies in 1977 and 1990. The consistently most important factors besides corporate profitability were differential tax rates, restrictions on repatriation of profits or dividends, and the competitive position of foreign subsidiaries.

Tax Considerations in Transfer Pricing Decisions

An insight into the tax considerations involved was given in a *Newsweek* article (April 15, 1991) by Larry Martz, entitled "The Corporate Shell Game." A hypothetical example was presented of a U.S. company that manufactured goods through its German subsidiary and sold them to its Irish subsidiary, which in turn sold the goods back to the U.S. parent company. The goods were manufactured at a cost of $80 by the German subsidiary and sold for the same amount to the Irish subsidiary. Even though the tax rate in Germany is 45 percent, there is no tax on the transaction. The Irish subsidiary turns around and sells the goods to the U. S. parent for $150, earning a profit of $70. Because the tax rate in Ireland is only 4 percent for that transaction, the Irish subsidiary pays only $2.80 in tax. The U. S. parent then sells the goods for $150, earning no profit and paying no tax, even though the U. S. tax rate is 35 percent. Thus, the U. S. company ends up paying only $2.80 in income taxes, and this amount is paid in Ireland.

U. S. Rules

In the United States, Section 482 of the Internal Revenue Code governs transfer-pricing rules. The code section permits the IRS to distribute, apportion, or allocate gross income, deductions, credits, or allowances between related enterprises if it feels that tax evasion is taking place. The IRS prefers that all transfers among related enterprises take place at arm's-length prices, which are defined as the prices that would be obtained between unrelated entities. As a result, the IRS is concerned about monitoring transfers in the following five areas: loans and advances, performance of services, use of tangible property, use of intangible property, and sale of tangible property.

In making the allocations, the key for the IRS is to try to establish what an arm's-length price should be. For the sale of tangible property, that price can be determined in one of six ways: as the comparable uncontrollable price method, the resale price method, the comparable profits method, the cost-plus method, the profits split method, and other methods. The first method uses the concept of a market price to

Table 6.4 Importance of Environmental Variables Influencing International Transfer Pricing Behavior

Ranking of Average Importance Score		Variables	Average Importance Score	
1990	1977		1990	1977
1	1	Overall profit to the company	4.04	3.94
2	4	Differentials in income tax rates and income tax legislation among countries	3.45	3.06
3	2	Restrictions imposed by foreign countries on repatriation of profits or dividends	3.32	3.24
4	3	The competitive position of subsidiaries in foreign countries	3.31	3.16
5	6	Rate of customs duties and customs legislation where the company has operations	3.04	2.99
6,7,8	8	Restrictions imposed by foreign countries on the amount of royalty or management fees that can be charged against foreign subsidiaries	2.90	2.85
6,7,8	11	Maintaining good relationships with host governments	2.90	2.75
6,7,8	9	The need to maintain adequate cash flows in foreign subsidiaries	2.90	2.83
9	7	Import restrictions imposed by foreign countries	2.71	2.89
10	5	Performance evaluation of foreign subsidiaries	2.69	3.01
11	16	The need of subsidiaries in foreign countries to seek local funds	2.61	2.40
12	12	Devaluation and revaluation in countries where the company has operations	2.44	2.71
13,14	15	Antidumping legislation of foreign countries	2.38	2.45
13,14	20	Antitrust legislation of foreign countries	2.38	2.14
15	17	The interests of local partners in foreign subsidiaries	2.36	2.30
16	10	Rules and requirements of financial reporting for subsidiaries in foreign countries	2.34	2.78
17	14	Volume of interdivisional transfers	2.31	2.53
18	13	Rates of inflation in foreign countries	2.24	2.57
19	19	Risk of expropriation in foreign countries where the company has operations	2.01	2.23
20	18	U. S. government requirements on direct foreign investments	1.94	2.27

Source: R.Y.W. Tang, "Transfer Pricing in the 1990s," *Management Accounting* (February 1992).

determine the transfer price. Of course, an external market for the same or very similar product must exist for this method to be used. The IRS also allows for differences resulting from reductions in variable expenses (such as selling expenses).

If it is impossible to use the comparable uncontrollable price method, the firm must then use the resale price method. Assume that the manufacturer in the United States sells a product to an independent distributor in Hong Kong, which sells the product directly to any other firm. The IRS would then take the price established by the distributor to outside customers and back out any costs to completion plus a normal profit margin to determine the transfer price from the manufacturer to the distributor.

The cost-plus method involves the costs of manufacturing the product plus a normal profit margin from the sales of similar products. Obviously, it is difficult to justify costs and normal profit margins. The other three methods are less common and are used as a last resort.

TAX PLANNING IN THE INTERNATIONAL ENVIRONMENT

As we have seen, the tax dimensions of international operations are very complex. The tax environment is unique in each national setting, and the advice of competent local staff who understand the tax situation is essential. In spite of the individual nature of each country, we can nevertheless use some general concepts as tax planning guides.

Choice of Methods of Servicing Foreign Markets

There are a variety of ways in which a firm can choose to service its foreign markets: exports of goods and services and technology, branch operations, and foreign subsidiaries.

Exports When exporting goods and services, a firm must decide whether to service the products from the parent country or from a foreign location. A U.S. firm needs to consider the benefits of operating through a sales office abroad. A foreign sales corporation (FSC) provides such an opportunity and can provide substantial tax benefits if the operations are legitimate ones that result in active rather than passive income. If the income is active, it makes sense to set up the sales office in a tax haven country where income can be sheltered. When the firm decides to license technology abroad, it must be aware of the withholding taxes and relevant tax treaties.

Foreign Branches Operating abroad through a branch has several distinct benefits. Because branch profits and losses are not subject to deferral, it is often beneficial to open a branch when first operating abroad since the initial years are normally loss years. The home office could use branch losses to offset home office income for tax purposes. Branch remittances are usually not subject to withholding taxes as are dividends from subsidiaries. For example, in Belgium there is a withholding tax on branch remittances, but a tax treaty with the United States eliminates that tax. Natural resource companies like to operate through branches abroad because the IRS allows branches to use the depletion allowance and other tax benefits relating to natural resources. These benefits come back directly to the parent company.

Foreign Subsidiaries A major tax benefit of operating abroad through a subsidiary is that its income is usually sheltered from taxation in the home country until a dividend is remitted. In the United States, that is true for all subsidiary income except the passive income of a CFC. This underscores the importance of making sure the operations of a CFC in a tax haven country are legitimate so the firm does not have to worry about the Subpart F provisions. The major problem with operating through a subsidiary is that any losses sustained cannot be recognized by the parent company. Thus, the subsidiary form of organization is much more valuable after the startup years, when the operations become profitable.

Location of Foreign Operations The location of foreign operations is influenced by three major tax factors: tax incentives, tax rates, and tax treaties. The importance of tax incentives was emphasized in the Brazilian and Mexican examples in the Tax Incentives section of this chapter. The existence of tax incentives can materially reduce the cash outflow required for an investment project, which will increase the net present value of the project. That tax effect could change the timing of an investment decision.

Because the determination of revenues and expenses for tax purposes is a function of tax law in most countries, it is important to be intimately familiar with local tax laws. This is almost impossible for someone in corporate headquarters, so it is necessary to have competent tax and legal help in each local country.

Tax treaties have a critical impact on the cash flows related to withholding taxes on dividends, interest, and royalties. Strict attention to tax treaties can help investors choose the location of their legal operations wisely (which may or may not be the same as the location of their managerial operations). For example, the withholding tax between the United States and the United Kingdom is 15 percent according to a bilateral treaty, whereas both countries have a 5 percent withholding agreement with the Netherlands. A U.S. company would be better off establishing a holding company in the Netherlands to receive dividends from its British operations, subject to a 5 percent withholding tax. The Dutch holding company could then remit a dividend to the U.S. parent subject to a 5 percent withholding tax, which would be better than the 15 percent withholding tax between the United States and the United Kingdom. This is just one example of the ways tax treaties can be used to improve the cash flows of foreign investors.

Transfer Pricing

As discussed earlier, transfer pricing is a method of equalizing taxes globally. This ability is limited by the increasing vigilance of tax authorities, particularly those of the United States, but possibilities exist. Care needs to be taken (as with other strategic issues) that in the final decision tax considerations do not crowd out important management control and other essential issues.

CONCLUSIONS

Most corporate entities in the world suffer some form of corporate income tax. The key to any form of multinational tax planning is to minimize this tax and other forms of taxation by careful planning and allocation. Governments, on the other hand, are devoted to the pursuit of their "fair share" of the taxes for companies based in their own country and those that are from other countries. This constant tussle is played out with the assistance of lawyers and accountants around the world. It is not the role of managers to learn all of the rules of taxation in the countries of the world but rather to understand the parameters that affect their ability to do business in a country and the overall return that will be earned from such business. It should be remembered at all times that those returns to individual providers of capital and the ability of the corporation to survive will in the long term be dependent not just on its net income but the cash flow that it is able to retain after taxes.

SUMMARY

1. The territorial approach to taxing income asserts that foreign source income should be taxed where earned and not mixed with domestic source income. The worldwide philosophy treats all income as taxable to the parent. This leads to double taxation, which can be minimized by the tax credit and tax treaties.

2. The classic system of corporate income taxation taxes income when it is received by each taxable entity, which leads to double taxation. The integrated system of taxation tries to eliminate double taxation through a combination of a split-rate system and tax credits.

3. Countries often collect a withholding tax on dividends, interest, and royalties paid to foreign investors. These levies can be reduced through tax treaties.

4. The value-added tax (VAT) or goods and services tax (GST) is an indirect tax that is an important source of revenue in many countries, especially in Europe. It is applied at each stage of the production process for the value added by the firm to goods purchased from the outside.

5. Tax treaties can specify that certain classes of income would not be subject to tax, reduce the rate on income and/or withholding taxes, and specifically deal with the issue of tax credits.

6. A tax haven is a country that has no income tax, taxes income at low rates, or exempts from taxation income from foreign sources.

7. In the United States, a controlled foreign corporation (CFC) is any foreign corporation that is majority-owned by U.S. shareholders. Income from a non-CFC is not taxed until a dividend is sent to the U.S. investor. Active income from a CFC also qualifies for the deferral privilege and is not taxed until remitted as a dividend.

8. Some countries provide tax holidays, such as the forgiveness of income taxes for a period, to attract foreign investors.

9. International tax planning requires that a firm take taxes into consideration when determining the type of operation to be followed in servicing international markets (exporting, licensing, branches, or subsidiaries) and the location of the operation (by considering tax incentives, tax rates, and tax treaties).

10. Companies set transfer prices for a variety of reasons, including tax minimization strategies, competition in the foreign country, market conditions in the foreign country, customs duties, exchange controls, price controls, import restrictions, and the desire to help the foreign affiliate earn a reasonable profit. The objective of tax law relating to transfer pricing is to ensure that each country earns a fair share of corporate income tax.

DISCUSSION QUESTIONS

1. A company has subsidiaries in host countries A and B. Country A has a statutory corporate tax rate of 30 percent, whereas country B's is 40 percent. What are some specific reasons that country B's effective tax rate might actually be more favorable to the firm?

2. Assume that a U. S. company wishing to shelter its foreign source income from U. S. taxes uses the Netherlands Antilles. Using a review of the literature outside the text, answer the following questions:

   a. Why is the Netherlands Antilles such a good tax haven country?

   b. What problems does the Netherlands Antilles face as a tax haven country?

   c. What impact could the repeal in the United States of the 30 percent withholding tax on interest from securities have on the use of the Netherlands Antilles as a tax haven country?

3. How does the existence of classic and integrated corporate tax systems affect the financing decisions of multinational corporations?

4. Why and how do tax authorities get involved in the transfer pricing situation?

5. According to the survey mentioned in this chapter, what are the most important factors companies consider in establishing transfer prices? What might cause this survey to provide less-than-accurate reasons for actual practices?

EXERCISES

1. Assume a VAT situation where the tax rate is 15 percent, with export sales exempt. The manufacturer does not purchase inputs on which VAT has been paid, and its net selling price to the wholesaler before VAT is £250. The wholesaler adds value of £300, and the retailer adds value of £500 to the consumer.

   a. What are the gross and net selling prices at the manufacturer, wholesaler, and retailer levels?

   b. How much in VAT is paid to the tax authorities at each level?

   c. What is the final amount that the domestic consumer pays, and how much of that is VAT?

   d. Would your answer to (c) be the same if the retailer were to export the goods instead of selling them to a domestic consumer?

2. ABC company has income from the following countries:

Country	Type of Operation	Gross Earnings	Income Tax Rate
United States	Parent	500,000	40%
X	Branch	(10,000)	25%
Y	Distribution	120,000	5%
Z	100%-owned	400,000	45%

   ABC's subsidiary in Z declares a 40 percent dividend; Z's withholding tax on dividends is 5 percent. Both the branch and the distribution facility, which is wholly owned, retain all earnings. The distribution earnings are considered to be foreign-based company sales income. What is ABC's final U. S. tax liability?

3. Puerto International has a branch in Mexico that manufactures a garage door alarm for people with mountain bike racks that fit on the top of their cars. The subsidiary earned 800,000 dollars in 2000 before tax, with Mexican corporate tax rates at 40 percent. Taxes were paid evenly throughout the year. How much income did Puerto have to include in its U. S. taxable income in 2000, and what was the tax credit?

4. In 2000, San Fernando drilling shipped 300 diamond drill bits to its subsidiary in Ecuador. The drill bits were shipped at San Fernando's cost of $1,000,000 each to avoid Ecuador's duty of 20 percent. In 2000, Ecuador's income tax on foreign subsidiaries was 35 percent and the U. S. corporate tax rate was 35 percent. In 2001 Ecuador proposes to raise the corporate tax rate to 45 percent, eliminate duties, and impose a 10 percent VAT. The U. S rate will remain the same.

   a. What action (if any) should San Fernando take on its export pricing?

   b. What possible U. S. government action may result from your decision in (a)?

5. As a U. S. congressman from South Carolina you are considering proposing a bill to eliminate a state income tax of 7 percent and a sales tax of 5 percent and replace it with a value-added tax of 10 percent. Discuss the pros and cons of such an action. You should note a typical South Carolina family spends about 80 percent of its taxable income on goods and services that would be covered by this tax.

CASE

Midwest Uniforms

Midwest Uniforms Inc. manufactures and sells cloth and disposable uniforms. The company also launders and delivers uniforms to hospitals, medical laboratories, and doctors' offices. The corporation is organized in the state of Michigan and operates three plants there—one that manufactures disposable uniforms and related supplies such as caps and masks; one that manufactures reusable cloth uniforms; and a plant that launders, presses, and delivers clean uniforms.

The company is owned by the Fulton family. Daniel Fulton, age 60, and his wife, Lauren, age 59, jointly own 40 percent of the corporation's one vote per share common stock. The Fultons' son, Michael, owns 20 percent of the common stock, their daughter, Meghan, owns 20 percent of the stock, and a family trust holds the remaining 20 percent for five grandchildren. Daniel manages the plant that manufactures disposable uniforms while Michael runs the cloth uniform plant, and Meghan manages the plant that launders and delivers uniforms.

During the early 1980s, the bulk of the demand for the company's disposable and cloth uniforms came from the midwest. In the late 1980s, the company saw increased demand for its disposable uniforms from outside the region and outside the United States. In the past few years, the company has started to supply disposable uniforms to companies in the hazardous waste cleanup industry. It expects its sales of disposable uniforms to hazardous waste companies to triple during the 1990s. The corporation had $4 million of revenue in 1992, of which $1,500,000 was attributable to the sale of disposable uniforms.

Midwest Uniforms' manufacturing plants are working at near capacity. The company has considered closing its laundering facility and converting it to a manufacturing plant. Many of its cloth uniform customers have indicated, however, that the company's ability to launder and deliver clean uniforms is one of the reasons they purchase uniforms from Midwest. The company also has considered expanding each of the manufacturing plants, since it has adequate land at each location. Because the demand for its cloth uniforms is still predominantly from the midwest while the demand for the disposable uniforms is becoming worldwide, Daniel Fulton has suggested that the company consider converting the disposable uniform plant to a cloth uniform plant and building a new disposable uniform manufacturing facility elsewhere.

Source: this case was prepared by Kathleen E. Sinning of Western Michigan University as a basis for class discussion rather than to illustrate either effective or ineffective handling of a situation. All rights reserved to the author. Permission to use this case was obtained from the author.

Daniel would like the company to build a disposable uniform plant in Puerto Rico. He and his wife are nearing retirement age and feel that if they located to a warmer climate, they would be able to work well beyond the age of 65. His estimates indicate that it would be less expensive to build the plant in Puerto Rico than in the midwest and that labor costs could be reduced by at least 25 percent and operating costs could be reduced by at least 20 percent.

The facility in Puerto Rico would operate as a branch of Midwest Uniforms. The raw materials would be shipped to Puerto Rico from the supplier in the United States and the uniforms, caps, masks, etc., that are manufactured would be shipped directly from the plant to customers worldwide. Daniel's research indicates that taxes are lower in Puerto Rico and that the United States provides a tax credit for foreign income taxes.

Michael Fulton is concerned about the potential labor unrest in Puerto Rico. He wants the company to organize a subsidiary in Hungary and call it Global Uniforms Inc. Since Hungary left socialism, it has been forced to deal with terrible pollution problems, as have other countries in the former eastern bloc. In fact, the pollution problems of these countries are a major obstacle to joining the Eastern Community (EC) since they must first comply with the environmental rules of the EC. Michael feels that by locating a plant in eastern Europe, the corporation will be able to take advantage of the emerging markets in that area and, as a result, more than triple its sales of disposable uniforms and supplies. His research also indicates that the corporation could cut labor costs by 30 percent and operating costs by 25 percent by locating to Hungary.

Michael is particularly interested in sheltering income from taxation so that the grandchildren in the family will have adequate funds to attend college and graduate school. He believes that organizing a foreign subsidiary would save the corporation taxes since his research indicates that a foreign corporation's U. S. shareholders are not taxed on the corporation's income until it is distributed to the shareholders as a dividend. He would like, if possible, to leave all the foreign earnings in the foreign company until the grandchildren are ready to attend college. He proposes that 20 percent of the stock of the subsidiary be owned by the family trust and 80 percent by Midwest Uniforms Inc.

Meghan, on the other hand, would like the corporation to expand the two existing manufacturing plants and continue to manufacture the disposable products in the United States. She is concerned that the U. S. taxation of worldwide income would actually result in a higher overall tax liability for the corporation. She believes that the corporation can increase its exports through sales offices located in foreign countries.

The current and projected revenue and expenses of Midwest Uniforms are included in Exhibit 1. The estimates assume that the plants will remain in the United States.

Tax Considerations of Doing Business In Puerto Rico[1]

In Puerto Rico, a corporation is considered to be a domestic corporation if it is organized under the laws of Puerto Rico and a foreign corporation if it is organized under the laws of another jurisdiction. A corporation is considered to be a resident of Puerto Rico if it is incorporated under the laws of Puerto Rico or, in the case of a foreign corporation, it is engaged in a trade or business in Puerto Rico. A Puerto Rican corporation is taxed on its worldwide income. A resident foreign corporation is taxed on all Puerto Rican source income and certain foreign income connected with Puerto Rican operations.

A corporation can use either a calendar or fiscal year in calculating its tax liability. Corporate tax is imposed at a flat rate of 22 percent. A surtax is imposed on taxable income, after a deduction of $25,000, at the rates indicated in Exhibit 2. There is no provision in Puerto Rico for filing consolidated returns. A controlled or affiliated group of corporations is limited to one surtax exemption that must be allocated among the members of the group.

---

[1] *Sources:* Price Waterhouse, New York (1991). *Corporate Taxes, A Worldwide Summary,* and Coopers & Lybrand (1991). *1991 International Tax Summaries, A Guide for Planning and Decision.* New York: Wiley.

Exhibit 1   Current and Projected Revenues and Expenses

Plant	1992	1993	1994	1995
Disposable uniforms				
Revenues	$1,500,0000	$2,000,000	$2,750,000	$3,500,000
CGS	400,000	550,000	745,000	945,000
Operating expenses	500,000	666,000	915,750	1,165,500
Cloth uniforms				
Revenues	2,000,000	2,500,000	2,750,000	3,000,000
CGS	600,000	750,000	825,000	900,000
Operating expenses	500,000	625,000	688,000	750,000
Laundry				
Revenues	500,000	550,000	600,000	650,000
CGS	100,000	110,000	120,000	130,000
Operating expenses	200,000	220,000	240,000	260,000

Exhibit 2   Corporate Surtax Rates in Puerto Rico

Surtax Net Income			
Over	Not Over	Tax on Column 1	Percentage on Excess
0	$75,000	—	6
$75,000	125,000	$4,500	16
125,000	175,000	12,500	17
175,000	225,000	21,000	18
225,000	275,000	30,000	19
275,000*		39,500	20

*In the case of a corporation whose net income subject to tax exceeds $500,000 for any taxable year, a tax of 5 percent of net income subject to tax in excess of $500,000 is imposed to phase out the benefits of the graduated tax rates.

A branch operating in Puerto Rico is taxed at the same rates as a corporation and is entitled to the same deductions and credits. Branches of foreign corporations are subject to income tax only on their Puerto Rican source income and on income effectively connected with a trade or business within Puerto Rico. In addition, foreign corporations doing business in Puerto Rico are subject to a branch profits tax (BPT). The BPT is 25 percent (10 percent for hotel, manufacturing, or shipping operations) and is applied to amounts deemed to be repatriated from the branch in Puerto Rico. The deemed dividend will generally be triggered if the branch has earnings and profits generated in Puerto Rico that are *not* reinvested in Puerto Rico. The BPT is not applicable to those corporations deriving at least 80 percent of their gross incomes from Puerto Rican sources.

To encourage industrialization in Puerto Rico, certain activities (basically manufacturing, export, maritime freight transportation, and certain service industries) may obtain partial exemption from income and property taxes and 60 percent exemption from municipal

Exhibit 3   Periods and Rates of Exemptions from Puerto Rico Taxes

Industrial Zones	1–5 Years	6–10 Years	11–15 Years	16–20 Years	21–25 Years
1. High industrial development	90%	90%	None	None	None
2. Intermediate industrial development	90%	90%	90%	None	None
3. Low industrial development	90%	90%	90%	90%	None
4. Vieques and Culebra	90%	90%	90%	90%	90%

license taxes. The municipal license taxes are 0.3 percent of gross receipts. The exemption can be obtained for a period of 10 to 25 years depending on the location of the business within the island. For purposes of the partial income exemption, Puerto Rico has been classified into four industrial zones. The periods and rates of exemption are included in Exhibit 3. In addition, the two principal harbors in Puerto Rico have been classified as foreign trade zones and foreign or domestic goods may be entered without a formal U. S. customs inspection and without the payment of any duties or excise taxes.

Tax Considerations of Doing Business in Hungary[2]

A company is considered a resident of Hungary if it is incorporated in and has its head office in Hungary. A foreign company cannot trade through a branch in Hungary, but it can open a representative office, a service office, or a construction site.

Resident corporations are taxed on their worldwide incomes. A business profits tax of 40 percent is levied on all Hungarian business entities. The tax rate is affected by tax incentives that are intended to encourage foreign investment in manufacturing corporations. The incentives are in the form of rebates. The tax rates after the rebates are included in Exhibit 4.

Entities subject to the business profits tax are not subject to other income taxes. Business entities of foreign ownership, however, are subject to an additional 4.5 percent levy on the business profits tax base.

A foreign company that trades in Hungary is subject to a corporate tax of 40 percent of the taxable income. The taxable income of a representative office is deemed to be 90 percent of the total of 6 percent of Hungarian sales made by its parent company and 90 percent of 5 percent of sales made outside Hungary if the representative office was involved.

[2] Ibid.

Exhibit 4   Business Profits Tax Rates in Hungary

Type of Entity	Rate
Standard rate for corporations	40%
Manufacturing entity owned more than 30% by foreigners	
First 5 years	16%
Second 5 years	24%
Manufacturing entity owned more than 30% by foreigners in a priority industry	
First 5 years	0
Second 5 years	16%

Questions

1. If the corporation builds a plant in Puerto Rico, can it use the foreign tax credit for any foreign taxes that it pays? Can the credit be used for taxes paid to Hungary?

2. If the corporation decides to build a plant in Puerto Rico, is there any other U.S. tax provision that it can use in lieu of or in addition to the foreign tax credit?

3. If the corporation organizes a subsidiary in Hungary, will the income of the corporation be subject to U.S. taxation? If so, when and how? Will the controlled foreign corporation rules apply to a subsidiary organized in Hungary?

4. What are the benefits of organizing a foreign sales corporation?

REFERENCES AND FURTHER READING

Anonymous. (1996). "Acceptable Transfer Pricing Methodologies." *International Tax Review* 7(2), 25.

Arpan, J. (1972). *Intracorporate Pricing: Non-American Systems and Views.* New York: Praeger.

Avi-Yonah, R. (1995). "The Rise and Fall of Arm's Length: A Study in the Evolution of U.S. International Taxation." *Virginia Tax Review* 15(1, Summer).

Baker, Al, M. Carsley, and R. O'Connor. (1997). "Two Approaches—One Result." *International Tax Review* 107–114.

Borstell, T. (1997). "Introduction to Transfer Pricing." *International Tax Review* (April): 3–8.

Burns, J. (1980). "Transfer Pricing Decisions in U. S. Multinational Corporations." *Journal of International Business Studies* (Fall): 23–39.

Cavusgil, S. (1996). "Transfer Pricing for Global Markets." *Columbia Journal of World Business* 31(4, Winter): 66–78.

Plasschaert, S. (1994). "The Multiple Motivations for Transfer Pricing Modulations in Multinational Enterprises and Governmental Counter-Measures: An Attempt at Clarification." *Management International Review* (34, First Quarter): 36–50.

Ruchelman, S.C., L. Schneidman, and F. B. Voght. (1998). "The Good, The Bad, and The Ugly: Recent Cases Addressing International Tax Transactions." *The International Tax Journal* 24(2, Spring): 1–35.

Tang, R. Y. W. (1992). "Transfer Pricing in the 1990s." *Management Accounting* (February): 22–26.

Tate, C. (1998). "Transfer Pricing: The New Tax Minefield." *Australian CPA* 68(6, July): 46–47.

Turner, R. (1998). "Proceed with Caution." *CA Magazine* 131 (6, August): 33–34.

SOME USEFUL INTERNET WEB SITES

1. KPMG Global Tax Services and Virtual Tax Library: *http://www.tax.kpmg.net/*
   This site provides access to a wide array of tax information for companies operating across borders, including the latest tax news from different countries and regions. Examples of stories early in 2000 include an extension of the U. S. /Mexico Maquiladora duty-free zone and a change to tax bases for Venezeula.

2. ISBC VAT Site: *http://www.isbc.com/isbc/business/vat-rates.cfm*
   A small business guide to VAT. Provides details on VAT rates in Europe.

3. VAT UK government site on VAT in Europe:
   http://www.hmce.gov.uk/bus/vat/info-vat.htm

4. OECD comparison of member tax rates by country.
   http://www.oecdwash.org/PRESS/CONTENT/incometaxrates.pdf

5. U.S. state personal income tax rates by state.
   http://www.taxadmin.org/fta/rate/ind_inc.html

6. U. S. state corporate income tax rates by state.
   http://www.fmsmpc.com/taxrates.html

CHAPTER SEVEN

GLOBAL FINANCIAL STATEMENT ANALYSIS

INTRODUCTION

This book emphasizes a management approach, with the view that managers must understand accounting and control issues as MNEs cross borders. The objective is to draw from these accounting systems the information that will allow managers to meet existing strategic objectives and refine different strategies. What is more, as global capital markets continue to broaden, all users of financial statements, be they private or financial analysts, need to understand something about international accounting in order to understand the financial reports of these companies.

Assuming the firm follows the classic international entry style, its first exposure to international accounting usually occurs as a result of an import or export opportunity. In its earliest trading opportunity a domestic company may receive an unsolicited inquiry or purchase order from a foreign buyer. Assuming the domestic company desires to make the sale, it needs to investigate the foreign buyer, particularly when the buyer asks for an extension of credit. This procedure is often not as easy as it appears. When the foreign company offers a balance sheet and income statement for analysis, several things immediately become evident. First, the language and currency are often different. Second, the terminology is different. Third, the types and amount of information disclosed are likely to be different. Also, the procedures that were followed to arrive at the final figures are likely to be different. Differences in approaches to valuation, recognition, or realization render the financial statements meaningless unless the analyst is familiar with the foreign country's accounting system.

Stage two of a global involvement strategy often involves foreign direct investment (FDI). Such FDI, if it involves the creation or purchase of a business entity in another country, usually requires that the parent take on the responsibility for the subsidiaries' financial statements. This involves home-based personnel analyzing and, in the years after the purchase, developing financial statements in each of the countries where it has operating subsidiaries. It must also prepare a set of financial statements consistent with accounting standards and practices in its home country for consolidation and reporting purposes.

As a firm enters the realm of a global MNE doing business in a large number of countries, it may choose for business and financial reasons to list in a global capital market such as New York or London. If this is neither the firm's home base nor a country whose accounting rules it uses, the aspiring capital raiser must either prepare accounts in the generally accepted accounting principles (GAAP) of the market in which it is raising capital or prepare a reconciliation to that GAAP. The best example of this is Form 20-F required by the SEC, which requires firms to reconcile their financial statements to U.S. GAAP.

In all of the circumstances described above, the ability to assess differences in accounting rules between countries is paramount. This chapter begins the examination of global diversity of financial reporting. Diversity or differences in *financial reporting practices* (FRPs) between countries affect both the users and preparers of financial statements.

Table 7.1 gives some idea of how the users and preparers of financial statements are impacted by the global diversity in financial reporting. About half of those responding to a survey by Choi and Levich (1997) claimed to be affected by such diversity. Of the affected groups, the issue that caused the most concern was the constant need to revalue investments and adjust calculations of required returns to reflect these revaluations. Microsoft, for example, makes its results electronically available in six different GAAPs, each with a different result. We replicate four of these in Table. 7.2.

Those who were unaffected by diversity in financial reporting, however, included many individuals who had created some form of coping mechanism. Some of these coping strategies included:

- Restating foreign statements to their own GAAP
- Learning about foreign GAAP
- Using other strategies/information

The creation of a coping mechanism is not free, however, and those who are unaffected due to the existence of a coping mechanism had incurred real costs to deal with accounting diversity.

Table 7.1   Capital Market Effects of Accounting Diversity: Summary Findings for Investors, Issuers, Underwriters, Regulators, and Others

	Yes	No	N.A.	Total
\multicolumn{5}{c}{Key question: Does accounting diversity affect your capital market decisions?}				
Investors	9	7	1	17
Issuers	6	9		15
Underwriters	7	1		8
Regulators	0	8		8
Raters and others	2	1		3
Total	24	26	1	51

Source: Choi and Levich (1997), *Handbook of International Accounting,* 6–17.

Table 7.2   Microsoft Corporation
Consolidated Statement of Earnings Year Ended June 30, 1999

	Australian GAAP	Canadian GAAP	U.K. GAAP	French GAAP
Net income—after tax foreign GAAP	$10,658	$10,794	$10,529	$7,783
Preferred stock dividends provided for or paid	-$28			
Acquired in-process technology	$0	$99		
Tax benefit of stock options	-$2,873	-$3,107	-$2,743	
Other adjustments unspecified	$29	$0	$0	$3
Net income—U.S. GAAP	$7,786	$7,786	$7,786	$7,786
NIBT	11,891	11,793	11,892	11,888

Note. Non-U.S. results are unaudited with convenience translations to U.S. dollars provided by the authors.
Source: http://www.eu.microsoft.com/msft/ar.htm.

ENVIRONMENTAL INFLUENCES ON FINANCIAL REPORTING

As with business in general, corporate financial reporting and information disclosure practices are influenced by a variety of economic, social, and political factors. The nature of the financial reporting systems at the country level will vary according to the relative influence of each of these environmental factors and such financial reporting systems will, in turn, tend to reinforce established patterns of behavior. The nature of these influences and how they are likely to operate is as follows:

- *Enterprise ownership.* The need for public accountability and disclosure will be greater where there is a broad ownership of shares compared to family ownership. Further, with state ownership, the influence of centralized control on the nature of financial reporting systems will tend to override the microeconomic objectives of the firm.

- *The activities of enterprises* will also influence the nature of the financial reporting system depending on whether the business is agricultural, extractive, or manufacturing; whether it is diversified; whether it is multinational; and whether it is a large group of companies or a small business.

- *The sources of finance* are another important influence. Clearly, there will be more pressure for public accountability and information disclosure when finance is raised from external shareholders rather than banks or family sources, where information will be available more directly.

- *Taxation* is a very important factor in situations where financial reporting systems are strongly influenced by state objectives. In countries like France, Germany, and Japan, public financial reports are used as a basis for determining tax liabilities. In the United States and the United Kingdom, on the other hand, the published accounts are adjusted for tax purposes and submitted separately from the reports to shareholders.

- *The level of development and independence of the auditing and financial reporting profession.* A more developed financial profession is more likely in a judgmentally based public financial reporting system rather than in more centralized and uniform systems. Furthermore, the development of professional financial reporting will depend on the existence of a sound infrastructure of financial reporting education and research, which is often lacking in, for example, developing countries.

- *The social climate,* that is, attitudes informing and consulting employees and toward environmental concerns, will also be influential. In Europe, for example, there is a much more positive approach to the disclosure of information relating to such matters than in the United States.

- *The stage of economic growth and development* will also be influential insofar as a change from an agricultural to a manufacturing economy will pose new financial reporting problems, such as the depreciation of machinery, leasing, and so on. In many countries, services are now becoming more important, and thus problems related to how to account for intangible assets such as brand names, goodwill, and human resources have become significant.

- *The legal system* is also important in determining the extent to which company law governs the regulations of financial reporting. In countries such as France and Germany, with a tradition of codified Roman law (or civil codes)—versus common law as in the United Kingdom and the United States—financial reporting regulations tend to be detailed and comprehensive. Furthermore, the influence of the financial reporting profession in setting financial reporting standards tends to be much less in such countries compared with countries such as the United Kingdom and the United States, where company law is supplemented by professional regulation.

- *The influence of culture* (i.e., societal or national values) on financial traditions and practices needs to be taken into account. Culture is "the software of the mind," the most basic values held by a society. Culture acts as a sounding board against which all changes in institutional or other arrangements are measured.

- Finally, *international factors* are also bringing about changes in the environment that are bringing about harmonization in international financial reporting in contrast to the constraining influences operating at national levels.

Naturally, the influence of each of these factors is dynamic and will vary both between and within countries over time. Moreover, an evolutionary process of some complexity appears to be at work, and this is reflected in a growing number of international and regional influences. These include the activities of MNEs and intergovernmental organizations as the International Accounting Standards Committee (IASC).

While there are many differences in national environments, with correspondingly varying effects on financial reporting systems, there are also many similarities. Attempts to classify countries and identify patterns or groupings appear to be a useful way to gain a better understanding of the key factors influencing the development of financial reporting systems and thus help us predict likely changes and their impact.

CLASSIFICATION OF FINANCIAL REPORTING SYSTEMS

There have been many academic attempts to classify and explain why countries are different in their financial reporting practices. Two models with somewhat different perspectives are those of Nobes (1983) and Gray (1988). Both of these models provide a basic idea of why accounting systems are different and how they might be expected to react to possible attempts to change them.

Nobes Model

In an article by Nobes (1983), a hierarchical scheme of classification is used to describe how the accounting world might be divided up (see Figure 7.1). This structure traces the origin and purpose of financial reporting in a small set of developed countries. Nobes made an initial basic distinction between classes of financial reporting systems using their origin and original purpose as the basis for allocating countries to one classification group or another.

Nobes envisaged two basic classes of financial systems: a microeconomic system (business oriented and designed to serve providers of capital), and a macroeconomic (government-oriented) system. Nobes proposed two further subclasses as follows:

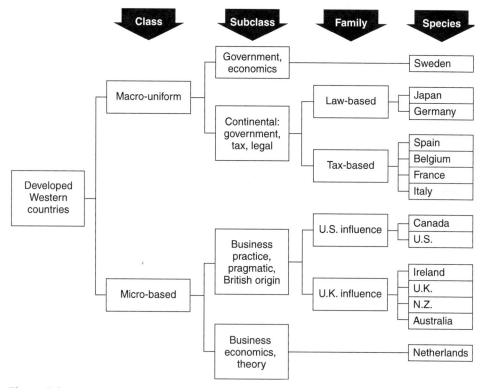

Figure 7.1   Nobes Classification Model

Source: C.W. Nobes, "A Judgmental International Classification of Financial Reporting Practices," *Journal of Business Finance and Accounting* (Spring 1983): 7.

1. The macroeconomic system, based on the use that is made by the government of accounting data (taxation or economic management)

2. The microeconomic system, where basic philosophy (pure microeconomic measurement vs. practitioner judgment) and historical origin (U.K. and U.S.) are the key determinants.

Nobes's list of factors that separate systems is also interesting in that it is a mix of practice and fundamental reasons. This list is contained in Table 7.3. A test of Nobes's model by Doupnik and Salter shows it, at least in 1993, to be fairly accurate in predicting patterns of actual financial reporting practice.

Gray Model

While many studies attempt to explain why financial reporting might be different cross-nationally, few had examined the question of how the fundamental values of a society might affect financial reporting. Further, the available studies were fairly unidimensional, concentrating on financial reporting practice rather than creating an overall picture of the elements that make up the financial reporting system.

Gray (1988) provided a more comprehensive model based on an analysis of accounting values. The model itself incorporated earlier work on societal values by Hofstede (1980). Gray's dimensions are contained in Table 7.4.

Reflect for a moment on the history and culture of two contrasting economic superpowers, the United States and Japan. The U.S. culture can be traced directly to American history and geography. America is a country founded by persons seeking to improve themselves and willing to take risks to do so. The relatively low population density and wide-open spaces that the new land offered supplemented this population influx effect. Settlement of this empty land required individuals who were self-sufficient. The American culture is thus one of high individualism and thrives on uncertainty, a culture where the rights of the individual are protected by the legal and economic structure. The values of individualism that are the basis of U.S. culture are reflected in the key documents of American history, such as the Declaration of Independence and the Constitution.

Table 7.3 Factors for Differentiation of Financial Reporting Systems

1. Type of users of the published accounts of the listed companies
2. Degree to which law or standards prescribe in detail and exclude judgment
3. Importance of tax rules in measurement
4. Conservatism/prudence (e.g., valuation of buildings, stocks, debtors)
5. Strictness of application of historic cost (in the historic cost accounts)
6. Susceptibility to replacement cost adjustments in main or supplementary accounts
7. Consolidation practices
8. Ability to be generous with provisions (as opposed to reserves) and to smooth income
9. Uniformity between companies in application of rules

Source: C.W. Nobes, "A Judgmental International Classification of Financial Reporting Practices," *Journal of Business Finance and Accounting* (Spring 1983): 7.

Table 7.4   Gray's Financial Reporting (Subculture) Values

---

1. *Professionalism versus statutory control:* This value reflects a preference for the exercise of individual professional judgment and the maintenance of professional self-regulation as opposed to compliance with prescriptive legal requirements and statutory control.

2. *Uniformity versus flexibility:* This value reflects a preference for the enforcement of uniform financial reporting practices between companies and for the consistent use of such practices over time, as opposed to flexibility in accordance with the perceived circumstances of individual companies.

3. *Conservatism versus optimism:* This value reflects a preference for a cautious approach to measurement that enables one to cope with the uncertainty of future events as opposed to a more optimistic, laissez-faire, risk-taking approach.

4. *Secrecy versus transparency:* This value reflects a preference for confidentiality and the disclosure of information about the business only to those who are most closely involved with its management and financing as opposed to a more transparent, open, and publicly accountable approach.

Thus we would expect the American financial reporting system to be one that demands protection of the individual through high levels of disclosure, a strong independent audit profession, and yet still reflects a relatively optimistic view of the future. This to a large measure is a good description of current U.S. GAAP and SEC disclosure rules.

While obviously it could be argued that culture can be partially offset by taxation and markets, it seems that even in these areas there appears to be an interaction as presented by Gray (1988). For example, in the United States there is a separation of GAAP financial reporting and financial reporting for taxes, where information and taxes do not mix.

If one examines Japan using the same model, we find a country with little geographic wealth, which is periodically battered by typhoons, and earthquakes and where survival required a group effort and there is little room for individual deviance. It also has a strong sense of honor and distance between rulers and ruled. Given this situation it is hardly surprising that a culture of communality led by strong leaders arose. In addition, it is again not surprising that financial reporting arises from the government and serves to provide information to the whole community in the form of government tax returns and certain other reports.

Individual shareholders are a secondary consideration and income measurement is conservative to permit the building of group wealth with a minimum of reduction through taxation. Given the sense of community among investors and companies, it is hardly surprising that auditors are, at best, viewed as unnecessary and, at worst, unwelcome.

In these extremes one can see the two ends of a cultural spectrum and how it impacts the elements of the financial reporting system. Culture, described by Hofstede as "software of the mind," is the sum of the most fundamental values that a society holds. It impacts on all levels of decision making, including accounting. Gray (1988) shows how culture may be formed and may impact on accounting by forming a set of accounting values.

Gray's model, like that of Nobes, has been tested empirically. Salter and Niswander (1995) concluded from an empirical study of twenty-nine countries that Gray's model "provided a workable theory to explain cross-national differences in financial reporting structure and practice which is particularly strong in explaining

Table 7.5   Salter and Niswander (1995)—A Test of Gray's Model (1988)

Hofstede Values	Individualism (IND)	Uncertainty Avoidance (UA)	Power Distance (PD)	Masculinity (MASC)
Gray's Subvalues				
Professionalism				
Proposed Relationship	Positive	Negative	Negative	N.S.
Result	N.S.	Negative	N.S.	N.S.
Uniformity				
Proposed Relationship	Negative	Positive	Positive	N.S.
Result	N.S.	Positive	N.S.	Negative
Conservatism				
Proposed Relationship	Negative	Positive	N.S.	Negative
Result	N.S.	Positive	N.S.	Negative
Secrecy				
Proposed Relationship	Negative	Positive	Positive	Negative
Result	Negative	Positive	N.S.	N.S.

Notes: N.S. means "not significant," i.e., not significant at p-05.
   Results are p-values with signs from the applicable parameter.
Source: S.B. Salter and F. Niswander (1995).

different financial reporting practices." Integrating the work of Salter and Niswander (1995) and Gray (1988), it would appear that societies that are individualist in nature (e.g., Australia, United Kingdom, and United States) will demand more disclosure and a stronger independent audit profession to ensure the rights of the individual investor. Other countries, such as Japan and Germany, that are relatively high in uncertainty avoidance may opt for extremely uniform accounting rules passing through the legal system. Finally, to explain professional and regulatory structures, Salter and Niswander suggested that the inclusion of variables such as the development of financial markets and levels of taxation enhance the explanatory power of the model. They note that both of these factors enhance the power of auditors and encourage increased disclosure and a more optimistic view of income. Higher tax rates, by contrast, encourage measures that will reduce income and the relative power of auditors. Gray's hypotheses and the results of Salter and Niswander are shown in Table 7.5.

FINANCIAL REPORTING VALUES AND INTERNATIONAL CLASSIFICATION

Drawing together the thoughts of Gray and Nobes, a useful distinction emerges in trying to understand financial reporting systems of other countries. Essentially there are two key parameters that define such systems:

1. *The authority for financial reporting systems*—that is, the extent to which such systems are determined and enforced by statutory control or professional means.

2. *The measurement and disclosure characteristics of financial reporting systems.* In this way, financial reporting values can be linked to specific financial reporting system characteristics.

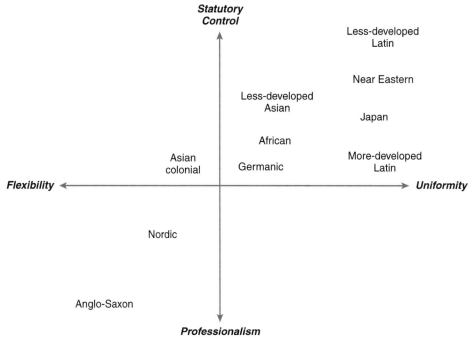

Figure 7.2   Accounting Systems: Authority and Enforcement

Source: S.J. Gray, "Towards a Theory of Cultural Influence on the Development of Accounting Systems Internationally," *Abacus* (March 1988): 12.

Gray's interpretation on how the countries of the world may be classified using these parameters is contained in Figures 7.2 and 7.3.

MAJOR DIFFERENCES IN FINANCIAL REPORTING

Financial reporting issues that separate countries can be divided into *format, measurement,* and *disclosure.* Let us look here primarily at the impact and differences caused by variations in format and measurement principles between countries. Disclosure issues will be discussed in some detail in the next chapter.

Format

The format of the financial statements includes the statements that are used and what they contain. Most countries have a statement that reports the income and expenses of the company, and another reporting the company's assets and liabilities. Less common statements include the *statement of cash flows/statement of changes in financial position,* and a separate *statement of retained earnings.* Some countries include management discussion, notes, and other items such as environmental or social data in their annual report.

Within the various statements, formats also considerably vary from country to country. The interested reader can obtain a good description of current financial reporting practices in a wide variety of countries by accessing the Marriott School of Management's International Accounting Practices Web page or the Fortune

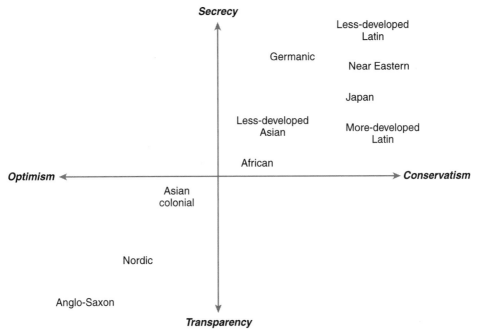

Figure 7.3   Accounting Systems: Measurement and Disclosure

Source: S.J. Gray, "Towards a Theory of Cultural Influence on the Development of Accounting Systems Internationally," *Abacus* (March 1988): 13.

Global 500 Web page. The listing at the end of the chapter contains these Web addresses and those of several major global corporations that provide their annual financial statements on the Web.

An examination of either of these sources of annual reports should include the following four questions on the format:

1. At what level is the company reporting? In the United Kingdom and the United States, consolidated accounts have been the rule for many years. In other countries this is a fairly recent arrival and some companies still provide separate statements for the parent and subsidiaries.

2. Which statements are present?

3. What is the flow of the statement, that is, reading from top to bottom, which items are first and which last?

4. Is there any netting or subtotals as we go along?

To give you a start, Table 7.6 compares H.J. Heinz (U.S.), Philips (Netherlands), and British Telecom (U.K.). Remember these companies all come from fairly similar cultures. You should notice the following from Table 7.6:

- The Europeans use the term *group accounts,* where group means *consolidated.* Many European companies will produce separate reports for the group and individual holding companies. Group accounts are now required by European Union rules. In some countries in Europe (e.g., France), group accounts can be produced using a substantially different

Table 7.6   A Comparison of Reporting at Three Major Companies

	H.J. Heinz	British Telecom	Philips
Entity Reported On	Consolidated	Group	Group
Statements reporting income and expenses	Consolidated statement of income and retained earnings	Group profit & loss account	Consolidated statement of income of group
Statements reporting assets, liabilities, and equity	Consolidated balance sheet	Group balance sheet	Consolidated balance sheet of group
Statements reporting cash flow	Consolidated statements of cash flows	Group cash flow statement	Consolidated statement of cash flows of the group
Other statements	Statement of retained earnings (part of income statement)	Group statement of total recognized gains and losses (separate)	None
Level of detail	High	Low—lots of summary headings	Lowest
Subtotals of income	Net income	Net income	Net income
Subtotals in the balance sheet	Assets; Liabilities and Owner's Equity	(1) Computation of Net Current Assets (2) Total Current Assets Less Liabilities No Bottom-line	Assets; Liabilities and Owner's Equity
Subtotals in the cash flow statement	Cash from various sources	Similar to United States	Similar to United States
Order/flow of statements income	Revenue>>>expenses	Turnover>>> expenses	Sales>>>expenses
Order/flow—balance sheet	Current>>> less current	Long term>>>short term>>>net	Long term>>> short term

set of financial reporting practices (FRPs) than those used at the individual company level.

- Heinz provides considerable detail on the face of its statements. British Telecom and Philips provide relatively less, with more information being left to the notes. The exception is the very detailed cash flow statement for Philips.

- Both European companies begin the balance sheet with long-term, relatively illiquid items (Fixed Assets) and then move to the more liquid items. The United States does the reverse.

- British balance sheets never arrive at a bottom line figure for Total Assets or Total Liabilities. Instead, Net Current Assets (Current Assets minus Current Liabilities) is computed. This item, in turn, is netted against Fixed Assets, and the total balanced against Shareholder Funds (Shareholders Equity). Both the U.S. and Dutch companies do arrive at the bottom line for total assets, which is balanced against Liabilities and Shareholders Equity.

Measurement

The second major source of differences is the issue of measurement of accounting items reported on the balance sheet, income statement, and the cash flow statements. Measurement describes how particular items that appear in the financial statements and notes are calculated and valued. Measurement is one of the key causes of accounting diversity. It should be remembered that even in a single country, a variety of measurement principles could exist. In the United States, for example, LIFO, FIFO, or even weighted average can represent inventory flow. Some general comments on measurement can be made for the groups defined according to cultural regions.

With respect to the measurement basis used, the conservative application of historical cost is generally required in the Germanic, Latin and certain Asian countries. Anglo-Saxon and Nordic countries tend to be more flexible, permitting considerable usage of current or market values in addition to historic cost. The United Kingdom and the Netherlands are examples of countries that fall within this category. Although often considered an Anglo country, the United States retains a conservative historical cost approach to fixed assets while permitting market valuations in very limited circumstances such as accounting for acquisitions and certain intangibles such as brands and publishing rights.

The following are brief descriptions of major areas of global financial reporting diversity:

- *Depreciation* in Anglo-Saxon and Nordic countries tends to be based on the concept of useful economic life, whereas in the Germanic, Latin, and Asian countries the tax rules generally encourage more accelerated methods.

- *Inventory measurement* is generally based on the principle of "lower of cost or market," with some variation in the meaning of market value in some countries, or cost in others. LIFO (last-in, first-out) is sometimes permitted for tax purposes (e.g., United States, Japan) but more often it is not (United Kingdom, Germany, France, Italy, Brazil).

- *Retirement benefits* are accounted for in different ways. In Anglo-Saxon and Nordic countries a liability is created on the basis of accrued and/or projected benefits likely to be payable to employees. In contrast, some Latin and Asian countries have a more pay-as-you-go approach.

- *Construction contracts* are generally accounted for using the percentage of completion method in Anglo-Saxon and Latin countries, but the completed contract method tends to be used in the Germanic countries.

- *Research and development* costs are usually expensed immediately in the Anglo-Saxon and Germanic countries, although capitalization of development expenses is permitted in the United Kingdom.

- *Accounting for taxation* is a major area of differentiation between Anglo-Saxon countries and the Germanic, Latin, and Asian countries. Since the latter groups' approach to the measurement of accounting income is strongly influenced by tax rules, they have little need for a detailed system of deferred income tax accounting. In contrast, in the United States, United Kingdom, and Canada, income for tax purposes often bears little or no resemblance to income related by GAAP. A detailed system of income tax allocation is thus required.

- *Business combinations* (mergers/acquisitions) and the resulting goodwill have been probably the largest sources of discord among the Anglo countries. While the purchase method is generally required, controversy centers on how to account for the treatment of that portion of the purchase price that cannot be accounted for by the value of assets received (goodwill). In the United States and Canada, goodwill is amortized over a period of time to income. In contrast, the Netherlands, for example, permits immediate writeoff of goodwill against equity. Thus, goodwill never directly impacts on the income statement.

Although there is a growing awareness of this diversity of measurement principles and practices internationally, there is much less known about the overall impact of accounting differences on earnings and shareholders' equity. After all, differences with respect to various aspects of measurement may well compensate for each other to the extent that their overall impact may not be significant. The important question is whether accounting differences systematically impact on measures of income. In other words, do these differences really matter?

IMPACT OF ACCOUNTING DIFFERENCES

In understanding the development of accounting internationally, conservatism is a dimension along which financial reporting practices in particular countries can be described. *Conservatism* philosophically reflects a preference for a cautious approach to measurement that enables one to cope with the uncertainty of future events as opposed to a more optimistic, laissez-faire, risk-taking approach. Gray (1980) has presented an idea of how conservatism might be measured in practice. Conservatism was defined as the extent to which, given the same basic accounting data, two companies would arrive at earnings numbers that are higher or lower. To the extent that one country's GAAP generated a higher net income than another's using the same base bookkeeping data, it may be seen to be less conservative and de facto more optimistic.

Beginning with Gray's (1980) methodology, we examine two "flexible" countries, the United States and the United Kingdom. Gray (1980) provides the following formula:

$$\text{Index of conservatism} = 1 - ((\text{RA} - \text{RD}) / |\text{RA}|)$$

where

> RA = adjusted earnings under the GAAP of the country we are using as our standard
>
> RD = disclosed earnings under the national GAAP of the country whose conservatism we are assessing
>
> |RA| = the absolute value of adjusted earnings under the GAAP of the country we are using as our standard

Using the United States as our base and comparing U.S. versus U.K. accounting principles, this becomes:

$$\text{Index of conservatism} = 1 - (\text{U.S. GAAP earnings} - \text{U.K. GAAP earnings}) / |\text{U.S. GAAP earnings}|$$

Table 7.7 Conservatism Index

	U.K. GAAP (£ million)	U.S. GAAP (£ million)	Conservatism Index
Earnings 1998	110	100	$1 - (100 - 110)/100 = 1.1$
Earnings 1997	90	100	$1 - (100 - 90/100) = .9$

Note: The data can also be restated in dollar terms as required.

An index value *greater than* 1 means that U.K. GAAP earnings are less conservative (more optimistic) than U.S. GAAP. U.K. GAAP would achieve a higher net income than U.S. GAAP would have with the same data. An index value *less than* 1 means that U.K. earnings are more conservative than the U.S. measure would have been. An index value *equal* to 1 indicates neutrality between the two systems with respect to the effect of accounting principles. The denominator has been taken as U.S. GAAP earnings to provide a benchmark against which U.K. GAAP earnings can be compared. Remember, both the U.S. and U.K. calculations begin with the same basic data. To illustrate the effect of the index, take the two examples in Table 7.7.

Having established an overall index of conservatism, it is then possible to establish the relative effect of the various individual adjustments by constructing partial indices of adjustment using the formula:

Partial index of conservatism = 1 − (partial adjustment/U.S. GAAP earnings).

Table 7.8 provides an example.

Conservatism and SEC Form 20-F

An opportunity to compare earnings resulting from any country's accounting principles with those that would have resulted under U.S. accounting principles is given by examining those non-U.S. corporations obliged to report to the Securities and Exchange Commission (SEC) in the United States using Form 20-F. The Form 20-F report to the SEC contains a reconciliation of foreign earnings with the earnings that would have been reported under U.S. GAAP. The effect of each accounting

Table 7.8 Partial Conservatism Index

Item	£ Million
U.K. GAAP Earnings	120
Adjustments to compute U.S. GAAP earnings	
Deferred taxation	(15)
Goodwill amortization	(5)
Adjusted earnings per U.S. GAAP	100
Overall index of conservatism	1.2
Partial index—deferred taxation	$1 - (-15/100) = 1.15$
Partial index—goodwill	$1 - (-5/100) = 1.05$

Note 18—United States Generally Accepted Accounting Principles

	Year Ended June 30 (in millions)		
	1996	**1997**	**1998**
Net income as reported in the consolidated statements of operations	A$ 1,020	A$ 720	A$ 1,682
Items increasing (decreasing) reported income before minority interest:			
Amortization of publishing rights, titles, and television licenses	(256)	(318)	(552)
Net deferred taxes related to the amortization of publishing rights, titles, and television licenses	(30)	(32)	(40)
Amortization of excess of cost over net assets acquired	16	13	17
Equity in earnings of associated companies	(51)	(235)	(288)
Revaluation of non-current assets	(76)	-	-
Developing business start-up costs	(59)	(239)	(145)
Other, net	(28)	(32)	(32)
Net decrease in reported income before minority interest	(484)	(843)	(1,040)
Approximate income before minority interest in accordance with accounting principles generally accepted in the United States	536	(123)	642
Minority interest	(53)	(76)	(87)
Approximate net income in accordance with accounting principles generally accepted in the United States	A$ 483	A$ (199)	A$ 555

Figure 7.4   The News Corporation Limited and Subsidiaries: Notes to Consolidated Financial Statements

policy, which differs between the two countries, is quantified separately. In addition to the quantified difference, the accounting policies as they affect the corporation are explained by way of notes, which occasionally give further insight into the difference between foreign and U.S. accounting practice. The SEC requires a report on Form 20-F where the foreign corporation sponsors an ADR (American depository receipt), which is traded on one of the national stock exchanges. An example of Form 20-F forms the basis of the case later in the chapter, British Telecom. See also News Corporation's U.S. GAAP reconciliation from Australian GAAP, which shows significantly lower profits and equity (Figure 7.4).

Other examples can be found on the Web by looking up any company's financial statements and searching for the words "U.S. GAAP." An interesting reverse opportunity to test conservatism can be obtained from Microsoft's Website, which provides its results in multiple GAAPs at the touch of a button.

The reconciliation disclosed in Form 20-F has been used to test whether a country's GAAP earnings before extraordinary items are systematically less conservative than they would be if the U.S. GAAP were applied. Weetman and Gray (1990), based on U.S. GAAP reconciliations of thirty-seven U.K. corporations from 1985 to 1987, concluded that U.K. earnings were, on average, between 9 and 25 percent higher than U.S. earnings, as a result of differences in accounting principles between the two countries, with a mean difference of 16.8 percent. The most

Note 18—United States Generally Accepted Accounting Principles

	As of June 30 (in millions)	
	1997	**1998**
Stockholders' equity as reported in the consolidated balance sheets	A$ 22,234	A$ 27,211
Items increasing (decreasing) reported equity:		
Publishing rights, titles, and television licenses:		
Revaluation and other	(4,188)	(5,366)
Amortization	(1,988)	(2,441)
Excess cost over net assets acquired:		
Effect of adopting SFAS No. 109 and other	1,991	2,397
Amortization	169	186
Accounts payable and other—noncurrent:		
Effect of adopting SFAS No. 109 and other deferred taxes	(2,445)	(2,923)
Other	(156)	(190)
Investments:		
Elimination of associated company's interest in TNCL	(530)	-
Associated companies reserve	(744)	(1,050)
Reclassification of minority interest in subsidiaries	(2,930)	(1,951)
Other	(121)	(160)
Net decrease in reported stockholders' equity	(10,942)	(11,498)
Approximate stockholders' equity in accordance with accounting principles generally accepted in the United States	A$ 11,292	A$ 15,713

Figure 7.4   (*Continued*)

common source of differences was the method used to account for goodwill and deferred taxes. A 1998 update (Weetman et al., 1998) finds that the United Kingdom was, if anything, more optimistic at 25.4 percent.

Drawing together a number of studies, Radebaugh and Gray (1997) have drawn up indices of conservatism for eight countries representative of most of the cultural groups defined in Gray (1988) (see Figure 7.5). Interestingly, although U.S. accounting textbooks are littered with references to the need to be conservative, Radebaugh and Gray's study would seem to indicate that U.S. GAAP would tend to generate a higher net income than any other major country except the United Kingdom.

GLOBAL HARMONIZATION

While a number of organizations around the world, including the UN and EU, have been concerned with harmonizing international differences in accounting and reporting, the most important body in recent years has been the International

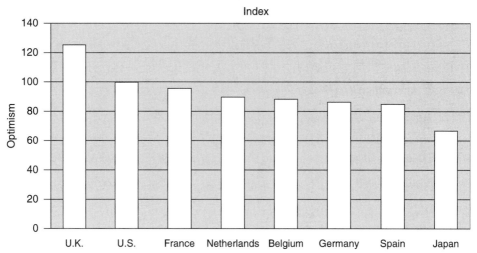

Figure 7.5 The Comparative Impact of International Accounting Differences on Earnings: Earnings Adjustment Index Based on U.S. GAAP

Accounting Standards Committee (IASC). The IASC was established in 1973 by leading professional accounting organizations in Australia, Canada, France, Germany, Ireland, Japan, Mexico, the Netherlands, the United Kingdom, and the United States. It now has a membership comprising 143 accounting organizations in 104 countries, including the founder members, most of whom maintain membership on the governing board and thus retain a significant measure of influence.

The main aim of international accounting standards has been to achieve a degree of comparability that will help investors make their decisions while reducing the costs of MNEs in preparing multiple sets of accounts and reports. It is also fair to say that IASC sees itself as having a major role to play in coordinating and harmonizing the activities of the many agencies involved in setting accounting and reporting standards. The IASC's standards are also intended to provide a useful model for developing countries wishing to establish accounting standards for the first time.

In the early days of IASC, international standards were developed allowing substantial flexibility to accommodate different national interests, but since the late 1980s, there has been growing pressure to develop more uniform standards to facilitate cross-border capital raisings and stock exchange listings. A core standards program to promote the development of more uniform and high-quality standards was initiated in cooperation with the International Organization of Securities Commissions (IOSCO) and was completed in 1998. The IASC is now hoping that IOSCO endorsement will lead to a greater recognition of international accounting standards (IASs) and the promotion of global harmonization at least among MNEs. The IASC has so far approved thirty-nine international accounting standards and has already gained acceptance by many stock exchanges around the world, although often subject to certain conditions (see Table 7.9). A growing number of companies are also electing to follow IASs (see Table 7.10), although compliance is not always as comprehensive in practice as claimed (Street, Bryant, and Gray, 1999).

The key question now is whether IOSCO members, and especially the United States, will accept IASs wholeheartedly as global standards with equal, if not greater, status compared to domestic standards. A crucial part of this acceptance is a re-

Table 7.9   IAS Financial Statements Allowed for Foreign Listed Companies: Selected Stock Exchanges

Argentina	**Buenos Aires Stock Exchange** Foreign companies may follow Argentine GAAP. Alternatively, they may follow IAS or their national GAAP, in which case they must include a reconciliation to Argentine GAAP.
Australia	**Australian Stock Exchange** Foreign listed companies may follow IAS.
Austria	**Wiener Börse (Vienna Stock Exchange)** Either IAS or U.S. GAAP financial statements must be used starting 2001 for domestic and foreign registrants listed on the A-Market or Austrian Growth Market. Listed companies not on the A-Market or AGM may use IAS or U.S. GAAP.
Canada	**Montreal Stock Exchange** Allows foreign companies to use IAS or U.S., U.K., or Australian GAAP, with advance permission and with a reconciliation to Canadian GAAP in the notes.
China (PRC)	**Shanghai Stock Exchange, Shenzen Stock Exchange** Companies that have issued B-Shares (these trade in China and overseas) must follow IAS. Companies that have issued H-Shares (these trade in Hong Kong only) may follow either IAS or Hong Kong accounting standards. Companies that have issued A-Shares (these trade in China only) must follow accounting standards promulgated by the PRC Ministry of Finance.
Europe	**EASDAQ (European Association of Securities Dealers Automated Quotation) Exchange** All listed companies, including domestic, may follow IAS.
Finland	**Helsinki Exchanges** Foreign listed companies may follow IAS or U.S. or U.K. GAAP or their national GAAP, with advance permission of the regulatory authority and with reconciliation to Finnish GAAP. Also, domestic listed companies may follow IAS if more than 50% of the shares are owned by foreigners or if the company is listed in an OECD country outside the European Economic Area, again with reconciliation to Finnish GAAP.
France	**Paris Stock Exchange** Foreign and domestic companies may follow IAS for consolidated financial statements, but only after IAS have been adopted by the Comité de la Réglementation Comptable.
Germany	**Deutsche Börse, Frankfurt Stock Exchange, Bavarian Stock Exchange, Stuttgart Stock Exchange** Foreign listed companies may follow German GAAP, IAS, or U.S. GAAP. Domestic companies also may follow IAS, U.S. GAAP, U.K. GAAP, or their national GAAP for consolidated financial statements. Neuer Markt companies must follow IAS or U.S. GAAP.
Hong Kong	**Stock Exchange of Hong Kong** Foreign listed companies may follow either Hong Kong GAAP or IAS with a reconciliation to Hong Kong GAAP. The Exchange allows some foreign companies to use U.K. GAAP, on a case-by-case basis. If the Stock Exchange of Hong Kong is the company's secondary listing, rather than primary listing, the company may follow the accounting principles of the market of primary listing. Domestic companies must follow Hong Kong GAAP.
Italy	**Rome Stock Exchange** Foreign and domestic companies may follow IAS for consolidated financial statements.

Table 7.9 IAS Financial Statements Allowed for Foreign Listed Companies: Selected Stock Exchanges (*Continued*)

Japan	**Tokyo Stock Exchange** Foreign listed companies may follow IAS if they use IAS financial statements for listing purposes in their home country or any other country, or otherwise the permission of the Ministry of Finance
Malaysia	**Kuala Lumpur Stock Exchange** Domestic listed companies must follow Malaysian GAAP. Foreign listed companies may follow Malaysian GAAP or IAS.
Netherlands	**Amsterdam Stock Exchange** Foreign companies may follow either IAS or U.S. GAAP without reconciliation to Netherlands GAAP. Domestic companies may follow Netherlands GAAP or IAS, U.S. GAAP, or U.K. GAAP with a reconciliation to Netherlands GAAP.
Singapore	**Stock Exchange of Singapore** Foreign listed companies may follow IAS (no reconciliation to Singaporean GAAP required) or U.S. GAAP (reconciliation to Singaporean GAAP is required).
South Africa	**Johannesburg Stock Exchange** A domestic listed company can follow South African GAAP or IAS. Under the listing requirements, a foreign listed company must follow "standards regarded by the [Exchange] as appropriate for listed companies." South African GAAP and IAS are the two examples cited as appropriate. As a result of a harmonization program, compliance with South African GAAP results also in compliance with IAS.
Switzerland	**Swiss Stock Exchange** All listed companies, including domestic, may follow IAS. Foreign listed companies may also follow their national GAAP but may have to add supplemental disclosures to meet requirements of Swiss GAAP.
Thailand	**Stock Exchange of Thailand** Foreign listed companies may follow Thai GAAP, IAS, or U.S. GAAP. Domestic listed companies must follow Thai GAAP or IAS if there is no Thai standard on the subject.
United Kingdom	**London Stock Exchange** Domestic listed companies must follow U.K. GAAP. Foreign listed companies may follow IAS or U.S or U.K. GAAP. Foreign companies may follow other national GAAP, in which case a reconciliation to U.K. GAAP may be required.
United States	**New York Stock Exchange, NASDAQ, American Stock Exchange, Arizona Stock Exchange, Boston Stock Exchange, Chicago Stock Exchange, Chicago Board Options Exchange, Pacific Stock Exchange, Philadelphia Stock Exchange** Foreign listed companies may use U.S. GAAP or IAS or their national GAAP. If not U.S. GAAP, a note reconciling income statement and balance sheet items to U.S. GAAP is required by regulation of the U.S. Securities and Exchange Commission. Domestic companies must follow U.S. GAAP.

Source: Adapted from *www.iasc.org.uk.*

Table 7.10 Examples of Major Companies Following International Accounting Standards

Companies Noting Full Compliance:

AGA (Sweden)	Jardine Matheson (Bermuda)
Alcan Aluminium (Canada)	Jelmoli (Switzerland)
Alusuisse-Lonza (Switzerland)	Moulinex (France)
Bayer (Germany)	Multi-Purpose Holdings (Malaysia)
Bongrain (France)	Nestlé (Switzerland)
Dominion Textile (Canada)	Pirelli (Italy)
Essilor (France)	Saurer (Switzerland)
Forbo (Switzerland)	Sika (Switzerland)
Heidelberger Zement (Germany)	Sulzer (Switzerland)
Holderbank (Switzerland)	Trelleborg (Sweden)

Companies Noting Full Compliance With Limited Exceptions:

Aerospatiale (France)	Metra (Finland)
AECI (South Africa)	Nokia (Finland)
Astra (Sweden)	Oerlikon-Buhrle (Switzerland)
Atlas (Sweden)	Olivetti (Italy)
Autoliv (Sweden)	Perstorp (Sweden)
Eridania Beghin-Say (France)	Renault (France)
Electrowatt (Switzerland)	Saint-Gobain (France)
Esselte (Sweden)	Schering (Germany)
Fiat (Italy)	South African Breweries (Germany)
Fujitsu (Japan)	Stora (Sweden)
Georg Fischer (Switzerland)	Toray (Japan)
Huhtamaki (Finland)	Usinor (France)
Kirin (Japan)	Valeo (France)
Kvaerner (Norway)	Vonroll (Switzerland)
Lafarge (France)	

Source: Street, Bryant, and Gray (1999).

structuring of the governance of IASC to make it a more independent body with a status consistent with the global authority required to set standards at this level. As of May 2000, IOSCO has recommended acceptance of IASs subject to supplemental treatments where necessary (see International Bulletin 7.1).

CONCLUSIONS

This chapter emphasizes the issues and problems arising from the global diversity in financial reporting. The multinational manager, whether analyzing a new client for credit or purchasing a company, needs to be aware that there may be significant differences between countries. The Microsoft Web site GAAP conversion shows that even very large companies may wish to provide data to investors in their own GAAP.

International Bulletin 7.1

IOSCO *Press Release* (Extract)
Sydney, Australia—May 17, 2000

Resolution Concerning the Use of IASC Standards for the Purpose of Facilitating Multinational Securities Offerings and Cross-border Listings.

The following resolution was approved by the Presidents Committee of IOSCO:

In order to respond to the significant growth in cross-border capital flows, IOSCO has sought to facilitate cross-border offerings and listings. IOSCO believes that cross-border offerings and listings would be facilitated by high quality, internationally accepted accounting standards that could be used by incoming multinational issuers in cross-border offerings and listings. Therefore, IOSCO has worked with the International Accounting Standards Committee (IASC) as it sought to develop a reasonably complete set of accounting standards through the IASC core standards work program.

IOSCO has assessed 30 IASC standards, including their related interpretations ("the IASC 2000 standards"), considering their suitability for use in cross-border offerings and listings. IOSCO has identified outstanding substantive issues relating to the IASC 2000 standards in a report that includes an analysis of those issues and specifies supplemental treatments that may be required in a particular jurisdiction to address each of these concerns.

The Presidents Committe congratulates the IASC for its hard work and contribution to raising the quality of financial reporting worldwide. The IASC's work to date has succeeded in effecting significant improvements in the quality of the IASC standards. Accordingly, the Presidents Committee recommends that IOSCO members permit incoming multinational issuers to use the 30 IASC 2000 standards to prepare their financial statements for cross-border offerings and listings, as supplemented in the manner described below (the "supplemental treatments") where necessary to address outstanding substantive issues at a national or regional level.

Those supplemental treatments are:

- **reconciliation:** requiring reconciliation of certain items to show the effect of applying a different accounting method, in contrast with the method applied under IASC standards;
- **disclosure:** requiring additional disclosures, either in the presentation of the financial statements or in the footnotes; and
- **interpretation:** specifying use of a particular alternative provided in an IASC standard, or a particular interpretation in cases where the IASC standard is unclear or silent.

In addition, as part of national or regional specific requirements, waivers may be envisaged of particular aspects of an IASC standard, without requiring that the effect of the accounting method used be reconciled to the effect of applying the IASC method. The use of waivers should be restricted to exceptional circumstances such as issues identified by a domestic regulator when a specific IASC standard is contrary to domestic or regional regulation.
The concerns identified and the expected supplemental treatments are described in the Assessment Report.

IOSCO notes that a body of accounting standards like the IASC standards must continue to evolve in order to address existing and emerging issues. IOSCO's recommendation assumes that IOSCO will continue to be involved in the IASC work and structure and that the IASC will continue to develop its body of standards. IOSCO strongly urges the IASC in its future work program to address the concerns identified in the Assessment Report, in particular, future projects.

IOSCO expects to survey its membership by the end of 2001 in order to determine the extent to which members have taken steps to permit incoming multinational issuers to use the IASC 2000 standards, subject to the supplemental treatments descibed above. At the same time IOSCO expects to continue to work with the IASC, and will determine the extent to which IOSCO's outstanding substantive issues, including proposals for future projects, have been addressed appropriately.

As such, managers need to understand how actual results may be significantly changed by differences in the financial reporting principles chosen and how to analyze financial statements from different GAAP perspectives.

While there are a number of influences that explain the development of financial reporting internationally and constrain global harmonization, it is noteworthy that recent progress by the IASC has been significant and promises at the very least more informed understanding of the impact of accounting differences.

SUMMARY

1. The significance of international accounting diversity for the global investment community has received increasing recognition.

2. International financial reporting classification helps to describe and compare financial reporting systems in a way that will promote improved understanding of the nature and sources of problems of financial reporting practice.

3. Although international classification research is still at an early stage, it is possible to identify some broad country groupings and patterns of financial reporting development. At the very least a macro/micro pattern can be observed. Within that framework, U.K., continental European, and U.S. models can be identified.

4. It is possible to identify key financial reporting values derived from societal cultural influences: professionalism, uniformity, conservatism, and secrecy. An international classification of financial reporting systems can be made on the basis of the link between financial reporting values, on the one hand, and financial reporting system characteristics, on the other.

5. There are many significant differences in financial statements and reporting practices around the world that impact on the presentation and calculation of items in the balance sheet and income statement.

6. Research into the quantitative impact of accounting measurement differences reveals that there is a hierarchy of conservatism with the United Kingdom and United States at the less conservative end of the spectrum compared with countries such as France, Germany, and Japan.

7. While global harmonization still has a long way to go and is constrained by different national accounting traditions and cultures, significant progress has been made recently by the International Accounting Standards Committee, the global standard-setting organization.

DISCUSSION QUESTIONS

1. Why has there been increasing recognition of the significance of international accounting diversity?

2. To what extent and in what ways are capital market participants, notably investors and corporations, affected by international accounting diversity?

3. Discuss the nature of Nobes's hierarchical classification scheme. What are the critical factors involved? How easy is it to fit countries into the categories suggested?

4. Critically evaluate the results of the empirical tests of Nobes's proposed classification scheme.

5. Discuss the nature and relevance of culture to financial reporting classifications, making special reference to the "financial reporting values" identified by Gray. By what process is culture likely to impact on financial reporting systems?

6. Critically evaluate Gray's proposed classification of culture areas according to the authority and enforcement aspects of financial reporting systems. How does your own country fit in with this classification scheme?

7. What are the major differences in measurement principles between the Anglo-Saxon, Nordic, Germanic, Latin, and Asian countries?

8. What is meant by the "index of conservatism"? How is it calculated in principle? How can it be used to assess the impact of specific accounting principles?

9. Of the countries named below, which is the most likely to have deferred taxation in the balance sheet?:

   a. USA

   b. France

   c. Austria

   d. Germany

10. Which of the following factors is most likely to cause the differences that separate Mexican accounting from the more traditional European systems?

    a. Tax rates

    b. Education level

    c. Language

    d. Inflation

11. Depreciation in Germany, like most German accounting practices, is based on:

    a. The Plan Comptable

    b. The Autobahn

    c. The rules laid out in the tax code

    d. GAAP as commonly agreed by accountants

    e. None of the above

12. What are the prospects for global harmonization using international accounting standards?

EXERCISES

Obtain the annual reports from a major U.S., European, and Asian company in the same or similar industry.

1. How do these reports differ in terms of format? You may wish to use Table 7.2 as a template.

2. What are the main differences in the accounting measurement policies used?

CASE

British Telecom

British Telecom: Notes to the Accounts
United States Generally Accepted Accounting Principles

The group's consolidated financial statements are prepared in accordance with accounting principles generally accepted in the U.K. (U.K. GAAP), which differ in certain significant respects from those applicable in the U.S. (U.S. GAAP). The following statements summarise the material estimated adjustments, gross of their tax effect, which reconcile net income from that reported under U.K. GAAP to that which would have been reported had U.S. GAAP been applied.

Net income	1999	1998	1997
YEAR ENDED 31 MARCH	£m	£m	£m
Net income applicable to shareholders under U.K. GAAP	2,983	1,702	2,077
Adjustments for:			
Pension costs	(104)	(66)	83
Redundancy charges	(284)	(253)	156
Capitalization of interest, net of related depreciation	(19)	(38)	(23)
Goodwill amortisation	(85)	(71)	(73)
Mobile licenses, software and other intangible asset capitalisation and amortisation, net	(226)	42	77
Investments	(6)	5	-
Deferred taxation	220	163	(148)
Other items	(60)	(37)	-
Net income as adjusted for U.S. GAAP	2,589	1,447	2,149
Basic earnings per American Depositary Share as adjusted for U.S. GAAP	£4.02	£2.27	£3.39
Diluted earnings per American Depositary Share as adjusted for U.S. GAAP	£3.93	£2.23	£3.36

Differences between United Kingdom and United States Generally Accepted Accounting Principles

The following are the main differences between U.K. and U.S. GAAP which are relevant to the group's financial statements.

(a) Pension costs

Under U.K. GAAP, pension costs are accounted for in accordance with U.K. Statement of Standard Accounting Practice No. 24, costs being charged against profits over employees' working lives. Under U.S. GAAP, pension costs are determined in accordance with the requirements of U.S. Statements of Financial Accounting Standards (SFAS) Nos. 87 and 88. Differences between the U.K. and U.S. GAAP figures arise from the requirement to use different actuarial methods and assumptions and a different method of amortising surpluses or deficits.

(b) Accounting for redundancies

Under U.K. GAAP, the cost of providing incremental pension benefits in respect of workforce reductions is taken into account when determining current and future pension costs, unless the most recent actuarial valuation under U.K. actuarial conventions shows a deficit. In this case, the cost of providing incremental pension benefits is included in redundancy charges in the year in which the employees agree to leave the group.

Under U.S. GAAP, the associated costs of providing incremental pension benefits are charged against profits in the period in which the termination terms are agreed with the employees.

(c) Capitalisation of interest

Under U.K. GAAP, the group does not capitalise interest in its financial statements. To comply with U.S. GAAP, the estimated amount of interest incurred whilst constructing major capital projects is included in fixed assets, and depreciated over the lives of the related assets. The amount of interest capitalised is determined by reference to the average interest rates on outstanding borrowings. At 31 March 1999 under U.S. GAAP, gross capitalised interest of £499m (1998 - £525m) with regard to the company and its subsidiary companies was subject to depreciation generally over periods of 2 to 25 years.

(d) Goodwill

Under U.K. GAAP, in respect of acquisitions completed prior to 1 April 1998, the group wrote off goodwill arising from the purchase of subsidiary undertakings, associates and joint ventures on acquisition against retired earnings. The goodwill is reflected in the net income of the period of disposal, as part of the calculation of the gain or loss on divestment. Under U.S. GAAP, such goodwill is held as an intangible asset in the balance sheet and amortised over its useful life and only the unamortised portion is included in the gain or loss recognised at the time of divestment. Gross goodwill under U.S. GAAP at 31 March 1999 of £1,957m (1998 - £925m) was subject to amortisation over periods of 3 to 20 years. Goodwill relating to MCI was unchanged for the period from 31 October 1997 when the investment ceased to have associated company status until disposal on 15 September 1998. The value of goodwill is reviewed annually and the net asset value is written down if a permanent diminution in value has occurred. Under U.K. GAAP, goodwill arising on acquistions completed on or after 1 April 1998 is generally accounted for in line with U.S. GAAP.

(e) Mobile cellular telephone licenses, software and other intangible assets

Certain intangible fixed assets recognised under U.S. GAAP purchase accounting requirements are subsumed within goodwill under U.K. GAAP. Under U.S. GAAP these separately identified intangible assets are valued and amortised over their useful lives.

(f) Investments

Under U.K. GAAP, investments are held on the balance sheet at historical cost. Under U.S. GAAP, trading securities and available-for-sale securities are carried at market value with appropriate valuation adjustments recorded in profit and loss and shareholder's equity, respectively. The net unrealised holding gain on available-for-sale securities for the year ended 31 March 1999 was £76m (1998 - £1,315m relating primarily to the investment in MCI, 1997 - £nil).

(g) Deferred taxation

Under U.K. GAAP, provision for deferred taxation is generally only made for timing differences which are expected to reverse. Under U.S. GAAP, deferred taxation is provided on a full liability basis on all temporary differences, as defined in SFAS No. 109.

At 31 March 1999, the adjustment of £1,424m (1998 - £2,095m) reconciling ordinary shareholders' equity under U.K. GAAP to the approximate amount under U.S. GAAP included the tax effect of other U.S. GAAP adjustments. This comprised an adjustment increasing non-current assets by £59m (1998 - £76m decrease); an adjustment increasing current assets by £50m (1998 - £68m increase); £nil adjustment (1998 - £184m decrease) to current liabilities; an adjustment decreasing minority interests by £11m (1998 - £3m decrease) and an adjustment increasing long-term liabilities by £1,544m (1998 - £2,274m increase).

(h) Dividends

Under U.K. GAAP, dividends are recorded in the year in respect of which they are declared (in the case of interim or any special dividends) or proposed by the board of directors to the shareholders (in the case of final dividends). Under U.S. GAAP, dividends are recorded in the period in which they are declared.

Questions:

Review the Form 20-F reconciliation from British Telecom (BT), a major U.K. company, and answer the following questions:

1. Compute a conservatism index for 1999, 1998, and 1997.
2. Which GAAP gives a more conservative net earnings figure?
3. For 1999 only, compute a partial conservatism index for each item.
4. Which items cause the largest difference between U.K. GAAP and U.S. GAAP for BT?
5. According to the notes to the 20-F, how do U.K. GAAP and U.S. GAAP differ on these issues?

REFERENCES AND FURTHER READING

Choi, F.D.S. and R.M. Levich. (1997). "International Accounting Diversity and Capital Market Decisions." In *Handbook of International Accounting*, F.D.S. Choi, Ed. New York: Wiley.

Doupnick, T.S. and S.B. Salter. (1993). "An Empirical Test of a Judgmental International Classification of Financial Reporting Practices." *Journal of International Business Studies* (First Quarter). Vol. 24, No. 1: 41–6.

Gray, S.J. (1980). "The Impact of International Accounting Differences from a Security Analysis Perspective: Some European Evidence." *Journal of Accounting Research* (Spring): 64–76.

Gray, S.J. (1988). "Towards a Theory of Cultural Influences on the Development of Accounting Systems Internationally." *Abacus* (March). Vol. 24 (1): 1–15.

Hofstede, G. (1980). *Culture's Consequences: International Differences in Work-Related Values.* Beverly Hills: Sage.

Nobes, C.W. (1983). "A Judgmental International Classification of Financial Reporting Practices." *Journal of Business Finance and Accounting* (Spring). Vol. 10, No. 1: 1–19.

Radebaugh, L.H. and S.J. Gray. (1997). *International Accounting and Multinational Enterprises*, 4th Ed. New York: Wiley, pp. 46–86.

Salter, S. and F. Niswander. (1995). "Cultural Influence on the Development of Accounting Systems Internationally: A Test of Gray's Theory." *Journal of International Business Studies.* (Second Quarter) 26(2): 379–397.

Street, D.L., S.M. Bryant, and S.J. Gray. (1999). "Acceptance and Observance of International Accounting Standards: An Empirical Study of Companies Claiming to Comply with IASs." *International Journal of Accounting* 34(1): 11–48.

Weetman, P. and S.J. Gray. (1990). "International Financial Analysis and Comparative Corporate Performance: The Impact of U.K. vs. U.S. Accounting Principles on Earnings." *Journal of International Financial Management and Accounting*, Vol. 2, Nos. 2 & 3 (Summer–Autumn): 111–129.

Weetman, P., E.A.E. Jones, C.A. Adams, and S.J. Gray. (1998). "Profit Measurement and U.K. Accounting Standards: A Case of Increasing Disharmony in Relation to U.S. GAAP and IASs." *Accounting and Business Research* 28 (3, Summer):189–208.

SOME USEFUL INTERNET WEB SITES

1. *http://www.byu.edu/c&i/cim/account/index.htm*
   Marriott School of Management international accounting site.

2. *http://www.fortune.com/fortune/global500/*
   Fortune Global 500.

3. *http://www.microsoft.com/msft/tools.htm#alternate*
   Microsoft annual financial statements in multiple GAAPs.

4. *http://lbce.ca/bce/e/investors/*
   Bell Canada

5. *http://www.bt.co.uk/report/fin/index.htm*
   British Telecom (U.K.).

6. *http://www.volvo.se/corpinfo/annual.html*
   Volvo (Sweden).

7. *http://www.sumitomocorp.co.jp/investl/index.html*
   Sumitomo (Japan).

8. *http://www.dtag.de/english/company/g_zahl/index.htm*
   Deutsche Bank (Germany).

9. *http://www.bhp.com.au/financ.htm*
   BHP (Australia).

10. *http://www.iaaer.org*
    This is the Web site of the International Association for Accounting Education and Research. It has useful links to academic assocations and professional accountancy organizations.

11. *http://www.iasc.org.uk*
    This is the Web site of the international Accouting Standards Committee (IASC). It provides updates on developments in International Accounting Standards.

12. *http://www.iosco.org*
    This is the Web site of the International Organization of Securities Commissions (IOSCO). There are useful links to other international regulatory and financial organizations.

CHAPTER EIGHT

GLOBAL TRANSPARENCY AND DISCLOSURE

INTRODUCTION

In the previous chapter we looked at financial reporting systems and discussed the analysis of financial statements internationally. In this chapter we look at differences in transparency and disclosure practices across countries. The lack of *transparency* of company accounts and reports is a major issue and concern in many countries around the world consistent with the growing need to attract and retain foreign capital and facilitate capital raisings internationally. This issue was recently highlighted with the Asian financial crisis and the suggestion that higher levels of disclosure would have helped to prevent the crisis occurring in the first place (see, for example, Choi, 1998). International Bulletin 8.1 provides an extract from a United Nations report that indicates the transparency issues involved.

DISCLOSURE IN CORPORATE REPORTS

The amount of information disclosed by MNEs in corporate reports has considerably expanded in recent years. The major source of pressure for increased disclosures has been the financial and investment community. Both MNEs and standard-setting bodies in countries with well-developed securities markets, such as the United States, the United Kingdom, France, Germany, and Japan, have been primarily concerned with responding to pressures from this direction.

There has also been something of an explosion in the demand for information by a wide range of other participant groups including, most importantly, governments, trade unions, employees, and the general public. In this chapter, we examine why disclosure is important, the incentives, the costs to management to make disclosure, and the available types of disclosure in different countries. Finally, we look at a type of disclosure that is of special concern to multinationals: segment disclosure (especially geographical segments).

International Bulletin 8.1

The Role of Accounting in the East Asian Financial Crisis: Lessons Learned?

An analysis of the immediate causes of the financial crisis that affected East Asian economies in the second half of 1997 raises serious questions about transparency, disclosure and the role of accounting and reporting in producing reliable and relevant financial information. While the trading, industrial and financial enterprises in the region grew fast and contributed to the "Asian Miracle," many of the very same enterprises collapsed and many others have become technically bankrupt.

What appears to have happened is that corporations and banks, operating within a weak reporting and regulatory framework, were unable to generate the necessary cash flows to meet their loan payments. A classic mismatch occurred between their short-term debts and long-term, unproductive investments. There was also the added problem that much of the debt was foreign short-term debt. The defaults sent warnings bells to investors and creditors who looked for ways to protect their own interests and panic ensued. Overseas banks refused to renew their loans; mutual fund investors sold their shares and converted their funds back into dollars. The frightened included local as well as foreign investors. This put tremendous pressure on local currencies, causing devaluation that in turn compounded the difficulty of debt repayment and gave rise to a vicious cycle of more capital flight, more panic, and contagion.

It is an accepted fact that an enterprise is open to the outsiders via the information it discloses in its financial statements. The information produced by the accounting system of an enterprise enables external parties to know about the financial performance of that enterprise. Investors, creditors and other stakeholders use accounting information as an input in the decision-making model. If a policy of complete and objective disclosure is not followed while preparing the financial statements, the users of accounting information are likely to be misled and therefore they may not be able to make the appropriate decisions in a timely fashion.

This assessment is consistent with normal market behavior as recently described by Arthur Levitt, Chairman of the U.S. Securities and Exchange Commission,[1]

> *The significance of transparent, timely and reliable financial statements and its importance to investor protection has never been more apparent. The current financial situations in Asia and Russia are stark examples of this new reality. These markets are learning a painful lesson taught many times before: investors panic as a result of unexpected or unquantifiable bad news.*

It seems that due to the lack of proper disclosure in the accounting reports of East Asian enterprises, the users of accounting information did not receive the early warning signals about the deteriorating financial conditions they should have and were therefore not able to make adjustments accordingly. It is difficult, if not impossible, to say to what extent disclosure deficiencies and non-transparency of financial statements were responsible for triggering the East Asian financial crisis, but there is general agreement that they played a crucial role. There is a general consensus amongst researchers, policy makers and practitioners that the East Asian financial crisis was mainly triggered by the micro-level problems that remained undetected for a long time. Although the international lenders and investors had access to various macro-level information, and aggregate data, lack of adequate disclosures in the financial statements deterred proper assessment of the risk exposures of the fund-seeking enterprises in the region.

[1]Arthur Levitt, *The "Numbers Game,"* presentation at the New York University Center for Law and Business, New York, September 28, 1998.

The president of World Bank, while analyzing the causes of the East Asian financial crisis, summarized disclosure problems as follows:[2]

> *The culture in the region has not been one of disclosure. If you go back further it was a culture of a smallish number of wealthy people. It was an agrarian society with a lot of people in the country and some significant factors of power. It is reflected in the chaebols. It is reflected in groups that come together. There were centers of power. There was little disclosure, and there was a familial structure in the industrial and in the financial sector just as there was in the ordinary sector.*

[2]James D. Wolfensohn (President, World Bank), *Address to the Overseas Development Council Conference on Asia's Coming Explosion,* Washington, D.C., March 19, 1998.

Source: Except from *Report for the UNCTAD,* by M. Zubaidur Rahman, December 17, 1998.

Importance of Information Disclosures

While there is no doubt about the continuing significance of accounting measurement issues, the importance of information disclosed in financial statements and accompanying reports is being increasingly recognized by multinational corporations. This information provides an important input to the financial analysis process of evaluating the *quality* of earnings and financial position, both current and prospective. A particularly important motivation for voluntary information disclosures by MNEs is that the annual report provides the opportunity to communicate more policy and future-oriented information about the corporation. This may better inform or influence investors in the increasingly globalized securities markets. It is interesting, for example, that more than 400 of the Fortune Global 500 firms provide financial and other corporate information on the Internet. This is a trend that is likely to have an increasing impact on the disclosure practices of stock exchange–listed companies around the world.

It is generally accepted that the costs of providing information should not exceed the benefits derived by the users of the information. In particular, the need for MNEs to maintain business confidentiality in sensitive areas and to avoid jeopardizing their competitive position should be taken into account. At the same time, this need must be weighed against the interests of analysts, investors, and the public in the transparency of multinational business operations. In practice, it appears that the more specific and the more future oriented—and especially the more quantitative—the information proposed for disclosure, the more sensitive becomes the attitude of MNEs toward its provision.

Managerial Incentives to Disclose Information

Management provides information, both voluntarily and in response to regulation. There may be incentives for the management of an MNE to disclose information voluntarily if it perceives it to be in its own interests, and those of the corporation, to respond to the information demands of users and participant groups. Research by Meek and Gray (1989) and others has shown, for example, that voluntary disclosures are forthcoming when corporations are competing for finance from investors, especially in a cross-border context. Where governments and trade unions exert an influence over the environment the MNE operates in, there will also be strong influences on the MNE to disclose information to compete with other MNEs for investment opportunities or to exchange it to maintain existing rights or avoid potential constraints on their operations.

On the other hand, if management decides that the information demands are unreasonable or inimical to its interests or those of the MNE (e.g., when the information is unfavorable or contains "bad news"), it must either achieve some compromise or accept the consequences, if any, of nondisclosure.

Costs of Information Production

The disclosure of information has a direct monetary cost. MNEs are understandably unwilling to incur increased costs through expanded disclosures unless they are required to do so or the potential benefits exceed the estimated costs. The direct cost of information disclosure to a corporation is the value of the resources used in gathering and processing the information as well as in its audit and communication.

The direct costs of such disclosures will preeminently depend on the internal structure of the MNE and information generated in order to manage this structure. The closer existing information is to the disclosure requested, the lower will be the actual direct cost of producing the information. Because the information needs of management are not always identical with those of other groups, the absence of complete harmony between internal and external information needs is inevitable.

Apart from the direct costs of disclosure there are the indirect costs relating to competitive disadvantage (see next section), with its associated disincentives to innovate or invest, as well as the costs resulting from interference or regulation by governments.

Competitive Disadvantage of Disclosure

The most frequently cited objection to increased disclosure requirements is that of competitive disadvantage (i.e., the use of the additional information by competitors to the detriment of the corporation disclosing the information). It is a major basis for the resistance to expanded disclosures. In some circumstances disclosure of information could be damaging to MNEs. As a general rule, the more specific or future oriented a disclosure is, the greater the potential competitive disadvantage for the disclosing corporation.

What of the relatively small percentage of possible disclosure that hypothetically could cause damage to the discloser? Should this danger definitely rule out its release? Information that allows competitors to increase their well being at the expense of the discloser is damaging for the latter but profitable for the former.

The dilemma is to distinguish between disclosures, which, for the economy as a whole, result in aggregate competitive advantages exceeding aggregate competitive disadvantages. What is detrimental or beneficial to the economy in the short term may, in some circumstances, have the opposite effect in the longer term. Increased competition through disclosure could lead to greater vigor in the economy. It could equally lead to a decline in business incentives as a result of the appropriation of rewards by competitors facilitated by expanded disclosures.

The relative importance of various possible costs of disclosure was explored in a study by Gray, Radebaugh, and Roberts in 1990. The study found general agreement by both U.S. and U.K. financial executives (see Table 8.1) that the indirect cost of competitive disadvantage was the most important cost factor constraining voluntary disclosures. However, the results of the tests showed that, overall, there

Table 8.1 Cost Factors Constraining Voluntary Information Disclosure as Perceived by U.K. and U.S. Financial Executives

	Rank	
	United Kingdom	United States
Cost competitive disadvantage	1	1
Cost or data collection and processing	2	2
Cost of auditing	3	3
Possibility of claims from employees or trade unions	4	9
Threat of takeover or merger	5	6
Cost of publication	6	5
Technical processing problems	7	3
Possibility of intervention by government agencies	8	8
Possibility of claims from political or consumer groups	9	10
Possibility of intervention by taxation authorities	10	7

Note: Items with higher ranks have greater constraints.
Source: S.J. Gray, L.H. Radebaugh, and C.B. Roberts, "International Perceptions of Cost Constraints on Voluntary Information Disclosures," *Journal of International Business Studies* (Winter 1990): 602.

were significantly different perceptions in the responses concerning the impact of several of the types of costs involved, including the possibility of claims from employees or trade unions and technical processing problems.

Managerial Attitudes to Voluntary Disclosures

Demands for additional information disclosures have come from both international organizations (in particular the UN, OECD, European Union, and IASC) and the host governments and societies in which MNEs operate. However, the growing globalization of capital markets indicates the presence of significant market pressures for additional information about MNE operations as well as the existence of prospects for and concern about the international coordination of capital market regulations. It is against this background that MNE management must weigh the costs and benefits of voluntary information disclosures.

Gray, Radebaugh, and Roberts (1990) also examined the extent to which there are perceived net costs or benefits for disclosing specific items of information voluntarily, the types of costs involved, and the significance of cost constraints with respect to specific disclosures. The results of the study showed that, on average, the respondents tended to perceive most voluntary or discretionary disclosure items as giving rise to a net cost (see Table 8.2). At the same time, there was a wide range of views depending on the specific item of information concerned. However, items perceived as giving rise to major net costs in both the United States and United Kingdom were inflation-adjusted profits, quantified forecasts, and narrowly defined segment information.

In terms of voluntary disclosure practices by MNEs, a study by Meek, Roberts, and Gray (1995) examined the factors influencing the voluntary disclosures of 226 MNEs from the United States, the United Kingdom, and continental Europe. A wide range of information disclosures were examined and categorized into three types: strategic, nonfinancial, and financial. A common benchmark of voluntary

Table 8.2   The Net Costs or Benefits of Disclosure of Specific Items as Perceived by U.K. and U.S. Financial Executives—Items with Highest Net Costs

	Rank	
	United Kingdom	United States
LOB profits; narrow definition	1	2
Describe major legal proceedings	2	9
Quantitative forecasts; sales and profits	3	7
LOB sales; narrow definition	4	4
Geographical profits; narrow definition	5	3
Inflation-adjusted profits	6	5
LOB segment transfers	7	12
Geographical segment transfers	8	13
Describe major patents and expiry rates	9	8
Foreign assets by country	10	10
Geographical sales data; narrow definition	11	6
Employment information	23	2
Value-added statements	24	1

Source: S.J. Gray, L.H. Radebaugh, and C.B. Roberts, "International Perceptions of Cost Constraints on Voluntary Information Disclosures," *Journal of International Business Studies* (Winter 1992): 602.

disclosures was established that would apply to all countries, and a disclosure score was calculated for each company. The means and standard deviations for all companies and for the United States, the United Kingdom, and the continental European groupings are shown in Table 8.3. Scores for these groupings are also given for the internationally listed and domestically listed samples; from these it can be seen that the internationally listed MNEs tend to disclose more information voluntarily.

Taken overall, the results show that all MNEs regardless of size or home country provide more information in their annual reports than the regulations require. With respect to the factors influencing voluntary disclosure, statistical support was found for size, international listing status, country or region of origin, and industry. A relatively weak multinationality effect was also detected. The results also indicate that the factors explaining voluntary annual report disclosures differ by information type. The largest MNEs are those that set the trends in providing voluntary disclosures of nonfinancial and financial information. There are also industry patterns to these two types of disclosures, suggesting that MNEs pay attention to what their closest competitors disclose when making decisions about such disclosures. Nonfinancial information is also a European phenomenon. Finally, strategic information disclosures are a special feature of continental European MNEs and, generally speaking, are also signficant for internationally listed MNEs.

INTERNATIONAL DISCLOSURE REGULATION AND REPORTING TRENDS

As indicated earlier, management's disclosure pattern may be set not only by its own preferences and cultural tendencies but also by regulation. International information disclosure requirements concerned specifically with the form and con-

Table 8.3 Voluntary Disclosure Scores by Multinationals

	Strategic Information		Nonfinancial Information		Financial Information		Overall Disclosures	
	Mean	Standard Deviation	Mean	Standard Deviation	Mean	Standard Deviation	Mean	Standard Deviation
All companies	21.03	13.81	18.06	11.01	16.62	8.89	18.23	7.49
U.S. All Companies	17.22	10.52	11.89	7.10	16.54	6.81	15.20	5.40
U. S. International	20.03	10.98	14.50	7.41	17.27	7.12	17.09	5.55
U. S Domestic	14.41	9.32	9.27	5.73	15.81	6.46	13.32	4.56
U.K. All Companies	16.83	8.52	25.70	9.15	14.58	9.30	18.73	6.78
U.K. International	17.41	9.70	25.71	10.28	16.92	10.44	19.87	7.95
U.K. Domestic	16.24	7.27	25.69	8.03	12.24	7.44	17.60	5.24
Cont. Euro. All Companies	36.52	16.56	23.01	12.41	19.67	11.83	25.16	8.30
Cont. Euro. International	36.51	17.54	21.87	13.28	23.19	9.34	26.23	8.36
Cont. Euro. Domestic	36.53	15.05	24.16	11.65	16.15	13.16	24.09	8.29

Source: G.K. Meek, C.B. Roberts, and S.J. Gray, "Factors Influencing Voluntary Annual Report Disclosures by U.S., U.K., and Continental European Multinational Corporations," *Journal of International Business Studies* (Third Quarter, 1995): 564.

tent of the directors' report in the EU center primarily on the Fourth (1978) and Seventh (1983) Directives on company annual accounts and consolidated accounts respectively. In the case of MNEs, the EU Seventh Directive, which has been implemented in all member countries, is especially relevant. Under Article 36 of the Directive, the annual report of the board of directors must include a "fair review of the development of the business" together with an indication of any important events that have taken place since the end of the year and any "likely future development." An indication must also be given of activities in the field of research and development. So far as individual companies, as opposed to groups of companies, are concerned, the Fourth Directive incorporates similar requirements.

Also relevant here are the information disclosure requirements in the United States. The SEC requires a *management discussion and analysis* of the financial statements to be provided in annual reports. This is expected to include discussion of the results of operations, liquidity and capital resources, and, preferably, the impact of inflation. In addition, the disclosure of future-oriented information is considered desirable. The discussion of these topics on a segmental basis for each business segment is also encouraged. The purpose of the SEC requirements is to provide a framework for discussion that allows management some flexibility to comment on the specific features of the corporation and its industry and that encourages innovation in presentation (e.g., the mixing of narrative commentary and quantitative data) to promote effective communication. The aim is to provide users with an understanding of management's own insights into strategy and performance. This example has been followed in the United Kingdom with the nonmandatory statement by the Accounting Standards Board recommending the provision of an "operating and financial review."

The relative strength of disclosure regulation internationally can be estimated using a 1992 study by Adhikari and Tondkar (see Table 8.4). This study revealed significant variations in the overall quantity and level of detail of disclosure (both financial and nonfinancial) that are required as part of the listing and filing requirements of stock exchanges around the world. Disclosure scores were calculated on a weighted as well as unweighted basis for a total of 35 stock exchanges. The weighted scores were based on the relative importance of the disclosures to stock market analysts. The New York Stock Exchange is clearly the leader in terms of disclosure requirements, with London not far behind.

The study found that size of the equity market was significant in determining the level of disclosure, and clearly those countries with more developed stock markets tend to have higher levels of disclosure regulation compared with those in some of the emerging economies (e.g., India and Pakistan), although Switzerland has one of the lowest levels of disclosure consistent with its reputation for secrecy. However, no significant relationships were found for the other variables examined, that is, degree of economic development, type of economy, activity on the equity market, and dispersion of stock ownership.

In the following review of trends, we will discuss the information disclosures in directors' reports in the context of three fairly well accepted categories of disclosure: we will label these the *corporate review,* the *operations review,* and the *financial review.* This chapter concludes with a discussion of additional information disclosures.

The *corporate review* includes information disclosures relevant to the overall performance of a corporation. This group of items includes:

1. The chairperson's statements
2. The review of corporate strategy and results

Table 8.4 Accounting Disclosure Requirements of Global Stock Exchanges:
Weighted and Unweighted Disclosure Scores

Stock Exchange (Country)	Disclosure Scores Weighted	Unweighted
1. Sydney (Australia)	74.60	74.64
2. Vienna (Austria)	54.17	53.52
3. Rio de Janiero (Brazil)	67.28	68.75
4. Toronto (Canada)	79.00	78.64
5. Bogota (Colombia)	54.58	54.48
6. Copenhagen (Denmark)	67.20	66.86
7. Cairo (Egypt)	49.02	48.02
8. Helsinki (Finland)	70.54	71.05
9. Paris (France)	76.20	76.16
10. Frankfurt (Germany)	67.20	66.86
11. Athens (Greece)	60.00	59.41
12. Hong Kong (Hong Kong)	77.04	75.77
13. Bombay (India)	58.23	58.84
14. Milan (Italy)	68.46	68.39
15. Tokyo (Japan)	77.68	77.68
16. Seoul (Korea)	71.43	72.00
17. Luxembourg (Luxembourg)	66.62	66.64
18. Kuala Lumpur (Malaysia)	75.69	75.41
19. Mexico (Mexico)	70.55	70.68
20. Amsterdam (Netherlands)	73.19	72.84
21. Wellington (New Zealand)	67.13	65.91
22. Oslo (Norway)	60.63	60.59
23. Karachi (Pakistan)	55.71	55.82
24. Lisbon (Portugal)	65.68	65.50
25. Singapore (Singapore)	80.89	80.32
26. Johannesburg (South Africa)	74.50	73.48
27. Madrid (Spain)	68.84	68.36
28. Stockholm (Sweden)	60.54	60.05
29. Zurich (Switzerland)	52.24	52.39
30. Taipei (Taiwan)	72.19	71.70
31. Bangkok (Thailand)	74.78	75.41
32. Istanbul (Turkey)	50.68	50.68
33. London (United Kingdom)	86.21	84.86
34. New York (United States)	90.31	90.75
35. Caracas (Venezuela)	73.67	73.32

Source: A Adhikari and R.H. Tondkar, "Evironmental Factors Influencing Accounting Disclosure Requirements of Global Stock Exchanges," *Journal of International Financial Management and Accounting* (Summer, 1992): 105.

   3. External and unusual events information

   4. Acquisitions and disposals information

   5. Human resources information (including information about manage-
      ment and organizational structure and labor employment information)

   6. Value-added information

   7. Social responsibility information

   8. Research and development information

   9. Investment program information

  10. Future prospects information

The *operations review* includes the following:

   1. A more detailed discussion and analysis of operations

   2. Activities disaggregated by business and geographical segment

The *financial review* includes the discussion and analysis of

   1. Results

   2. Liquidity and capital resources

   3. Asset valuations and inflation

Corporate Review

The corporate review is a review of the business activities of the corporation as a
whole and is consistent with the scope of the requirements of the EU Fourth
(1978) and Seventh (1983) Directives. The content of corporate review typically includes the following:

   1. *The chairperson's statement.*   The statement nevertheless provides a platform
      for insights from the chairperson or chief executive in his or her leader-
      ship role about the overall performance and prospects of the corporation.

   2. *A review of corporate strategy and results (possibly including a mission statement).*
      MNEs invariably provide some narrative commentary and data that are
      relevant to a review of corporate strategy and results. A mission statement
      or statement of objectives is sometimes included. More information tends
      to be disclosed in this review of corporate strategy and results when stock
      market pressures exert themselves (e.g., when corporations are changing
      their strategy or are subject to the threat of a takeover bid). The merger of
      Daimler with Chrysler, for example, in 1998 prompted substantial discus-
      sion in the DaimlerChrysler annual report about the strategy of the new
      company and gave rise to a new mission statement (see Figure 8.1).

   3. *Comments on external and unusual events.*   MNEs also tend to provide some
      commentary on the impact of external events such as exchange rates, in-
      terest rates, government policy, market conditions, foreign competition,
      and so on. Many corporations also report unusual events affecting the cor-
      poration, such as factory explosions, fraud, and litigation.

   4. *Acquisitions and disposals information.*   Discussion and analysis of acquisi-
      tions and disposals is not widespread. While disclosure levels are relatively
      high in the United States and United Kingdom, information on acquisi-
      tions and disposals is rarely comprehensive or well presented elsewhere.

OUR PURPOSE
is to be a global provider of automotive and transportation products and services, generating superior value for our customers, our employees and our shareholders.

OUR MISSION
is to integrate two great companies to become a world enterprise that by 2001 is the most successful and respected automotive and transportation products and services provider.

We will accomplish this by constantly delighting our customers with the quality and innovation of our products and services, resulting from the excellence of our processes, our people and our unique portfolio of strong brands.

Figure 8.1   Daimler Chrysler

5. *Human resources information.*   Many MNEs provide information that is relevant to an assessment of human resources. This area of disclosure often includes information about management and organizational structure as well as labor and employment. Information about senior management (e.g., names, experiences, responsibilities, but excluding the directors) and organizational structure tends to be provided by only a minority of MNEs. However, disclosure levels for these areas are relatively high in Australia and New Zealand, France, Sweden, and the United States.

Disclosures about labor and employment are made by a majority of MNEs, with disclosure levels relatively high in France, Germany, the Netherlands, Sweden, Switzerland, and the United Kingdom. The nature and extent of narrative commentary and data vary considerably and include such topics as labor relations, training, welfare benefits, and safety. It is interesting to note that France requires a separate *bilan social* (social balance sheet or social report) containing details of pay structure, health and safety conditions, hours worked, absenteeism, strikes, industrial relations, and so on. This encourages some French MNEs, for example, Pernod Ricard, to include employment information in their annual reports.

6. *Value-added information.*   While it is regarded by U.S. companies as a costly disclosure, value-added information often proves quite interesting and useful reading. Value-added statements show, in financial terms, the contribution of all stakeholders, and especially employees, to business performance. A minority of MNEs—primarily European firms—provide this information. An example of a value-added statement is given by Electrolux (Sweden) (see Figure 8.2).

The purpose of the value-added statement, which shows the value added to materials and services purchased externally, is to present the results of a corporation's operations that are attributable to the efforts of a more broadly defined group of participants, rather than just the investor group, and to show the distribution of wealth created to all stakeholders.

7. *Social responsibility information.*   The term *social responsibility* refers to accountability to society as a whole with respect to matters of public interest such as community welfare, public safety, and the environment. An increasing number of MNEs disclose social responsibility information such as environmental protection and cleanup information. This information

Statement of Added Value

Added value represents the contribution made by a company's production, i.e., the increase in value arising from manufacture, handling, etc. within the company. It is defined as sales revenues less the costs of purchased goods and services.

Sales revenues for the Electrolux Group in 1997 totalled SEK 113,000m (110,000). After deduction of purchases of goods and services, the value added by the Group amounted to SEK 32,977m (35,309), a decrease of 7%(–4) from the previous year. The decrease refers mainly to the provision for the restructuring program. During the past five years, added value has increased at an average annual rate of 4.5% (5.8).

In 1997, SEK 3,628m (5,536) of the value added remained within the Group and was utilized among other things for capital expenditure as well as product development and marketing Dividend payments to shareholders accounted for 3% (3) of added value in 1997, or 4% (3) of the Group's total payroll costs.

The added value generated within the Group over the past two years and its distribution are shown in the tables below.

CALCULATION OF ADDED VALUE	1997 SEKm	%	1997 per employee, SEK '000	1996 SEKm	%
Total revenues	113,000	100	1,067	110,000	100
Cost of purchased goods and services	–80,023	–71	–756	–74,691	–68
Added value	32,977	29	311	35,309	32

DISTRIBUTION OF ADDED VALUE	1997 SEKm	%	1997 per employee, SEK '000	1996 SEKm	%
To employees					
Salaries	19,883	60	188	20,249	58
Employer contributions	6,185	19	58	6,174	17
	26,068	79	246	26,423	75
To State and municipalities					
Taxes	944	3	9	1,237	3
To credit institutions					
Interest, etc.	1,422	4	13	1,198	3
To shareholders					
Dividend payments (1997; Proposed)	915	3	9	915	3
	3,281	10	31	3,350	9
Retained in the Group					
For wear on fixed assets (depreciation)	4,255	13	40	4,438	13
Other	–627	–2	–6	1,098	3
	3,628	11	34	5,536	16
Added value	32,977	100	311	35,309	100

Figure 8.2   Electrolux

is also often available from other sources. Figure 8.3 gives an example of environmental disclosure from SmithKline Beecham (UK).

8. *Research and development (R&D) information.*   It is generally accepted that R&D is a critical element of corporate success in the longer term. Information about R&D activities is disclosed by only a small majority of MNEs. While the nature and extent of the information, both narrative commentary and data, varies substantially, disclosure levels are relatively high in

ENVIRONMENT AND SAFETY

As we manufacture and deliver high-quality healthcare products around the world, we are committed to conducting ourselves in a manner that protects both people and the environment. To manage that commitment, we work according to established environment and safety practices and policies that are integrated into the very fabric of our business. Key achievements during 1999 include:

Environmental Goals After a detailed review of our long-term environmental performance goals, we identified new opportunities for improvement, including a ten-fold increase in the amount of waste recycled. The revised goals, based on specific facility projects, are detailed in our Environment and Safety Report.

Behavioural Safety Programme Our Behavioural Safety Programme empowers employees to encourage and counsel each other on safe work practices. The programme has been formally launched and will be phased into all manufacturing operations. We expect this innovative approach to safety to help SB achieve further reductions in lost time injury and illness incidence rates, which have been reduced by more than 20% each year over the last three years for a total improvement of 59%.

Control Matrices In support of our manufacturing processes, we introduced structured control systems that provide a standardised approach for categorising hazards and defining the corresponding level of administrative and engineering controls required for safe and environ-mentally responsible handling and production of SM materials.

Environment and Safety Management Implementation of our Environment and Safety Management System, which assists and supports compliance with SB and legislative requirements, continues on schedule. With implementation nearing completion at most of our sites, we will explore the possibility of external company-wide certification. We also continued to integrate environment and safety issues into key business processes such as research and development, capital review, contract manufacturing and site acquisition and divestiture.

Sustainable Development At SB, we believe that it is important to continue to move toward sustainable business practices. We integreate innovative product design and development, excellent economic performance, demonstrated social responsibility and strong commitment to safety and the environment into the fabric of our business. Doing so enables us to maintain a strong competitive advantage and achieve our goal of helping to make people's lives everywhere healthier.

Performance Corporate Environment and Safety reviews cite performance on a three-year schedule using a new scored system. An Environment and Safety Report is available and posted on the World Wide Web at www.sb.com. The report highlights SB's environment and safety activities and key performance indicators.

Environmental emission reduction goals
ten year goals 1996 to 2005

Organic discharges to wastewater	75% reduction
Organic emissions in air	70% reduction
Hazardous waste	23% reduction
Energy consumption	18% reduction

Lost time injury and illness incidence rate
incidents with one or more lost work days per 100,000 work hours

1996 0–93	
1997 0–69	
1998 0–50	
1999 0–40	

Figure 8.3 SmithKline Beecham

Germany, Japan, the Netherlands, Switzerland, the United Kingdom, and the United States.

9. *Investment program information.*   It is generally accepted that the quality of a corporation's capital expenditures, as opposed to acquisitions of ongoing businesses from other corporations, is a critical factor in corporate success in the longer term. However, information about the corporation's investment program, including the nature, location, and significance of capital expenditure, tends to be provided by only a small majority of MNEs. Disclosure levels are relatively high in Australia and New Zealand, the Netherlands, Switzerland, and the United Kingdom.

10. *Future prospects information.*   While users are interested in improving their understanding of the current and past activities of MNEs, they are also, often primarily, interested in the corporation's future prospects. Information about future business prospects is disclosed by a majority of MNEs. However, this information is usually provided in the form of narrative commentary—as might be expected given the sensitive nature from a competitive disadvantage perspective of quantitative, future-oriented information. The nature and extent of the information provided varies substantially and is often general and very limited. Disclosure levels, however, are relatively high in Germany, Hong Kong, the Netherlands, the United Kingdom, and the United States.

Operations Review

The operations review relates to the activities of the various segments of the corporation's operations. This is where a more detailed review of business activities is provided on a disaggregated basis. Segmental reporting is now a well-established practice in information disclosures by MNEs, but the focus of attention has been on quantitative rather than qualitative information. In practice, the majority of MNEs provide additional narrative commentary, and sometimes quantitative data, on a segmental basis in their operations review.

1. *Review of business segments.*   It is common practice for MNEs to provide a review of operations categorized by business segment, and a substantial majority of them do so. These reviews are often extensive, containing both narrative commentary and quantitative data. In countries where requirements governing the disclosure of quantitative segmental data only recently have been introduced or do not exist (e.g., Italy, Japan, Switzerland), this data often has been voluntarily incorporated into the operations review. The United States and Canada have recently provided for segmental disclosure on a management basis with disclosure being provided along the lines of the corporate organization.

   In countries where quantitative disclosure requirements are effective, the business segments reviewed tend to be consistent with the quantitative data disclosed, and in some cases the operations review provides even more desegregated and extensive information.

2. *Review of international operations and geographical segments.*   In contrast to business segments, a review of operations categorized by geographical segment is less common in practice. However, a discussion of activities on a geographical basis is frequently incorporated into the analysis of business segments. Some MNEs provide a review of international or geographical

segment operations in addition to a review of business segment operations. Whether or not this information is provided seems to depend on the organizational structure of the corporation or the directors' aim of emphasizing international operations, which, for example, seems quite common in the case of Japan.

The discussion and analysis of international operations is an important area of information because the business activities of MNEs are becoming increasingly complex and geographically diversified.

Financial Review

The financial review relates to the discussion and analysis of the financial results and position of the corporation as a whole. The topics discussed include results, liquidity and capital resources, and asset valuations and inflation. The scope of this review is broadly consistent with the requirements in the United States to provide a management discussion and analysis of matters relevant to an improved understanding of the factors influencing a corporation's performance. Items included are as follows:

1. *An analysis of results.*   U.S. MNEs, consistent with SEC requirements, generally provide a more extensive discussion of events with a potential impact on earnings. Also included are the correlation of past trends with current sales and earnings, the reconciliation of underlying causes and economic influences with any changes in sales in the current year, and the disclosure of any matters that are expected to impact future operations.

2. *An analysis of liquidity and capital resources.*   Disclosure levels are relatively high in France, Germany, Italy, the Netherlands, the United Kingdom, and the United States. Notably, U.S. MNEs generally provide a more extensive discussion, consistent with SEC requirements, and funding obligations under existing contracts and expectations regarding future contracts, including the funding of projected business expansions, are usually discussed. Plans to remedy liquidity problems are also discussed by some corporations.

3. *An analysis of asset values and inflation.*   Apart from South America, requirements in the area of asset values are limited, despite some experience of inflation accounting in a number of countries. A discussion of asset valuations and the impact of inflation are provided in practice by only a small majority of MNEs. It is noteworthy, however, that disclosure, in terms of both narrative commentary and data, is especially evident in the Netherlands, Sweden, Switzerland, and the United Kingdom.

SEGMENTAL REPORTING

As discussed earlier, a unique aspect of MNEs is that they operate in a variety of geographical as well as *line-of-business* (LOB) segments. One disclosure consequence is that they are often required to provide so-called *segmental* or *disaggregated data*. This section discusses the pros, cons, and regulations in this area.

Users and Uses of Segmental Information

Investors are likely to be interested in the future cash flows they may obtain by investing in a company as well as the risk of uncertainty of those cash flows. They are, therefore, interested in the performance of an MNE as a whole rather than the performance of any specific element of the corporation's activities. However, this does not mean that only consolidated information is valuable to them.

Both the size and uncertainty of future cash flows are likely to be affected by many factors, including those related to the industries and countries in which an MNE operates. Different industries and different countries have a variety of profit potentials, degrees, types of risk, and growth opportunities. Different rates of return on investment and different capital needs are also likely to exist throughout the various segments of a business.

Segmental information is likely to help investors by allowing them to combine company-specific information with external information, thus allowing a more accurate assessment of both the risk and the potential for future growth. In addition, investors can gain an idea of the success of past operations by comparing them with the performance of similar corporations.

Because of this diversification of operations, there has been a demand for MNEs to report key items of disaggregated information, especially turnover and profits. Such disaggregated or segmental data is typically provided for both geographical areas and lines of business.

Benefits of Segmental Reporting

The possible benefits of segmental data have been examined using a variety of research techniques. Such tests are of two types: (1) predictive ability (forecasting) tests, and (2) stock market reaction tests (i.e., how the market views the information disclosed).

Predictive ability tests compare the accuracy of forecasts of future sales or earnings based on consolidated data with that of forecasts based on disaggregated data. Research studies concerned with the prediction of earnings have all concluded that forecasts are most accurate if they are based on line-of-business (LOB) segmental data rather than consolidated earnings. In addition, there is some evidence that the relative accuracy of segment-based forecasts may depend on the size of the corporation, with such disclosures being more useful for smaller corporations. There have been few prediction studies relating to geographical segmental disclosures, but research by Roberts in 1989, using U.K. data, and Balakrishnan, Harris, and Sen in 1990, using U.S. data, found similar results to those involving LOB disclosures (i.e., segment-based outperformed consolidated-based forecasts).

With respect to stock market studies, there is evidence that disclosure of both LOB and geographical segment data, results in a decrease in market assessments of risk of the disclosing corporation. With regard to geographical disclosures, recent research using both U.K. and U.S. data has shown a significant relationship between such disclosures and market risk assessments.

Costs of Segmental Reporting

Several arguments against segmental disclosures have been put forward; some apply to all corporations, others only in certain situations. It has been argued that the cost of compiling, processing, and disseminating such information will exceed the benefits. However, no evidence is available regarding either the costs of disclosure or any precise quantification of benefits.

As discussed earlier, the potentially more serious costs is that of disseminating information likely to benefit existing or potential competitors. While this cost may apply at the corporation level, especially if the same requirements do not apply to corporations of other nationalities, it may not be a problem at the level of the entire economy. If such information aids competition and investor evaluation, it might be considered an advantage rather than a cost to society.

The major argument against segmental information is that in some cases it may be inappropriate and therefore potentially misleading. The disclosure of segmental information implicitly assumes that the segments reported are relatively autonomous and independent of each other. This means that the figures reported for any one segment can be assessed independently of a consideration of the performance of the rest of the company. If, instead, the company is highly integrated, not only are relatively large transfers between the segments likely, but the segment results cannot be understood or considered in isolation from the rest of company. At the extreme, if the company is highly integrated, any disaggregated results may be arbitrary enough to be meaningless.

U.S. Requirements

To date, the United States has the most extensive accounting requirements in the world. The SEC has required LOB segmental disclosures since 1969. In 1976, the FASB introduced SFAS 14, "Financial Reporting for Segments of a Business Enterprise." This standard formed the basis of reporting for segments for many years. Unfortunately, its impact was limited by the lack of a clear definition of geographical or line-of-business segments. Thus, reporting would often be vague and unduly aggregated.

In June 1997, after considerable debate and revision, the FASB issued SFAS 131, "Disclosures About Segments of an Enterprise and Related Information." This standard took effect for financial statements for periods beginning after December 15, 1997 and applied both to financial year-end and interim reporting.

This statement requires that a public business enterprise report financial and descriptive information about its reportable operating segments. Operating segments are components of an enterprise about which separate financial information is available that is regularly evaluated by the chief operating decision maker in deciding how to allocate resources and in assessing performance. Generally, financial information is required to be reported on the basis that it is used internally for evaluating segment performance and deciding how to allocate resources to segments. Reportable segments may be based on LOB, geographic location, or a combination of LOB and geographic location.

For each reportable segment, information must be disclosed about segment profit or loss, certain specific revenue and expense items, and segment assets.

Additional information is required about the geographic areas of operations if the reportable segment disclosures do not provide it. This second tier of reporting is referred to as enterprisewide disclosures. While sales and assets disclosures are required at this level, profits disclosures are not, thus resulting in a loss of information compared to SFAS 14 (Nichols, Street, and Gray, 2000).

U.K. Requirements

Following the EU Fourth and Seventh Directives, the U.K. Companies Acts of 1981 and 1989 (now incorporated in the 1985 Companies Act, as amended) require the disclosure of geographical segmental turnover, together with LOB disclosure of both sales and profit before tax. Geographical profits disclosures were not required although they were specified as a required disclosure, albeit with some flexibility, by the London Stock Exchange. The Companies Act also states that if any market or class of business is immaterial (a term not defined), it may be combined with another. Even more discretion is given to companies by the additional statement that "if disclosure is seriously prejudicial to the interest of the company that information need not be disclosed" (Schedule 4, para. 55[5]), it being sufficient instead to state that such disclosures have not been made. The only guidance the Companies Act provides regarding segment identification is the statement, "the directors of the company should have regard to the manner in which the company's activities are organized" (para. 55[3]). The most important new requirement is that such information should be provided in the notes to the accounts, thus falling within the scope of the audit.

More recently, SSAP 25, "Segmental Reporting," was issued in 1990 following approval by the Accounting Standards Committee. This extended existing requirements by requiring the disclosure of segment net assets for both LOB and geographical segments. In addition, geographical segmentation of sales was required, both by source, that is, location of production or service facilities, and destination.

Requirements Around the World

Many other countries also require segmental information (see Table 8.5). Notably, Australia, and Canada have requirements similar to those in the United Kingdom and the Unites States. In the EU, the Fourth (1978) and Seventh (1983) Directives have set a minimum requirement of disclosure (i.e., sales by line of business and geographical area). While the United Kingdom goes well beyond this, most European countries have adopted a less transparent approach. However, many major MNEs voluntarily disclose segmental information that is well up to world standards (see Philips [Netherlands] segment disclosures for 1999 in Figure 8.4).

In Japan, segmental reporting requirements were introduced only in 1990 and were limited to sales, profits, and assets disclosures by line of business. With regard to a geographical analysis, geographically segmented profits were not required to be disclosed until 1997.

In practice, there are differing approaches to geographical segment identification in various countries. For example, U.S. and U.K. MNEs tend to aggregate sales and profits by continent. However, there have also been cases of multicontinental aggregation, referring, for example, to Europe, the Middle East, and Africa as one segment. Such an approach is unlikely to be informative given the different economic and political environments and risk factors involved. In contrast, MNEs in some continental European countries voluntarily disclose additional segmental data, at least with respect to sales and employees, on a much more disaggregated geographical basis.

IASC Requirements

The IASC issued a standard (IAS 14) in 1981 that fairly closely followed the requirements in the United States. Thus, it required (for both LOB and geographical segments) information on sales, with internal and external revenues shown separately; operating results and identifiable assets, in either absolute or relative terms; and a reconciliation statement to the consolidated accounts. In 1995, following a review of IAS 14, the IASC issued a proposal, consistent with the FASB in the United States, to limit the scope for managerial discretion on segment identification. The ISAC approach was broadly similar to the U.S. approach in that it looked

Table 8.5   Segmental Disclosure Requirements

	Line of Business			Geographical		
	Sales	**Profits**	**Assets**	**Sales**	**Profits**	**Assets**
Australia	Yes	Yes	Yes	Yes	Yes	Yes
Brazil	No	No	No	No	No	No
Canada	Yes	Yes	Yes	Yes	Yes	Yes
China	Yes	Yes	Yes	Yes	Yes	Yes
France	Yes	No	No	Yes	No	No
Germany	Yes	No	No	Yes	No	No
Greece	Yes	No	No	Yes	No	No
Hungary	Yes	No	No	Yes	No	No
India	No	No	No	No	No	No
Italy	Yes	No	No	Yes	No	No
Japan	Yes	Yes	Yes	Yes	Yes	No
Kenya	No	No	No	No	No	No
Netherlands	Yes	No	No	Yes	No	No
Nigeria	Yes	Yes	Yes	Yes	Yes	Yes
Philippines	Yes	Yes	No	Yes	Yes	No
Saudi Arabia	No	No	No	No	No	No
Singapore	Yes	Yes	Yes	Yes	Yes	Yes
South Africa	Yes	Yes	Yes	Yes	Yes	Yes
Spain	Yes	No	No	Yes	No	No
Sweden	Yes	Yes	No	Yes	No	No
Switzerland	No	No	No	No	No	No
Thailand	Yes	Yes	No	Yes	Yes	No
United Kingdom	Yes	Yes	Yes	Yes	Yes	Yes
United States	Yes	Yes	Yes	Yes	Yes	Yes
European Union	Yes	No	No	Yes	No	No
IASC	Yes	Yes	Yes	Yes	Yes	Yes
UN	Yes	Yes	Yes	Yes	Yes	Yes

to a company's organization structure and internal reporting system as the basis for identifying segments. However, in contrast to the U.S. proposals, the IASC permitted a modification of this "management approach" to reflect circumstances where such an approach does not provide evidence of the source and nature of a company's *risk and returns* relating to its LOB and geographical segments.

In July 1997, a revised IAS 14 was issued. The key elements of this standard, which was effective for financial years beginning on or after July 1, 1998, are as follows:

- Segments are organizational units for which information is reported to the board of directors and CEO unless those organizational units are not along product/service or geographical lines, in which case use the next lower level of internal segmentation that reports product and geographical information.

Figure 8.4   Philips—Segmental Data (1999)
Data by product sector
(the data included in this report are unaudited)

Sales, sales growth, and number of employees by product sector				1999
	sales (to third parties)	% growth		number of employees
		nominal	comparable	
Lighting	4,548	2	1	47,453
Consumer Products	12,437	0	6	47,970
Components	3,754	(2)	3	41,709
Semiconductors	3,796	18	5	29,952
Professional	5,186	15	4	25,187
Origin	1,056	0	0	16,690
Miscellaneous	682	(27)	(11)	11,181
Unallocated				6,732
Total	**31,459**	**3**	**4**	**226,874**

Product sectors					1999
	segment revenues	Ebitda*	income (loss) from operations	as % of segment revenues	income (loss) from operations**
Lighting	4,597	772	602	13.1	631
Consumer Products	12,781	847	555	4.3	519
Components	5,325	661	286	5.4	311
Semiconductors	4,557	1,195	614	13.5	612
Professional	5,479	261	100	1.8	125
Miscellaneous	769	(9)	(91)	(11.8)	(83)
Unallocated		(365)	(412)		(416)
Total	**35,243**	**3,555**	**1,751**		**1,796**
Intersegment revenues	**(3,784)**				
Sales	**31,459**				
Income from operations as a % of sales			5.6		5.7

* In Philips' definition, Ebitda represents income from operations before depreciation and amortization charges

** Excluding restructuring

Figure 8.4   Philips—Segmental Data (1999) (*continued*)

Product sectors					1999
	total assets	net operating capital	(in)tangible fixed assets	capital expenditures	depreciation
Lighting	2,849	1,875	1,275	176	161
Consumer Products	4,500	1,689	884	296	285
Components	5,179	2,078	3,197	259	364
Semiconductors	5,188	3,194	2,917	622	467
Professional	3,432	1,780	916	99	84
Origin	683	240	275	56	68
Miscellaneous	913	318	328	68	79
Unallocated	6,752	(728)	362	86	40
Total	**29,496**	**10,446**	**10,154**	**1,662**	**1,548**

Data by geographic area
(the data included in this report are unaudited)

Sales, sales growth, and number of employees by main country				1999
	sales (to third parties)	% growth		number of employees
		nominal	comparable	
Netherlands	1,619	(2)	(1)	43,153
United States	7,535	5	9	26,282
Germany	2,727	(2)	2	13,964
France	1,962	(6)	(8)	12,521
United Kingdom	2,281	18	16	7,938
China (incl. Hong Kong)	2,023	8	4	22,097
Other countries	13,312	3	2	100,919
Total	**31,459**	**3**	**4**	**226,874**

(*continued*)

Figure 8.4 Philips—Segmental Data (1999) (*continued*)

Geographic areas					1999
	segment revenues	Ebitda*	income (loss) from operations	as % of segment revenues	income (loss) from operations**
Netherlands	12,452	927	513	4.1	565
Europe excl. Netherlands	16,600	1,118	611	3.7	622
USA and Canada	9,310	507	82	0.9	60
Latin America	1,642	15	(41)	(2.5)	(31)
Africa	107	3	1	0.9	1
Australia and New Zealand	424	4	1	0.2	1
Total	**51,723**	**3,555**	**1,751**		**1,796**
Interregional revenues	**(20,264)**				
Sales	**31,459**				
Income from operations as a % of sales			**5.6**		**5.7**

* In Philips' definition, Ebitda represents income from operations before depreciation and amortization charges

** Excluding restructuring

Main countries					1999
	total assets	net operating capital	(in)tangible fixed assets	capital expenditures	depreciation
Netherlands	7,452	2,439	1,811	435	370
United States	5,139	2,839	2,476	249	228
Germany	1,558	86	632	134	147
France	1,118	164	392	92	113
United Kingdom	1,041	607	321	55	53
China (incl. Hong Kong)	1,570	635	635	91	123
Other countries	11,618	3,676	3,887	606	514
Total	**29,496**	**10,446**	**10,154**	**1,662**	**1,548**

- The primary basis of reporting, LOB or geographical, is determined by the dominant source of company risks and returns normally indicated by the system of internal reporting (i.e., the management approach). If LOB segments are the primary basis of reporting, then more extensive disclosures are required compared with the secondary basis, geographical segments, and vice versa.

- The following should be disclosed for each primary segment:
  — Revenue (external and intersegment shown separately)
  — Operating result (before interest and taxes)
  — Carrying amount of segment assets
  — Carrying amount of segment liabilities
  — Cost to acquire property, plant, equipment, and intangibles
  — Depreciation and amortization
  — Non-cash expenses other than depreciation
  — Share of profit or loss of equity and joint venture investments
  — The basis of intersegment pricing

- The following should be disclosed for each secondary segment:
  — Revenue (external and intersegment shown separately)
  — Carrying amount of segment assets
  — Cost to acquire property, plant, equipment, and intangibles
  — The basis of intersegment pricing

- Segments should never be constructed solely for external reporting purposes.

- A 10 percent materiality threshold applies for each segment.

- Segments much equal at least 75 percent of consolidated revenue.

Note that similar to the United States, there is a loss of information about profits for secondary segments. An example of reporting under the new IAS 14 is given by Danisco, the Danish industrial group, which early adopted the new standard in 1997. In line with the management approach, the primary basis of reporting is by line of business with secondary reporting on a geographical basis defined as Denmark, other EU, rest of Western Europe, Eastern Europe, North America, Latin America, and Rest of World.

CONCLUSIONS

There is growing pressure around the world to promote greater transparency and disclosure consistent with the importance of cross-border capital raisings and the growth of world trade and investment. Disclosure regulation varies internationally and there is often a lack of transparency especially in the emerging economies.

While many MNEs tend to be willing to disclose additional information, a growing number of major MNEs are more enlightened and perceive it to be often in their own interests to make voluntary disclosures likely to be relevant to external stakeholders, particularly investors. However, the nature of the disclosures would seem to depend not only on international capital market factors but also on local national concerns and traditions. The IASC is endeavoring to raise the standard of disclosure globally. One of the most important areas concerns segmental disclosures, where the latest standard endeavors to reveal the returns and risks of MNE operations on a more strategic and hence more insightful basis.

SUMMARY

1. Information disclosure in MNE annual reports is an important complement to the financial statements. Additional information helps users to better understand the nature and effects of the activities of MNEs and to better analyze and assess the quality of earnings and financial position.

2. At the same time, MNEs need to consider the costs involved, maintain business confidentiality in sensitive areas, and avoid jeopardizing their competitive position. In practice the more specific and future oriented the item of information disclosure, the less likely are MNEs to want to make disclosures.

3. There are significant variations in the overall quantity and level of detail of disclosure required by stock exchanges around the world.

4. In practice, MNEs voluntarily disclose a wide range of additional narrative and quantitative information, though this tends to vary in volume, type, and quality according to the size of the MNE, its international stock exchange listing status, the geographical location of its headquarters, and the nature of its business operations.

5. The largest MNEs tend to be the trendsetters in providing voluntary disclosures of nonfinancial and financial information. There are also industry patterns to these two types of disclosure. Nonfinancial information disclosure is also a European phenomenon. Strategic information disclosures are a special feature of continental European MNEs and are also significant for internationally listed MNEs in general.

6. Additional voluntary information disclosures by MNEs in their annual reports relate to a wide range of information disclosed in the corporate review. Examples include information relevant to the overall performance and prospects of a corporation, including the chairperson's statement, corporate strategy and results, external and unusual events, acquisitions and disposals, human resources, social responsibility, R&D, investment program, and future prospects.

7. Information disclosed by MNEs in the operations review often includes a discussion and analysis of operations disaggregated by business and geographical segment.

8. Information disclosed in the financial review often includes a discussion and analysis of results, liquidity, and capital resources, and asset valuations and inflation.

9. Segmental reporting regulation is in considerable flux with new standards from the U.S. FASB and the IASC. Both these standards require segments to be defined in terms of corporate organizational structure and management with differential disclosures according to the primary and secondary basis of reporting.

DISCUSSION QUESTIONS

1. To what extent are information disclosures by MNEs in directors' annual reports, as opposed to the financial statements, likely to be useful to financial analysts and investors?

2. What are the likely costs and benefits to MNEs of making additional voluntary information disclosure?

3. In which countries are stock exchange disclosure regulations most stringent? Least stringent? What are the reasons for this?

4. What is the likely effect of international stock exchange listing status on the voluntary disclosures of MNEs?

5. Discuss the kinds of information you would expect to see in the corporate review, the operations review, and the financial review sections of an MNE's directors' report.

6. Discuss the relevance to financial analysts and investors of additional disclosures by MNEs with regard to corporate strategy and related issues.

7. To what extent are additional disclosures about human resources likely to be significant to financial analysts and investors?

8. What is meant by a *value-added* statement? To what extent is it likely to provide information over and above that already available in the income statement?

9. Why is information relevant to future prospects likely to be of interest to financial analysts and investors? What are the constraints on MNEs providing such voluntary disclosures in practice?

10. Discuss the usefulness of the SEC requirement in the United States to provide a *management discussion and analysis* of the financial statements.

11. Compare and contrast the U.S. and IASC approaches to segmental disclosure.

12. Is the standard of segmental reporting likely to improve following the recent changes to IAS 14?

13. To what extent and for what reasons do you think disclosure levels in stock markets around the world are likely to change during the next ten years? In the context of increasing competition for finance in international capital markets, what types of information should MNEs consider disclosing more of voluntarily? To what extent will an MNE's home country be an important factor in this decision?

14. What is your view of the major deficiencies/weaknesses in disclosure by MNEs today? In answering this, make clear your objectives and provide arguments to support your claims.

CASE

Nestlé

Key Figures by Management Responsibility and Geographic Area
(in millions of Swiss francs)

	1999
Sales	
Food:	
• Europe	27,098
• Americas	22,045
• Africa, Asia, and Oceania	13,611
Other Activities	11,906
	74,660
Results	
Food:	
• Europe	2,671
• Americas	2,799
• Africa, Asia, and Oceania	2,185
Other Activities	1,675
	9,330
Unallocated items[a]	(1,416)
Trading Profit	7,914

Capital Expenditure

Food:

• Europe	923
• Americas	718
• Africa, Asia, and Oceania	381
Other Activities	665
	2,687
Unallocated items[b]	119
	2,806

(a)   Mainly corporate expenses, research and development costs as well as amortisation of intangible assets.

(b)   Corporate and research and development fixed assets.

Key Figures by Product Group
(in millions of Swiss francs)

	1999
Sales	
• Beverages	20,859
• Milk products, nutrition and ice cream	19,411
• Prepared dishes and cooking aids (and miscellaneous activities)	20,185
• Chocolate and confectionery	10,195
• Pharmaceuticals	4,010
	74,660
Results	
• Beverages	3,764
• Milk products, nutrition and ice cream	2,168
• Prepared dishes and cooking aids (and miscellaneous activities)	1,850
• Chocolate and confectionery	882
• Pharmaceuticals	1,077
	9,741
Unallocated items[a]	(1,827)
Trading profit	7,914
Capital Expenditure	
• Beverages	618
• Milk products, nutrition and ice cream	366
• Prepared dishes and cooking aids (and miscellaneous activities)	464
• Chocolate and confectionery	280
• Pharmaceuticals	91
	1,819
Administration, distribution, research and development	987
	2,806

(a)   Mainly corporate expenses, research and development costs, amortisation of intangible assets as well as restructuring costs.

Questions:

Examine the segmental data reported by Nestlé in the company's 1999 annual report and accounts as given above. Nestlé claims to have prepared its report in accordance with IAS 14 (revised 1997). Please answer the following questions based on your study of these disclosures:

1. What is the primary basis and what is the secondary basis of segmental reporting by Nestlé?
2. To what extent has Nestlé complied with IAS 14?
3. To what extent has Nestlé voluntarily disclosed information beyond the requirements of IAS 14?

REFERENCES AND FURTHER READING

Adhikari, A. and R.H. Tondkar. (1992). "Environmental Factors Influencing Accounting Disclosure Requirements of Global Stock Exchanges." *Journal of International Financial Management and Accounting.* Vol. 4(2): 75–105.

Balakrishnan, H., T. Harris, and P.K. Sen. (1990). "The Predictive Ability of Geographic Segment Disclosures." *Journal of Accounting Research* (2): 305–325.

Choi, F.D.S. (1998). "Financial Reporting Dimensions of Asia's Financial Crisis." *Indian Accounting Review* 2(2): 1–11.

Chow, C.W. and A. Wong-Boren. (1987). "Voluntary Financial Disclosure by Mexican Corporations." *Accounting Review* (July) Vol. 62, No. 3: 533–541.

Cooke, T.E. (1991). "An Assessment of Voluntary Disclosure in the Annual Reports of Japanese Corporations." *International Journal of Accounting.* Vol. 26(3): 174–189.

European Community. (1978). *Fourth Directive for the Co-ordination of National Legislation Regarding the Annual Accounts of Limited Liability Companies* (Brussels: EC); European Union, *Seventh Council Directive on Consolidated Accounts* (Brussels: EC, 1983).

Gray, S.J. and C.B. Roberts. (1989). "Voluntary Information Disclosure and the British Multinationals: Corporate Perceptions of Costs and Benefits." In *International Pressures for Accounting Change*, A.G. Hopwood, Ed. Englewood Cliffs, NJ: Prentice-Hall.

Gray, S.J. and H.M. Vint. (1995). "The Impact of Culture on Accounting Disclosures: Some International Evidence." *Asia-Pacific Journal of Accounting* (December) Vol. 2: 33–43.

Gray, S.J., L.H. Radebaugh, and C.B. Roberts. (1990). "International Perceptions of Cost Constraints on Voluntary Information Disclosures: A Comparative Study of U.K. and U.S. Multinationals." *Journal of International Business Studies.* Vol. 21, No. 4: 597–622.

International Accounting Standards Committee. (1983). *International Accounting Standards Committee, Objectives and Procedures.* London: IASC, January.

Meek, G.K. and S.J. Gray. (1989). "Globalization of Stock Markets and Foreign Listing Requirements: Voluntary Disclosures by Continental European Companies Listed on the London Stock Exchange." *Journal of International Business Studies* (Summer). Vol. 20, No. 2: 315–336.

Meek, G.K., C.B. Roberts, and S.J. Gray. (1995). "Factors Influencing Voluntary Annual Reports Disclosures by U.S., U.K. and Continental European Multinational Corporations." *Journal of International Business Studies* (Third Quarter). Vol. 26, No. 3: 555–572.

Nichols, N., D.L. Street, and S.J. Gray. (2000). "Geographical Segment Disclosures in the United States: Reporting Practices Enter a New Era." *Journal of International Accounting, Auditing and Taxation* (Summer). Vol. 9, No. 1: 27–63.

Roberts, C.B. (1989). "Forecasting Earnings Using Geographic Segment Data: Some U.K. Evidence." *Journal of International Financial Management and Accounting* 1(2): 130–151.

Saudagaran, S.M. and G.C. Biddle. (1995). "Foreign Listing Location: A Study of MNC's and Stock Exchanges in Eight Countries." *Journal of International Business Studies* Vol. 26, No. 2: 319–342.

United Nations. (1988). *Conclusions on Accounting and Reporting by Transnational Corporations.* New York: UN: revised 1994.

SOME USEFUL INTERNET WEB SITES

1. *http://www.DaimlerChrysler.com*
2. *http://www.nestle.com*
3. *http://www.hoechst.com*
4. *http://www.sb.com*
5. *http://www.electrolux.com*
6. *http://www.philips.com*
7. *http://www.sec.gov*
   This is the SEC's home page; it offers SEC standards and all divisions of the SEC. This would be helpful to detail one of the organization's regulating financial statements. This site also offers links to other sites.
8. *http://www.iosco.org*
   This is the International Organization of Securities Commission's (IOSCO) home page. It offers the organization's standards for stock exchanges around the world, member countries, and its annual report.
9. *http://www.iasc.org.uk*
   This is the Web site of the International Accounting Standards Committee (IASC). It provides updates on the latest developments in international accounting standards.
10. *http://www.carol.uk*
    CAROL (Company Annual Reports On Line) is a free service offering access to European corporate reports.
11. *http://www.businessdirectory.dowjones.com*
    This site provides ratings and reviews of many business-related Web sites.
12. *http://www.hoovers.com*
    This site provides free information including press releases, links to company Web sites, and other information for both U.S. and non-U.S. companies.

CHAPTER NINE

FOREIGN CURRENCY ACCOUNTING AND EXCHANGE RATE CHANGES

INTRODUCTION

In Chapter 2 we introduced you to issues relating to foreign currencies and exchange risk management. Currencies continuously change in value. This in turn leads to three major risk types: transaction, translation, and economic risk. Economic risk is taken care of almost totally in the context of the strategy of the firm. The results of transaction and translation risks are reflected directly and promptly in the accounts and financial reports of the firm. Thus they have direct impacts on return on investment (ROI) and in turn on the rewards of the managers and units being evaluated. Accordingly, global managers need to understand these impacts. We begin with accounting for transactions.

ACCOUNTING FOR FOREIGN EXCHANGE TRANSACTION RISK

Foreign currency transactions are transactions denominated in a currency other than the reporting currency of the firm. The reporting currency is the currency in which the firm's financial statements are issued. For example, a sale by a U.S. firm to a Canadian firm for which payment is to be received in Canadian dollars is considered to be a foreign currency transaction for the U.S. firm. If the payment were to be received in U.S. dollars, the transaction would not be a foreign currency transaction, even though the buyer is not a U.S. firm. Interestingly, more than two-thirds of international financial transactions are in U.S. dollars (see International Bulletin 9.1). Foreign currency transactions may also involve the buying and selling of goods and services, the borrowing or lending of funds, or the receipt or payment of dividends.

When a transaction is denominated in a foreign currency, the firm needs to resolve five accounting problems:

1. The initial recording of the transaction
2. Recording of the value of foreign currency balances at subsequent balance sheet dates

International Bulletin 9.1

International Currency Zones

The emergence of the Euro as a competitor to the United States dollar for the role of world reserve currency may eventually lead to three global currency zones (the third being a "yen zone"). More than two-thirds of world's financial transactions are in U.S. dollars, yet the U.S. economy is only 20% of the world economy. In the words of former French president Charles de Gaulle, this allowed the U.S. to be indebted to foreign countries free of charge.

The emergence of a new reserve currency may reduce the need for derivative activity (many European banks are beginning to reduce their staff in this area). The head of the Monetary Union Unit for the European Commission, Peter Becx, says that most multinational companies are preparing to deal in the Euro, forcing smaller companies to follow suit. "It is likely the Euro will lead to fundamental changes, but only gradually."

Meanwhile, participants are hoping that emerging economies will learn to play by Western rules of money. But it is doubtful that they can do this even if they have the political will. Many Asian countries, including those that are mature, have poor account-keeping systems. Communist-influenced nations like China and Russia, which until recently did not even consider such notions as return on investment, are even further behind."

Source: Business Review Weekly, November 16, 1998.

---

3. Treatment of foreign exchange gains or losses
4. Recording the settlement of foreign currency receivables and payables when due
5. Accounting for hedges (forward contracts, etc.)

The initial recording of any transaction is common to all countries. Assuming there are no derivatives involved, the spot rate between local currency and the foreign currency on the day of the transaction is the local currency/unit of foreign currency multiplied by the value of the transaction in foreign currency. The result (product) represents the amount of the transaction. If the transaction involves a payable or receivable and the rate of exchange continues to vary, the value of that item, while the same as the sale initially, will vary in subsequent periods.

Most countries account for changes in the rate of exchange after the initial transaction using what is called the *two-transaction approach*. This method assumes:

- The sale is one transaction completed at delivery.
- The creation of the financial instrument (e.g., accounts receivable/payable) represents a decision to extend credit and is a separate and second transaction.
- The changes in the value of the foreign currency are reflected in changes in the value of the financial instrument (e.g., accounts receivable/payable).
- These changes in asset value are recorded on the income statement (profit and loss account) as foreign exchange gains or losses.
- These gains and losses are either taken immediately or deferred until the transaction is complete.

The following is an example of a simple series of bookkeeping entries for a sale from a U.S. company to a German company of products valued at one million Euros.

Aloha Company Problem

Aloha Company (a U.S.-based company) sells 1,000 units of Product X to a customer in Berlin, Germany at a price of 1,000 Euros each. The goods are shipped on December 15, 2000; payment will be received 30 days later on January 15, 2001. Aloha company will close its books at fiscal year-end (FYE) on December 31, 2000.

12/15/2000   Aloha Company has an account receivable and sale of 1,000,000 Euros. As a U.S.-based company, Aloha keeps its books in U.S. dollars; therefore the Euros must be *translated* into U.S. dollars.

U.S. Dollars per Euro	
Date	Spot Rates
12/15/2000	$1.05/Euro
12/31/2000	$1.00/Euro
1/15/2001	$1.03/Euro

Two-Transaction/Immediate Recognition Method

12/15/2000   Accounts Receivable $1,050,000
                       Sales $1,050,000
To record a sale of 1 million Euros on credit at Euro1 = $1.05

12/31/2000   Foreign Exchange Loss $50,000
                       Accounts Receivable $50,000
To record the effect of a change in exchange rates 12/15–12/31: 1 million × (01.05-1.00)

1/15/2001   Cash (or Foreign Currency) $1,030,000
                       Accounts Receivable $1,000,000
                       Foreign Exchange Gain $30,000
To record the receipt of 1 million Euros in payment of Accounts Receivable due.

Table 9.1 provides a generic guide to entries that arise from movements in foreign currencies.

Comparative National Differences

The method used in the Aloha example is the two-transaction/immediate recognition method. In this method, both gains and losses would be recognized every time the company closes its books, which for most large companies would be at least monthly. Table 9.2 outlines the approach used in accounting for foreign exchange transactions in a number of key countries. From this it can be seen that there are a variety of approaches in practice. However, the immediate recognition method is required only by the United States and IASC. In France and Germany, losses are recognized immediately but not gains. In Canada, long-term gains and losses are deferred.

Table 9.1 Entries for Movements in Foreign Exchange

Transaction	Resulting Balance Sheet Item	Direction of FC in US$/FC	
		Increase in the Number of HC per FC Results in:	Decrease in the Number of HC per FC Results in:
1. Export sale	FC Receivable	FX gain	FX loss
2. Granting of a loan to a customer in FC	FC Note Receivable	FX gain	FX loss
1. Import purchase	FC Payable	FX loss	FX gain
2. Borrowing in an FC	FC Note Payable	FX loss	FX gain

Note: FC—foreign currency; HC—home currency; FX—foreign exchange.

Hedging and Derivatives for Foreign Currency Transactions

Give the risks described above that net income of a firm could vary considerably with foreign exchange rates, it seems reasonable that managers will take actions to protect themselves from foreign exchange transaction risks. While it is theoretically possible that managers could price only in their own currency, unless the customer is so small or the risk so great that the corporation is willing to walk away from the business, this is not an option. Managers therefore attempt to reduce the risk inherent in most transactions by trying to lock in the value of the foreign exchange they are about to receive through hedging.

Hedging foreign currency transactions involves setting up an offsetting series of transactions to cover a particular foreign exchange risk. A hedge is a foreign exchange contract designed to offset any existing foreign exchange exposure. A

Table 9.2 Accounting for Foreign Exchange Transactions: Comparative View

Country	Base Method	Gains and Losses
United States—GAAP	Two transaction	Recognize immediately.
United States—IRS	Two transaction	Defer until the transaction is complete.
Canada	Two transaction	Recognize immediately, but for long-term items the resulting gains and losses are deferred and amortized over the underlying.
France	Two transaction	Recognize losses immediately but not gains for some options.
Japan	Two transaction	Recognize immediately, but long-term items are carried at the original exchange rate.
Germany	Two transaction	Recognize losses immediately but not gains.
IASC	Mixed (one transaction for severe devaluation)	Recognize immediately in income of the current period; in the case of severe devaluation add to the value of the asset subject to a Lower of Cost and Market test.

hedge is usually carried out through the use of a foreign exchange derivative that will move in the direction opposite to the risk inherent in the "real" or physical transaction. A simple forward contract guaranteeing the right to buy (or sell) foreign currency at a fixed price and date in the future is often used, but futures, options, swaps, and other more exotic forms of derivatives may be used. The key is to cover the risk of the underlying physical transaction. See Table 9.3.

Accounting for Hedges and Derivatives: U.S. Approach

In accounting for hedging there are two key questions: How do we value the derivatives that are used as hedges and where do the gains and losses go? The U.S. Financial Accounting Standards Board, perhaps more than many institutions, has wrestled with these issues and continues to do so. In 1981, the FASB issued Statement of Financial Accounting Standards, No. 52 (SFAS 52) on foreign currency translation. Statement 52 required that foreign currency receivables or payables including foreign exchange forward contracts be translated at the current exchange rate with any gains or losses being taken to income. Where foreign exchange forward contracts were used as hedges a special procedure was applied that effectively allowed the offset of gains and losses between the gains or losses on the physical transaction and resulting instrument and the gains and losses on derivatives.

Effective June 15, 2000, a new standard, SFAS 133, updated SFAS 52 to account for derivative instruments and hedging. SFAS 133 requires:

- That an entity recognize all derivatives as either assets or liabilities in the statement of financial position and measure those instruments at fair value.

- If certain conditions are met, a derivative may be specifically designated as (a) a hedge of the exposure to changes in the fair value of a recognized asset or liability or an unrecognized firm commitment; (b) a hedge of the exposure to variable cash flows of a forecasted transaction.

- The accounting procedures in this standard as they apply to hedges are as follows:

  - For a derivative designated as hedging the exposure to changes in the fair value of a recognized asset or liability or a firm commitment (referred to as a *fair value hedge*), the gain or loss is recognized in earnings in the period of change together

Table 9.3 Accounting for Foreign Exchange Derivatives

Transaction	Resulting Balance Sheet Item	Risk	Derivative Solution
1. Export sale	FC Receivable	FX loss as the foreign currency falls	FX forward contract, option, or future to sell the FC at an exchange rate at an agreed time (contract payable in FC)
2. Granting of a loan to a customer in a FC	FC Note Receivable		
1. Import purchase	FC Payable	FX loss as the foreign currency rises	FX forward contract, option, or future to buy the FC at a exchange rate at an agreed time (contract receivable in FC)
2. Borrowing in an FC	FC Note Payable		

Note: FC—foreign currency; FX—foreign exchange.

with the offsetting loss or gain on the hedged item attributable to the risk being hedged. The effect of that accounting is to reflect in earnings the extent to which the hedge is not effective in achieving offsetting changes in fair value.

- For a derivative designated as hedging the exposure to variable cash flows of a forecasted transaction (referred to as a *cash flow hedge*), the effective portion of the derivative's gain or loss is initially reported as a component of other comprehensive income (outside earnings) and subsequently reclassified into earnings when the forecasted transaction affects earnings. The ineffective portion of the gain or loss is reported in earnings immediately.

In both cases the gains and losses on the derivative go to part of the income statement. In the case of cash flow hedges, gains and losses from the derivative end up in the second part of the new U.S. comprehensive income statement, which accounts for changes in value and for most U.S. companies would be considered below the line (i.e., not part of the companies' regular income).

Comparative National Practices

The British approach to accounting for derivatives is similar to that of the United States. If the derivative is held for trading purposes, the normal treatment is to mark the derivative to market and recognize gains and losses immediately. If the derivative qualifies for hedge accounting, the goal is to achieve symmetry between its profit recognition and that of the item being hedged. The qualifications for a hedge are basically the same as those described above in the U.S. case, and anticipated future events are available for hedge accounting if they are relatively certain.

The Japanese approach to accounting for financial instruments is not highly regulated and relies more on industry practice and tax law than on specific accounting standards. Trading derivatives—especially for banks—tend to be marked to market, but that is not the practice for institutions other than banks. Those companies tend to use hedge accounting similar to what one would find in the United States. In addition, it is unlikely that full mark-to-market accounting will take place for some time, even though that is highly likely both in the United States and at the level of the IASC.

The Canadian practice provides for disclosure but very little measurement. However, recent changes to the basis of GAAP practiced in Canada mean that the Canadian and U.S. systems will de facto be identical.

International Accounting Standards

In December 1998, the IASC passed IAS 39, "Financial Instruments: Recognition and Measurement," to take effect on January 1, 2001. This standard is for all practical purposes identical to SFAS 133, except that for a cash flow hedge, changes in the value of the hedge are retained and used by the IASC to adjust the value of the final asset rather than going to comprehensive income as in SFAS 133. A comparison of the IASC and FASB standards can be found at the IASC Web site www.iasc.org.uk.

ACCOUNTING FOR FOREIGN EXCHANGE TRANSLATION RISK

Translation risk arises solely because in most countries firms must prepare their financial statements (i.e., balance sheet and income statement) in a single currency. As firms go through the natural progression of a company engaged in international business from export and import goods and services through to investment overseas, they tend to create legal entities outside their own country, doing business in a currency other than their own. Thus the firms' foreign subsidiaries and joint ventures have financial statements expressed in foreign currencies that must be restated in the domestic currency.

Two terms important to the discussion of translation are *functional currency* and *reporting currency*. The functional currency is the currency of the primary economic environment in which the subsidiary company operates. The reporting currency is the currency in which the parent company prepares its financial statements.

The process of translation involves restating an account from one country to another. If the exchange rate used to translate the account from one country to another were the rate in effect when the original transaction took place (such as the acquisition of property, plant, and equipment), that rate would be called the *historical* exchange rate. If the exchange rate used were the one in effect at the balance sheet date, it would be considered the *current* or *closing* rate.

The translation of foreign currency financial statements involves dealing with two key issues:

1. The exchange rates at which various accounts are translated from one currency into another (translation methods)
2. What to do about the treatment of gains and losses

Translation Methodologies: Overview

In the process of translation, all foreign currency balance sheet and income statement accounts are restated in terms of the reporting currency by multiplying the foreign currency amount by the appropriate exchange rate. The major methods that have been used in the translation process are the *temporal* and the *current rate* methods. See Table 9.4.

Temporal Method

The temporal method requires cash, receivables, and payables (both current and concurrent) to be translated at the current rate. Other assets and liabilities may be translated at current or historical rates, depending on their characteristics. Assets and liabilities carried at past exchange prices are translated at historical rates. For example, a fixed asset carried at the foreign currency price at which it was purchased would be translated into the reporting currency at the exchange rate in effect when the asset was purchased. Assets and liabilities carried at current purchase or sales exchange prices or future exchange prices would be translated at current rates. For example, inventory carried at market would be translated at the current rather than the historical rate.

The attractiveness of the temporal approach lies in its flexibility. If a country were to change from historical cost accounting to current value accounting, the temporal method would automatically translate all assets and liabilities at current rates.

Current Rate Method

The current rate method is the easiest to apply because it requires that all assets and liabilities be translated at the current exchange rate. This approach is easier to use than the others because a company would not have to keep track of various historical exchange rates. The current rate approach results in translated statements that retain the same ratios and relationships that exist in the local currency. For ex-

Table 9.4 Exchange Rates Used for the Current Rate and Temporal Translation Methods

	Current Rate	**Temporal**
Cash	C	C
Current Receivables	C	C
Inventories		
Cost	C	H
Market	C	C
Long-Term Receivables	C	C
Long-Term Investment		
Cost	C	H
Market	C	C
Property, Plant, and Equipment	C	H
Intangible Assets (long-term)	C	H
Current Liabilities	C	C
Long-Term Debt	C	C
Pain-in Capital	H	H
Retained Earnings	B	B
Revenues	A	A
Cost of Goods Sold	A	H
Depreciation Expense	A	H
Amortization Expense	A	H

Notes:
A = Average exchange rate for the current period.
C = Current exchange rate at balance sheet date.
H = Historical exchange rate.
B = Balancing (residual or plug) figure.

ample, the ratio of net income to sales in local currency is rarely the same under other translation approaches because a variety of current, historical, and average exchange rates is used to translate the income statement. Because all accounts would be translated at a single exchange rate under the current rate method, the ratio at net income to sales would remain the same in the reporting currency as in the foreign currency.

Translation Process: Temporal Method

Earlier in this chapter, we mentioned that the translation process has to deal with two issues: which exchange rate (current or historical) must be used to translate each individual account in the financial statements and how the resulting translation gain or loss is to be recognized in the statements.

Assume that Russian Radiators is the Russian subsidiary of a U.S. firm and that the functional currency is defined as the U.S. dollar rather than the Russian ruble. The use of the temporal method requires that we do the following:

1. Remeasure cash, receivables, and liabilities at the current balance sheet rate.

2. Remeasure inventory (which is carried at historical cost in this case), fixed assets, and capital stock at the appropriate historical exchange rates.

Table 9.5   Russian Radiators Inc. Exchange Rates

Relevant exchange rates are as follows:

	U.S. $/Ruble		U.S. $/Ruble
Historical rate	0.0880	Avg. during 1999	0.0025
December 31, 1998	0.0056	Avg. 4th Q 1998	0.0080
December 31, 1999	0.0009	Avg. 4th Q 1999	0.0013

3. Remeasure most revenues and expenses at the average rate for the year; costs of sales and depreciation expense are translated at the appropriate historical exchange rates.

4. Take all remeasurement gains or losses directly to the income statement.

To accomplish these purposes, it is easier to remeasure the balance sheet before the income statement. Table 9.5 shows the relevant exchanges rates. Table 9.6 shows the rates applied in the translation process. Notice here that there is no exchange rate beside retained earnings. This is because the retained earnings amount is the difference between total assets and liabilities less the other stockholders' equity accounts (in this case, just capital stock). Thus, the retained earnings balance must be $932 at the end of 1999.

Table 9.6   Russian Radiators Inc. Balance Sheet

	Dec. 31, 1998 Russian Rubles	Exchange Rate $/Ruble	Dollars	Dec. 31, 1999 Russian Rubles	Exchange Rate $/Ruble	Dollars
Cash	20,000	0.0056	112	14,000	0.0009	126
Accounts receivable	40,000	0.0056	224	110,000	0.0009	99
Inventories	40,000	0.008	320	30,000	0.0013	39
Fixed assets	100,000	0.088	8800	100,000	0.088	8800
Accumulated depreciation	−20,000	0.088	−1760	−30,000	0.088	−2640
Total	180,000		7,696	224,000		6,311
Accounts payable	30,000	0.0056	168	50,000	0.0009	45
Bonds	21,247	0.0056	119	21,247	0.0009	19
Loan	44,000	0.0056	246.4	39,000	0.0009	35
Capital stock	60,000	0.088	5,280	60,000	0.088	5280
Retained earnings	24,753		1,883	53,753		932
	—		—	—		—
Total	180,000		7,696	224,000		6,311

Notes 1999:

Opening RE	24,753	1,883
Net Income/Loss	29,000	-1,038
Translation Gain		87
Closing RE	53,753	932

Table 9.7 Russian Radiators Inc. Income Statement

	Dec. 31, 1999 Russian Rubles	Exchange Rate $/Ruble	Dollars
Sales	230,000	0.0025	575
Expenses			
CGS	110,000	(see note)	531
Depreciation	10,000	0.088	880
Other	50,000	0.0025	125
Taxes	6,000	0.0025	15
Foreign Exchange Loss	25,000	0.0025	62
	—		—
Total Expenses	201,000		1,613
Net Income Before Translation Gain			–1,038
Translation Gain			87
	—		—
Net Income	29,000		–951
Calculating Cost of Goods Sold Under the Temporal Method			
Beginning Inventory	40,000	0.008	320
Purchases	100,000	0.0025	250
	—		—
	140,000		570
Ending Inventory	30,000	0.0013	39
	—		—
Cost of Goods Sold	110,000		531

The remeasured statement of income and retained earnings is found in Table 9.7. Notice that in the income statement, cost of sales and depreciation expense are not remeasured at the same exchange rate, as are other revenues and expenses. In the case of cost of sales, different rates are used for beginning inventory, purchases, and ending inventory. Depreciation expense is translated at the historical rate in effect when assets were purchased. In the case of ending inventory, it is useful at this point to briefly explain more specifically how the remeasurement process works. U.S. GAAP adheres to the lower-of-cost-or-market concept, so those two amounts must be calculated before determining which is the correct inventory figure. Cost is determined by multiplying the historical cost in the foreign currency by the exchange rate in effect when the inventory was acquired. Market is determined by multiplying the market value in the foreign currency by the current exchange rate (actually the exchange rate in effect when market is determined). The lower-of-cost-or-market test is then conducted in dollars. It is important to note that the test is not performed in the foreign currency but *is* performed in the reporting currency.

The income statement has a translation gain of $87. That figure is derived by working backward. We know from the balance sheet in Table 9.6 that the ending retained earnings balance must be $932. Because we were provided the beginning

Table 9.8 Russian Radiators Key Ratios

Ratio	Ruble Data 1999	U.S. $ Data 1999
Return on Investment	12.95%	−15.07%
Return on Sales	12.61%	−165.43%
Debt to Equity	52.96%	0.87%

retained earnings (RE) balance, we can derive the net income (NI) figure for the year (ending RE − beginning RE = NI). All the other accounts were remeasured, so the translation gain is the amount that must be incorporated to arrive at the net income figure. The important thing to note here is that the translation gain is taken directly to the income statement rather than to the balance sheet. Also notice in terms of ratios (Table 9.8) that Russian Radiators goes from an apparently profitable state with an average level of debt to one that has a very negative ROI and ROS but almost no debt.

Translation Process: Current Rate Method

The current rate method is far easier to negotiate. It is used when the functional currency is defined as the foreign currency. To accomplish the translation process, the following steps must be performed:

1. All assets and liabilities are translated at the current exchange rate.
2. Stockholders' equity accounts are translated at the appropriate historical exchange rates.
3. All revenue and expense items are translated at the average exchange rate for the period.
4. Dividends are translated at the exchange rate in effect when they were issued.
5. Translation gains and losses are taken to a special accumulated translation adjustment account in stockholders' equity.

Our example here is Pillai Auto and the relevant exchange rates in Table 9.9. Tables 9.10 and 9.11 show the income statement and balance sheet for Pillai Auto. Pillai is a subsidiary of a U.S. company, but one that is independent and where the functional currency is the local currency of the Republic of Trinidad and Tobago, the Trinidad and Tobago (TT) dollar. In the current rate method, it is better to translate the income statement before translating the balance sheet because the translation gain or loss becomes a balance sheet balancing amount rather than an

Table 9.9 Pillai Auto Exchange Rates TT$/US$

December 31, 1998	0.1935
December 31, 1999	0.1875
Historical rate	0.1600
Rate when equity was issued	0.16

Table 9.10 Pillai Auto Income Statement 1999

	TT$	TT$/US$	US$
Sales	31,500	0.1750	5,513
Expenses			
Cost of Goods Sold	(18,000)	0.1750	(3,150)
Depreciation	(2,750)	0.1750	(481)
Other	(4,500)	0.1750	(788)
Taxes	(1,500)	0.1750	(263)
Net Income	4,750		831
Dividends	2,375	0.1750	416
			415

income statement balancing amount as in the temporal method. Notice that in Table 9.10 all income statement accounts are translated at the average exchange rate for the period. The beginning retained earnings balance was provided, and dividends are translated at the exchange rate in effect when they were paid. Thus, the ending retained earnings balance is derived from the other figures rather than a balancing amount in the balance sheet.

Table 9.11 Pillai Auto Balance Sheet 1998 and 1999

	Dec. 31, 1998 (TT$)	TT$/US$	U.S. Dollars	Dec. 31, 1999 (TT$)	TT$/US$	U.S. Dollars
Cash	1,000	0.1935	194	2,000	0.1875	375
Accounts Receivable	3,900	0.1935	755	4,725	0.1875	886
Inventories	3,600	0.1935	697	4,700	0.1875	881
Fixed Assets	27,500	0.1935	5,321	27,500	0.1875	5,156
Accumulated Depreciation	(2,750)	0.1935	(532)	(5,500)	0.1875	(1,031)
Total	33,250		6,434	33,425		6,267
Accounts Payable	6,500	0.1935	1,258	6,000	0.1875	1,125
Long-Term Debt	12,500	0.1935	2,419	10,800	0.1875	2,025
Capital Stock	6,200	0.1600	992	6,200	0.16	992
Retained Earnings	8,050		1,765	10,425		2,181
Accumulated Translation Adjustment	—		—	—		(56)
Total	33,250		6,434	33,425		6,267

In Table 9.11 all assets and liabilities are translated at the current exchange rate. Capital stock is translated at the exchange rate in effect when it was issued, and retained earnings are picked up from Table 9.10. All that is left is the accumulated translation adjustment—$56 loss that makes the balance sheet balance. Also notice that the ratios of Pillai (Table 9.12) are almost identical in TT and US dollars. Thus if the local manager is rewarded based on ROI then he or she will be rewarded on operating performance rather than the performance of the country's currency. In contrast, the result for the manager at Russian Radiators will be quite different.

TRANSLATION PROCESS: GLOBAL OVERVIEW

United States

In the United States, foreign currency translation is conducted under SFAS 52 (as amended by SFAS 133). This standard requires firms to select a functional currency for each subsidiary. The functional currency is selected on the basis of operating criteria established by management. If the firm wishes to change the functional currency, it can do so only because the operating criteria used in the initial selection have changed. This was designed so that companies do not change functional currencies capriciously to take advantage of the differences in the financial statements that result from the different translation methods. Figure 9.1 sets out the SFAS 52 guidelines in chart form.

The actual translation process depends on which currency the books and records of the foreign entity are kept in and on how the parent defines the functional currency of the foreign entity. If the functional currency is not the same for parent and subsidiary then the subsidiary's books are translated into U.S. dollars using the current rate method. The standard used the current rate method as its predominant mode of reporting.

If the parent's activities are so intertwined with that of the subsidiary that the subsidiary has no independent existence but is essentially an extension of the parent, the subsidiary's functional currency is deemed to be the U.S. dollar, whatever currency the books are kept in. For such a subsidiary, the temporal method is used. Similarly, if the subsidiary operates in a country where there is a cumulative inflation rate of approximately 100 percent over a three-year period, the functional currency is deemed to be the U.S. dollar and the temporal method is used.

Up to this point, we have tried to focus on practices in the United States. However, the general rules of translation described in the temporal and current rate methods are essentially the same worldwide. Despite this, there are some interesting differences in practice.

Table 9.12 Pillai Auto Key Ratios

Ratio	TT$ Data 1999	U.S.$ Data 1999
Return on Investment	14.21%	13.26%
Return on Sales	15.08%	15.07%
Debt to Equity	64.96%	63.82%

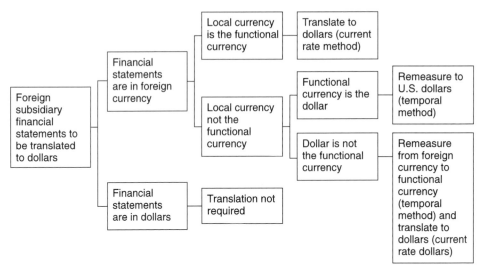

Figure 9.1   Choices of Functional Currency and Translation Method

Europe in General

The Fourth Directive, on the format and content of financial statements in the European Community, and the Seventh Directive, on consolidated financial statements, do not contain any guidance on accounting for foreign currency transactions and the translation of foreign currency financial statements. Some countries, such as the United Kingdom, Ireland, and the Netherlands, have standards. Others, such as France and Germany, have no standards or laws, so there is a great variance in practice. Whereas SFAS 52 in the United States requires that transaction gains and losses be taken to the income statement, there is no such uniform practice in Europe. Although European firms tend to take losses to income, gains are often deferred until payment is settled, which is the practice of the Internal Revenue Service in the United States.

Although both the current rate and temporal methods are allowed in most European countries, most tend to use the current rate method. The notable exception is Germany, where firms tend to use a form of the temporal method. The Germans do not make a distinction in translation methodology based on the functional currency, as is the case in the United States.

The French use the temporal method for integrated foreign companies (similar to using the reporting currency as the functional currency) and the current rate method for self-sustaining foreign entities (similar to using the foreign currency as the functional currency). Gains and losses are treated in the same way as in Statement 52. In the case of foreign entities in highly inflationary countries, however, the French allow firms to restate financial statements for the effect of inflation.

United Kingdom

In April 1983, the Accounting Standards Committee (now Accounting Standards Board) of the United Kingdom issued Statement of Standard Accounting Practice No. 20 (SSAP 20), "Foreign Currency Translation." Prior to that time, the method of translation most widely used in the United Kingdom was the current rate method (known as the *closing rate method* in the United Kingdom). However, SSAP 20 allows the use of the closing rate method or the temporal method, depending on the operating relationship that exists between the investor and investee. This is similar to the concept of the functional currency described in Statement 52.

In spite of the similarities between the standards of the United States and the United Kingdom, some important differences also exist.

- SSAP 20 does not deal with foreign currency transactions. It comments in the foreword to the standard that foreign currency transactions must be translated into the reporting currency, but it does not deal with many of the issues covered in Statement 52.

- In terms of terminology, the British use the closing rate rather than current rate.

- The current rate is also permitted for the translation of revenues and expenses.

- Statement 52 requires the use of the temporal method to translate the financial statements of operations in highly inflationary economies. SSAP 20 recommends that companies, where possible, adjust financial statements to current price levels before translating them.

- SSAP 20 does not require the level of disclosure on translation gains and losses that is required in Statement 52. In addition, British firms do not have to set up a separate section in stockholders' equity to hold translation adjustments since they already use a reserve account for a variety of adjustments. SSAP 20 requires disclosure of the movement on reserves during the year. It requires that somewhere the net amount of exchange gains and losses included in equity and in net income for the period be disclosed.

A reading of SSAP 20 reveals two interesting points. The first is that the vast majority of firms affected by the standard did not have to change their practices materially insofar as it has been estimated that over 90 percent of the British multinationals were using the closing rate method when the standard was adopted. The experience in the United States was just the opposite when Statement 52 was issued: essentially all firms were using the temporal method. The other point is that the British standard seems to have more flexibility built in than does the U.S. standard.

Canada

The Canadian standard on foreign currency translation was adopted in July 1983. That standard, which dealt with both transactions and translation, has elements that are similar to as well as different from the United States and British standards.

For translating foreign currency financial statements, the temporal and current rate methods can be used depending on the operating characteristics of the foreign operations. If the reporting enterprise is an integrated foreign operation, the temporal method for translation must be used. This is similar to defining the functional currency as the reporting currency in Statement 52. Translation gains and losses are taken to income unless they relate to long-term debt. As noted earlier, those gains and losses can be deferred and amortized.

If the reporting enterprise is a self-sustaining foreign operation, the current rate method must be used. This is similar to defining the functional currency as something other than the reporting currency in Statement 52. Translation gains and losses are taken to a separate section in stockholders' equity rather than taken to income, which is consistent with Statement 52.

If the foreign operation is in a highly inflationary country, its financial statements should be translated into the reporting currency using the temporal method. This is consistent with Statement 52 but inconsistent with SSAP 20, which requires the adjustment for price-level changes before translation using the closing rate method.

International Accounting Standards

International Accounting Standard No. 21, "The Effects of Changes in Foreign Exchange Rates" (IAS 21), was first issued in 1983 but revised in 1993 (effective 1995). As one can tell from the dates, the British, Canadian, and international standards were all completed about the same time and within a few years of the issuance of Statement 52 in the United States. IAS 21 is a fascinating standard because it was obviously written to accommodate the British and Americans, and it also contains a few ideas relevant to some of the developing countries.

IAS 21 contains provisions for both transactions and translation of financial statements. In the case of translating foreign currency financial statements, the closing rate and temporal methods are used, depending on the operating characteristics of the foreign operations. When using the closing rate method and translating the income statement, the average rate must be used. Operations in highly inflationary countries must be adjusted for local inflation before translation into the reporting currency. Translation gains and losses are taken to stockholders' equity.

CONCLUSIONS

One of the major environmental challenges faced by the global firm is the changing value of the world's currencies relative to its own. For financial accounting, the challenge is to account for changes in the value of foreign currency assets and liabilities arising from transactions and investments abroad. The key questions that arise are how we measure the value of an asset or liability and, when these values change, how we account for the result (i.e., is this income or not?). In the United States and a few other countries, this situation has been made somewhat easier by the creation of a separate comprehensive income statement, which measures the result of unrealized changes in the value of assets and liabilities as pseudo-income. Nonetheless, the fact that the U.S. FASB has now issued three major statements on valuing foreign exchange assets and liabilities (and two peripheral ones) in the last twenty years indicates that this issue is both difficult and important.

SUMMARY

1. For foreign currency transactions, a variety of methods of income recognition are used around the world. The immediate recognition method is required by the United States and IASC.

2. Hedging and the use of derivatives is an effective way to reduce foreign currency transaction risk.

3. The translation of foreign currency financial statements involves dealing with the issues of which exchange rates are to be used and the treatment of gains and losses.

4. Under the current rate method, assets and liabilities are translated at the current exchange rate, stockholders' equity is translated at the historical rate, net income is translated at the average rate, and translation gains and losses are taken to a special account in stockholders' equity.

5. Under the temporal method, cash and amounts receivable and payable in cash are remeasured at the current rate. Assets carried at past exchange rates are remeasured at historical rates. Assets carried at current exchange prices are remeasured at the current rate. Revenue and expense items are remeasured at the average rate except for cost of sales and depreciation expense, which are translated at their relevant historical rates. Translation gains and losses are taken to the income statement.

6. Translation methodologies vary around the world but there is some consensus that the method used should depend on the operating characteristics of the firm's foreign operations. In general, the current rate method tends to be the predominant method of currency translation used in practice.

DISCUSSION QUESTIONS

1. When it comes to translating the financial statements of entities in highly inflationary countries, which of the following approaches makes more sense and why?

   a. Remeasure using the temporal method, even though the functional currency is the local currency for operating purposes.

   b. Restate for inflation and translate using the current rate method.

2. Why do currency differences affect foreign exchange reporting?

3. Why do German and French approaches to reporting foreign exchange gains and losses differ from those in the United Kingdom?

4. What difference has the introduction of a comprehensive income statement made to U.S. accounting for foreign exchange?

5. Choose a country and prepare a report on its foreign exchange risk. How do you think accountants should deal with this?

6. Why do you think it has been so difficult for accounting regulators to deal with accounting for foreign exchange over the last twenty-five years?

EXERCISES

Assume the following exchange rates between the U.S. dollar and the British pound sterling:

Spot	April 1	1.6290
Three-month forward	April 1	1.6095
Spot	April 30	1.6275
Spot	May 31	1.6005
Spot	June 30	1.5950

1. On April 1, a U.S. manufacturer enters into a commitment to sell equipment to a British importer with the sale denominated in pounds sterling £500,000. The goods are to be delivered the same day and paid for on June 1.

   a. Assuming that no forward contract is entered into, what would be the journal entries for the U.S. exporter on April 1, April 30, May 31, and June 30? Assume the books are closed each month.

    b. Assuming that a forward contract is entered into on April 1, what would be the journal entries for the U.S. exporter on April 1, April 30, May 31, and June 30?

2. On April 1, a British manufacturer enters into a commitment to sell equipment to a U.S. importer for £100,000. The goods are to be delivered on April 1 and paid for on June 30.

    a. Assuming that no forward contract is entered into, what would be the journal entries for the U.S. importer on April 1, April 30, May 31, and June 30?

    b. Assuming that a forward contract is entered into on April 1, what would be the journal entries for the U.S. importer on April 1, April 30, May 31, and June 30?

3. On April 1, a U.S. manufacturer sells equipment to a British importer. The sale is denominated in pounds sterling £250,000.

    a. Assuming that no forward contract is entered into, what would be the journal entries for the U.S. exporter on April 1, April 30, May 31, and June 30?

    b. Assuming that a forward contract is entered into on April 1, what would be the journal entries for the U.S. exporter on April 1, April 30, May 31, and June 30?

4. If the sale were denominated in U.S. dollars at the April 1 exchange rate, what would be the journal entries for parts (a) and (b) of Exercise 3 in pounds sterling for the British importer?

CASE

Piparo International

On June 1, a British software developer sells software to Piparo International, a U.S.-based software company, for £500,000, with payment to be made on June 30. Because of concern over the possible foreign exchange risk, Joan Tan, Piparo's chief foreign exchange trader, got the following information from her commercial and investment banks:

    $1.5970 spot rate on June 1

    $1.5969 forward rate for June 30 delivery

Questions:

1. What would Piparo's journal entries be on June 1 and June 30 if Joan Tan decided to enter into the forward contract, and the spot rate on June 30 were $1.6500?

2. How would your answer for Question 1 differ if the spot rate on June 30 were $1.5500?

3. Based on this case, what are the strengths and weaknesses of using forwards and options as hedging devices?

CASE

Yarmouth Woolens

Yarmouth Woolens is a Canadian processor of wool fibers and manufacturer of a variety of intermediary wool products such as yarns and carpet fibers. Located in Halifax, Nova Scotia, Yarmouth Woolens purchases unprocessed fleece, and manufactures in Canada, Scotland, Australia, Greece, and Uruguay. The Canadian and Scottish operations are responsible for most of the North American and European sales, while the Greek and Uruguayan operations sell primarily back to the Canadian plants. The Australian plant manufactures and sells in the local Australian market.

All five manufacturing plants are in areas where unprocessed fleece is readily available. Each plant buys locally and then processes the wool into yarns and carpet fibers. While the Canadian home company is over 40 years old, the foreign operations are all less than 10 years old, the newest acquisition being the Greek plant in 1988.

As a result, Yarmouth is not very experienced in multinational ventures and has had a lot of troubles with their foreign operations. They have experienced labor difficulties in the United Kingdom both from labor strikes and heavy employee turnover. They have encountered bureaucratic government controls in Greece, in spite of Greece dropping most of these as part of joining the European Community in 1981. Additionally, inflation in Greece has been 14 to 15 percent in 1988–1989. They have been pleasantly surprised by the welcoming attitude expressed in Uruguay and have found that Uruguay is a country that welcomes foreign direct investment. However, Uruguay has had severe inflation problems: 83 percent in 1985, 69 percent in 1988, and nearly 100 percent in 1989. This has caused a lot of problems with the financial statements of the Uruguayan company. Last, the Australian company has been a source of financial problems. The distance from Halifax has been blamed for unresolved disputes between Australian management and Yarmouth. As a result, Yarmouth has not been happy with their apparent lack of control.

Each foreign operation is a 100 percent wholly owned subsidiary. The ability to own 100 percent of all foreign stock in each of these countries was an important consideration in deciding to make the foreign investments. While different amounts of control were allowed for each foreign operation, it was thought that 100 percent ownership would allow Yarmouth to step in if necessary.

Foreign Currency Translation

The Australian and British subsidiaries have conducted their affairs quite independently and in their own currencies. The Uruguayan company has been tightly controlled by the Canadian operation, although sales to the home company have always been denominated in Uruguayan new pesos, so that the Canadian operation could extend its payments in less expensive pesos by purchasing them at the last minute with Canadian dollars. This has been part of their strategy to combat inflation. The Greek subsidiary also has been tightly controlled, exporting primarily to the United Kingdom. Those sales have been denominated usually in U.K. pounds, since the inflation rate has been considered less of a concern.

Yarmouth, being a Canadian company, translated the results of its foreign operations into Canadian dollars using the temporal and current rate methods as required under the Canadian Institute of Chartered Accountants *CICA Handbook*, Section 1650. The procedures are substantially similar to those of the United States as outlined in Financial Accounting Standards Board Statement No. 52: *Foreign Currency Translation*. Both of these statements are consistent with International Accounting Standards Statement No. 21: *Accounting for the Effects of Changes in Foreign Exchange Rates*.

As a result, the following translation methods into Canadian dollars were used for each of the foreign operations:

Australia	Current rate
United Kingdom	Current rate
Greece	Temporal
Uruguay	Temporal

Exhibit 1 shows the balance sheets and income statements of the four foreign operations in local currencies, but in accordance with Canadian accounting principles for 1990. Exhibit 2 displays exchange rates used for the translation of financial statements. Exhibit 3 shows the four foreign operations after appropriate translation has taken place. Yarmouth uses both untranslated and translated information to assess local foreign performance and make comparisons with its Canadian operations.

Exhibit 1   Untranslated Financial Statements for Yarmouth Subsidiaries

	Balance Sheet December 31			
	1989 Australia Aus $ (in thousands)	**1990 Australia Aus $ (in thousands)**	**1989 U.K. £ (in thousands)**	**1990 U.K. £ (in thousands)**
Assets				
Cash	3,000	1,750	7,000	14,500
Receivables	9,000	8,250	3,000	4,500
Inventory*	4,000	6,000	6,000	2,000
Property, plant, & equipment	19,000	19,000	27,000	27,000
Accumulated depreciation	(6,000)	(9,000)	(6,000)	(9,000)
Total assets	29,000	26,000	37,000	39,000
Liabilities and equity				
Accounts payable	6,000	6,000	4,000	4,000
Short-term debt	10,000	11,000	12,000	12,000
Common stock	11,000	11,000	8,000	8,000
Retained earnings	2,000	(2,000)	13,000	15,000
Total equities	29,000	26,000	37,000	39,000

Income Statement Year Ending December 31, 1990		
Sales	17,000	12,000
Cost of sales	12,000	6,000
Gross margin	5,000	6,000
Expenses		
Depreciation	3,000	3,000
Other	6,000	1,000
Total	9,000	4,000
Net income	(4,000)	2,000
Retained earnings 12/31/89	2,000	13,000
Retained earings 12/31/90	(2,000)	15,000

*Inventory is valued at last in, first out. Although LIFO is acceptable in Canada, it is a minority method and is used here in anticipation of sale to a U.S. company.

Exhibit 1   Untranslated Financial Statements for Yarmouth Subsidiaries (*continued*)

Cash Flow Statement
Year Ending December 31, 1990

Cash from operations	(4,000)	2,000
Net income	3,000	3,000
Add depreciation	(1,000)	5,000
Receivables change	750	(1,500)
Inventory change	(2,000)	4,000
Payables change	0	0
	(2,250)	7,500
Investment: property	0	0
Financing	1,000	0
Change in cash	(1,250)	7,500

Balance Sheet
December 31

	1989 Greece drachma (in millions)	1990 Greece drachma (in millions)	1989 Uruguay new pesos (in millions)	1990 Uruguay new pesos (in millions)
Assets				
Cash	1,140	1,290	1,520	1,712
Receivables	2,190	3,440	2,860	3,408
Inventory†	1,010	1,310	540	440
Property, plant, & equipment	3,720	3,720	6,120	6,420
Accumulated depreciation	(600)	(1,200)	(720)	(1,260)
Total assets	7,460	8,560	10,320	10,720
Liabilities and equity				
Accounts payable	820	820	2,120	2,120
Short-term debt	4,070	3,870	6,210	6,310
Common stock	2,050	2,050	550	550
Retained earnings	520	1,820	1,440	1,740
Total equities	7,460	8,560	10,320	10,720

†Inventory is valued at last in, first out. Although LIFO is acceptable in Canada, it is a minority method and is used here in anticipation of sale to a U.S. company.

(*continued*)

Exhibit 1   Untranslated Financial Statements for Yarmouth Subsidiaries (*continued*)

<table>
<tr><td colspan="3" align="center">**Income Statement**
Year Ending December 31, 1990</td></tr>
<tr><td>Sales</td><td align="right">12,000</td><td align="right">2,060</td></tr>
<tr><td>Cost of sales</td><td align="right">6,300</td><td align="right">830</td></tr>
<tr><td>Gross margin</td><td align="right">5,700</td><td align="right">1,230</td></tr>
<tr><td>Expenses</td><td></td><td></td></tr>
<tr><td>Depreciation</td><td align="right">600</td><td align="right">540</td></tr>
<tr><td>Other</td><td align="right">3,800</td><td align="right">390</td></tr>
<tr><td>Total</td><td align="right">4,400</td><td align="right">930</td></tr>
<tr><td>Net income</td><td align="right">1,300</td><td align="right">300</td></tr>
<tr><td>Retained earnings, 12/31/89</td><td align="right">520</td><td align="right">1,440</td></tr>
<tr><td>Retained earnings, 12/31/90</td><td align="right">1,820</td><td align="right">1,740</td></tr>
</table>

<table>
<tr><td colspan="3" align="center">**Cash Flow Statement**
Year Ending December 31, 1990</td></tr>
<tr><td>Cash from operations</td><td></td><td></td></tr>
<tr><td>Net income</td><td align="right">1,300</td><td align="right">300</td></tr>
<tr><td>Add depreciation</td><td align="right">600</td><td align="right">540</td></tr>
<tr><td></td><td align="right">1,900</td><td align="right">840</td></tr>
<tr><td>Receivables change</td><td align="right">(1,250)</td><td align="right">(548)</td></tr>
<tr><td>Inventory change</td><td align="right">(300)</td><td align="right">100</td></tr>
<tr><td>Payables change</td><td align="right">0</td><td align="right">0</td></tr>
<tr><td></td><td align="right">350</td><td align="right">392</td></tr>
<tr><td>Investment: property</td><td align="right">0</td><td align="right">(300)</td></tr>
<tr><td>Financing</td><td align="right">(200)</td><td align="right">100</td></tr>
<tr><td>Change in cash</td><td align="right">150</td><td align="right">192</td></tr>
</table>

Exhibit 2 Exchange Rates: Cost in U.S. Dollars of One Foreign Currency Unit

	Canada	Uruguay	Greece	Australia	United Kingdom
Canadian acquisition date	$0.8382	$0.00223	$0.00677	$0.8540	$1.8085
December 31, 1989	$0.8635	$0.00126	$0.00640	$0.7899	$1.6140
Average for 1990	$0.8628	$0.00095	$0.00633	$0.7812	$1.7720
U.S. acquisition date/ December 31, 1990	$0.8621	$0.00063	$0.00627	$0.7725	$1.9300
Average for 1991	$0.8638	$0.00052	$0.00599	$0.7663	$1.8998
December 31, 1991	$0.8654	$0.00041	$0.00571	$0.7600	$1.8695

Exhibit 3 Financial Statements for Yarmouth Subsidiaries Translated into Canadian Dollars (Current Rate Method) (Dollars in Thousands)

	Balance Sheet December 31			
	1989 Australia Can. $	1990 Australia Can. $	1989 U.K. Can. $	1990 U.K. Can. $
Assets				
Cash	2,744	1,568	13,084	32,463
Receivables	8,233	7,393	5,608	10,075
Inventory (LIFO)	3,660	5,377	11,215	4,477
Property, plant, & equipment	17,382	17,026	50,468	60,447
Accumulated depreciation	(5,489)	(8,065)	(11,215)	(20,149)
Total assets	26,530	23,299	69,160	87,313
Liabilities and equity				
Accounts payable	5,489	5,377	7,477	8,955
Short-term debt	9,148	9,857	22,430	26,866
Translation adjustment	(1,452)	(1,658)	(6,056)	2,075
Common stock	11,292	11,292	17,260	17,260
Retained earnings	2,053	(1,569)	28,049	32,157
Total equities	26,530	23,299	69,160	87,313

	Income Statement Year Ending December 31, 1990			
Sales		15,394		24,648
Cost of sales		10,866		12,324
Gross margin		4,528		12,324
Expenses				
Depreciation		2,717		6,162
Other		5,433		2,054
Total		8,150		8,216
Exchange gain/loss		0		0
Net income		(3,622)		4,108
Retained earnings, 12/31/89		2,053		28,049
Retained earnings, 12/31/90		(1,569)		32,157

(continued)

Exhibit 3 Financial Statements for Yarmouth Subsidiaries Translated into Canadian Dollars (Current Rate Method) (Dollars in Thousands) (*continued*)

Cash Flow Statement
Year Ending December 31, 1990

Cash from operations		
Net income	(3,622)	4,108
Add translation gain/loss	0	0
Add depreciation	2,717	6,162
	(905)	10,270
Receivables change	679	(3,081)
Inventory change	(1,811)	8,216
Payables change	0	0
	(2,037)	15,405
Investment: property	0	0
Financing	905	0
Change in cash before translation	(1,132)	15,405
Exchange rate effect	(44)	3,974
Change in cash	(1,176)	19,379

Balance Sheet
December 31

1989 Greece	1990 Greece Can. $	1989 Uruguay Can. $	1990 Uruguay Can. $	Can. $
Assets				
Cash	8,550	9,420	2,280	1,369
Receivables	16,425	25,109	4,290	2,727
Inventory (LIFO)	8,181	10,401	1,512	1,232
Property, plant, & equipment	30,132	30,132	17,136	17,481
Accumulated depreciation	(4,860)	(9,720)	(2,016)	(3,528)
Total assets	58,428	65,342	23,202	19,281
Liabilities and equity				
Accounts payable	6,150	5,986	3,180	1,696
Short-term debt	30,525	28,251	9,315	5,048
Translation adjustment	0	0	0	0
Common stock	16,605	16,605	1,540	1,540
Retained earnings	5,148	14,500	9,167	10,997
Total equities	58,428	65,342	23,202	19,281

Exhibit 3 Financial Statements for Yarmouth Subsidiaries Translated into Canadian Dollars (Current Rate Method) (Dollars in Thousands) (*continued*)

Income Statement
Year Ending December 31, 1990

Sales	88,800	2,369
Cost of sales	46,620	1,120
Gross margin	42,180	1,249
Expenses		
Depreciation	4,860	1,512
Other	28,120	448
Depreciation	4,860	1,512
Total	32,980	1,960
Exchange gain/loss	152	2,541
Net income	9,352	1,830
Retained earnings, 12/31/89	5,148	9,167
Retained earnings, 12/31/90	14,500	10,997

Cash Flow Statement
Year Ending December 31, 1990

Cash from operations		
Net income	9,352	1,830
Add translation gain/loss	(152)	(2,541)
Add depreciation	4,860	1,512
	14,060	801
Receivables change	(9,247)	(631)
Inventory change	(2,220)	280
Payables change	0	0
	2,593	450
Investment: property	0	(345)
Financing	(1,480)	115
Change in cash before translation	1,113	220
Exchange rate effect	(243)	(1,131)
Change in cash	870	(911)

Exhibit 4 Untranslated Financial Statements for U.S.-Owned Subsidiaries

Balance Sheets
December 31

	1990 Australia Aus. $ (in thousands)	1991 Australia Aus. $ (in thousands)	1990 U.K. £ (in thousands)	1991 U.K. £ (in thousands)
Assets				
Cash	1,750	1,538	14,500	10,842
Receivables	8,250	11,962	4,500	6,158
Inventory (LIFO)	6,000	5,000	2,000	3,000
Property, plant, & equipment	19,000	19,000	27,000	33,000
Accumulated depreciation	(9,000)	(12,000)	(9,000)	(12,000)
Total assets	26,000	25,500	39,000	41,000
Liabilities and equity				
Accounts payable	6,000	6,000	4,000	4,000
Short-term debt	11,000	9,000	12,000	10,000
Common stock	11,000	11,000	8,000	8,000
Retained earnings	(2,000)	(500)	15,000	19,000
Total equities	26,000	25,500	39,000	41,000

Income Statement
Year Ending December 31, 1991

Sales		26,000		14,200
Cost of sales		15,600		5,940
Gross margin		10,400		8,260
Expenses				
Depreciation		3,000		3,000
Other		5,900		1,260
Total		8,900		4,260
Net income		1,500		4,000
Retained earnings, 12/31/89		(2,000)		15,000
Retained earnings, 12/31/90		(500)		19,000

Exhibit 4 Untranslated Financial Statements for U.S.-Owned Subsidiaries (*continued*)

Cash Flow Statement
Year Ending December 31, 1991

Cash from operations		
Net income	1,500	4,000
Add depreciation	3,000	3,000
	4,500	7,000
Receivables change	(3,712)	(1,658)
Inventory change	1,000	(1,000)
Payables change	0	0
	1,788	4,342
Investment: property	0	(6,000)
Financing	(2,000)	(2,000)
Change in cash	(212)	(3,658)

Balance Sheets
December 31

	1990 Greece drachma (in millions)	1991 Greece drachma (in millions)	1990 Uruguay new pesos (in millions)	1991 Uruguay new pesos (in millions)
Assets				
Cash	1,290	1,345	1,712	1,919
Receivables	3,440	3,985	3,408	3,821
Inventory (LIFO)	1,310	910	440	540
Property, plant, & equipment	3,720	4,020	6,420	6,120
Accumulated depreciation	(1,200)	(1,800)	(1,260)	(1,800)
Total assets	8,560	8,460	10,720	10,600
Liabilities and equity				
Accounts payable	820	820	2,120	2,120
Short-term debt	3,870	3,620	6,310	6,110
Common stock	2,050	2,050	550	550
Retained earnings	1,820	1,970	1,740	1,820
Total equities	8,560	8,460	10,720	10,600

(*continued*)

Exhibit 4 Untranslated Financial Statements for U.S.-Owned Subsidiaries (*continued*)

Income Statement
Year Ending December 31, 1990

Sales	9,500	1,970
Cost of sales	5,700	886
Gross margin	3,800	1,084
Expenses		
Depreciation	600	540
Other	3,050	464
Total	3,650	1,004
Net income	150	80
Retained earnings, 12/31/89	1,820	1,740
Retained earnings, 12/31/90	1,970	1,820

Cash Flow Statement
Year Ending December 31, 1990

Cash from operations		
Net income	150	80
Add depreciation	600	540
	750	620
Receivables change	(545)	(413)
Inventory change	400	(100)
Payables change	0	0
	605	107
Investment: property	(300)	300
Financing	(250)	(200)
Change in cash	55	207

The Sale of Foreign Operations

Yarmouth has never been comfortable with operations abroad, and mediocre and mixed performances of these companies along with their small size relative to the Canadian operations prompted them to search for a buyer of all the subsidiaries. After close to a year of searching, they located Lawrence Fibers in Massachusetts and concluded a transaction involving four separate prices, one for each company.

The purchase was completed December 31, 1990. The assets of each company were considered fairly valued at their book values and any difference between Lawrence's cost and the book value was due to goodwill. Goodwill, of course, is carried on the books of Lawrence.

The new owner, however, was informed by Yarmouth of its difficulties in controlling some of the operations. As a result, Lawrence decided to tightly control both the British and Australian subsidiaries. Considerable profit repatriation has been made from these operations, and both managements have been replaced by U.S. expatriate management. The results of this policy have been mixed. While the Australian company is now very responsive to the home office, the Scottish company is still experiencing labor problems. Furthermore, the Scottish firm has made it clear that it does not like being controlled by Lawrence. Both, however, are now profitable.

The Uruguayan operation continues as before except that sales are now satisfied with U.S. dollars, although local management is involved in more of the day-to-day decisions. The management in Lawrence has found that the heavy control over the U.K. and Australian subsidiaries uses a lot of their resources, especially since they must also closely monitor Uruguay. As a result, Lawrence found that it is necessary to let the subsidiary in Greece operate autonomously, conducting its sales and purchases in Greek drachmas and serving the European Community market along with the U.K. operation. This strategy, while due to depleted resources by which to control the company, is also helpful in letting them explore the new free markets of eastern Europe where they are geographically so close.

The Foreign Operations After The Sale

The results for 1992 for the four companies in their currencies are shown in Exhibit 4. United States generally accepted accounting principles are used which are substantially similar to those of Canada. Because of the different roles these companies play for the U.S. company, the following methods were used for currency translation:

Australia	Temporal
United Kingdom	Temporal
Greece	Current rate
Uruguay	Temporal[1]

References

Beaver, W., & Wolfson, M. (1984, March–April). Foreign currency translation gains and losses: What effect do they have and what do they mean? *Financial Analysts Journal*, pp. 28–36.

Canadian Institute of Chartered Accountants (1983, June). *CICA handbook. Section 1650. Foreign currency translation* (pp. 401–423).

Financial Accounting Standards Board (1981, December). *Foreign currency translation* (Statement of Financial Accounting Standards No. 52) (par. 5–14).

International Accounting Standards Committee (1983, July). *Accounting for the effects of changes in foreign exchange rates* (International Accounting Standard No. 21).

Price Waterhouse (1984). *Doing business in Greece*. New York.

Price Waterhouse (1992). *Doing business in Uruguay*. New York.

Questions:

1. Perform financial statement analysis for Yarmouth's foreign subsidiaries using Exhibit 1 and 3. Your analysis should include income/sales, return on investment, working capital, current ratio, quick ratio, and debt/equity.

    a. Explain why some of these ratios are changed after translation.

    b. Should Yarmouth evaluate their foreign operations before or after translation?

    c. Could translation have any effect on management behavior?

2. Translate the newly owned U.S. foreign subsidiaries using appropriate methods and perform the financial statement analysis from 1 above.[2]

    a. Does the new reporting currency have an impact on the presentation of the companies?

    b. What effect does the change in translation methods have on the presentation of the subsidiaries?

---

[1]Though the functional currency of the Uruguayan company is now less clear, the country is experiencing hyperinflation and must, therefore, use the temporal method, regardless of any change in its control of operations.

[2]*Note:* Students may find that creating a spreadsheet program to produce results in the format shown in Exhibit 3 may be useful. Alternatively, the results can be done manually using the exchange rates in Exhibit 2.

REFERENCES AND FURTHER READING

Bartov, Eli. (1997). "Foreign Currency Exposure of Multinational Firms: Accounting Measures and Market Valuation." *Contemporary Accounting Research* 14 (4, Winter): 623–652.

Bartov, Eli and Gordon M. Bodnar (1995). "Foreign Currency Translation Reporting and the Exchange-Rate Exposure Effect." *Journal of International Financial Management & Accounting* 6 (2, Summer): 93–114.

Cooper, Kerry, Donald R. Fraser, and Malcolm R. Richards. (1978). "The Impact of SFAS #8 on Financial Management Practices." *Financial Executive* 46 (6, June): 26–40.

Choi, Frederick D. S. and Ronald R. Gunn. (1997). "Hyperinflation Reporting and Performance Assessment." *Journal of Financial Statement Analysis* 2 (4, Summer): 30–38.

Pourciau, Susan and Thomas F. Schaefer. (1995). "The Nature of the Market's Response to the Earnings Effect of Voluntary Changes in Accounting for Foreign Operations." *Journal of Accounting, Auditing & Finance* 10 (1, Winter): 51–70.

PriceWaterhouse Coopers. (1998). *The New Standard on Accounting for Derivative Instruments and Hedging Activities.* New York: PriceWaterhouse Coopers.

Wilson, Arlette C. and Sarah Stanwick. (1995). "Alternatives to Current Accounting for Derivative Instruments." *CPA Journal* 65 (12, December): 48–49.

SOME USEFUL INTERNET WEB SITES

1. CPE Online: *http://www.cpeonline.com/cpenew/aasems.asp*
   A U.S. commercial online training program for accountants.

2. *http://www.2g.biglobe.ne.jp/~ykamur/n990718c.htm*
   Business Accounting Deliberation Council (Japan) policies on foreign exchange accounting.

3. *http://www.x-rates.com/*
   X-Rate currency conversion service.

4. FX Net Statement of Recommended Accounting Practice of Derivatives:
   http://www.fxfxnet.com/members/treasury/srapd.htm#top
   FXFXNET, Ltd. Provides specific foreign exchange information to global FX traders and corporate treasurers.

5. Micromash: *http://www.micromash.com/description/der2.htm*
   A continuing professional education service unit on "Accounting for Derivatives."

6. International Treasurer: *http://www.intltreasurer.com/deraccabr.htm*
   The *Journal of Treasury and Risk Management* article on accounting for derivatives and subsequent updates.

CHAPTER TEN

AUDITING AND THE MULTINATIONAL ENTERPRISE

INTRODUCTION

Auditors have traditionally practiced internationally, both as individuals and as firms. The main impetus behind this movement has been the globalization of business, which has accelerated especially in recent years. As enterprises became multinational, they asked that their financial advisors be equally multinational. As a result, professional accountants have organized themselves into global organizations, providing a wide range of services throughout the world. This chapter examines the role of the external auditor in its interaction with the multinational. It also examines the largest auditors in their roles as global service corporations and some of the unique problems they experience.

The external auditor is an independent professional who works closely with clients to provide global value-added services such as tax advice, training, review of financial control systems, and, in more remote locations, basic accounting services. Given that audit firms often have offices and correspondents in a larger number of countries than any single multinational firm, external auditors have also become repositories of information about operating conditions for firms wishing to move into a particular location.

THE GLOBAL AUDIT

Services of the Global Audit Firm

Although each firm is different, the services provided by the global audit firm include:

- Audit/attestation and assurance services
- Tax advisory and compliance services
- Consulting/management advisory services

The services described in Table 10.1 provide a broad taxonomy that applies equally well to domestic and global firms. What is different about the global corpo-

Table 10.1 Taxonomy of Global Auditing

	Attestation	**Assurance**	**Consulting/Tax**
Result	Written conclusion about the reliability of the written assertions of another party.	Better information for decision makers. Recommendations might be a byproduct.	Recommendations based on the objectives of the engagement. Tax documents for the government. Tax advice.
Objective	Reliable information.	Better decision making.	Better outcomes.
Independence	Required by standards.	Included in definition.	Not required.
Substance of auditor output	Conformity with established or stated criteria.	Assurance about reliability or relevance of information. Criteria might be established, stated, or unstated.	Recommendations; not measured against formal criteria.
Form of auditor output	Written.	Some form of communication.	Written or oral.

ration is the complexity of these functions and the number of potential audit locations. Procter & Gamble (P&G) operates in 140 countries, each with its own unique reporting rules, currency, and taxes. Their auditors have to review their operations in each of these countries plus in many of them file a tax return. They also have to prepare a consolidated return in P&G's home base in the United States.

CHALLENGES TO AUDITING THE MULTINATIONAL ENTERPRISE

Although audit responsibilities are similar for international and domestic operations, there are some unique challenges in the foreign environment, such as local accounting practices, foreign currency, local legal and business practices, language and customs, and distance. Although most large companies attempt to standardize their accounting practice worldwide, it does not happen everywhere. Local records may be kept according to local accounting procedures, which makes it difficult to use a standardized audit package. Also, the infrequency of audits (because of distance) may mean that there are insufficient accounting data to provide a clear audit trail. Some of the factors making auditing a challenging task include:

- Local business practices and customs
- Differences in currency, language, and law between countries
- Distance and organizational issues
- Availability of suitable personnel

Audit Challenges: Local Business Practices and Customs

Audit and assurance procedures employed by audit firms are designed to verify past transactions, assess the quality of the control system, and determine future areas of risk. Local business practices and customs can make this a challenging process owing to:

1. *Predominance of cash.* Paying expenses by cash, rather than check, is common practice in many countries, particularly emerging market economies, but it makes record keeping of expenses and revenue control difficult. Japan provides a good example of some of the challenges that arise in cash management. It is very common for the Japanese to use cash instead of checks for some transactions. To send cash in the mail, they use money envelopes carried in special pouches by the mail carrier. Larger businesses use checks, but banks often provide only computerized lists of transactions rather than cancelled checks. This makes it difficult to check the signature and authorization of actual checks during the audit. Because of the interlocking nature of banks, many payments are made by bank transfers directly from one back account to another. The only verification of the transfers is a computer printout. Some firms use a variety of transfers to keep the government from verifying earnings for a tax base.

2. *Inability to confirm accounts receivable.* In most cases, the confirmation letter itself must be translated into another language. Relying on the customer to return the confirmation is another challenge because foreign customers lack experience with confirmations. It may not be the custom for local auditors to send confirmations for accounts receivable or even to confirm year-end bank balances. The mail service may also be inefficient and unreliable, and it may take weeks before the customer receives the confirmation letter, if the customer receives it at all. In emerging markets where qualified staff are rare, audit confirmations are often seen as an intrusion and responded to with caution. This is particularly true in countries where auditors must by practice or law report to the government without necessarily telling their clients.

Audit Challenges: Currency, Language, and Law

Foreign Currency   Foreign currency restrictions and transfer requirements should be known for each country in which the auditor works. In addition, the auditor must be aware of corporate procedures for translating financial statements and recording foreign currency transactions so that reports sent to the parent in its own currency are prepared properly. Management must determine which translation methodology is to be used, and the auditor needs to determine if the choice is based on the right criteria, using the appropriate accounting standard.

Language and Culture   Ignorance of the local language can be a fatal handicap when the auditor deals with bilingual personnel. Having to rely on a translator may mean that the auditor is not getting the full story. In many countries, the financial statements must be kept in the local language and currency, so knowledge of that language is essential. Sometimes, knowing the language can be useful for getting information in touchy situations. For example, two auditors of the Brazilian subsidiary of a large multinational energy company noticed that a purchasing agent was driving a relatively expensive car. Because the two auditors spoke the local language, they were able to go to the man's home and interview his father. They found out from the proud father that his son was so important he received a 5 percent commission on everything he bought for the company. Needless to say, the purchasing agent did not last long in his position.

Interaction of Home Country and Local Law   Home countries occasionally have laws that extend to subsidiaries of their domestic companies that operate abroad.

These laws may contradict or conflict with laws in the host country. Examples include boycotts on doing business with certain countries or anti-boycott legislation where the auditor must certify that no country is being discriminated against. Other examples include human rights or other social disclosure. Perhaps one of the most intrusive of such extraterritorial laws is the U.S. Foreign Corrupt Practices Act, which not only forbids most forms of bribes but also specifies what minimum accounting controls must be in place.

Audit Challenges: Distance and Organization for Providing Audit Services

The auditor of a large multinational corporation has a very difficult time organizing the firm's services properly. For example, Coca-Cola, the U.S. beverages company based in Atlanta, Georgia, has operations all over the world. Its auditor, Ernst & Young, also has an office in Atlanta, which is responsible for the audit. One of the partners in the Atlanta office is assigned as the partner in charge of the worldwide audit. That partner must decide on the scope of the audit, taking into consideration such factors as

- the countries where Coca-Cola has subsidiaries
- the materiality of each subsidiary vis-à-vis the corporation as a whole
- the existence of a branch, subsidiary, or correspondent of the auditor in the country or city of each major subsidiary

A major challenge of auditing outside the home base is distance. Far-flung operations are not audited as frequently or as thoroughly as the domestic operations, which makes the foreign audit even tougher. It is often impossible to conduct pre-audit and post-audit visits; so most communication has to be by telephone, telex, fax, or mail. The earlier example on confirming accounts receivable illustrates the difficulty of distance. When post-audit problems arise, it may be impossible to get an answer quickly or to communicate adequately.

Given the need to cover clients in widely dispersed areas, how do public accounting firms service their multinational clients? The simplest way is for a professional to travel from the home office to service a client abroad. This would be sufficient as long as the foreign sector was a small part of the client's overall operations. However, this approach is unsatisfactory in the long run because of the complexity of the international audit and tax environments and the increasing internationalization of most of the firm's larger clients.

Beyond the traveling auditor approach the firm must make an increasing commitment to physical or legal presence on the ground overseas. The lowest level of commitment uses a variety of relationships with host-country correspondent firms. These can range from very weak to very strong.

At one end of the scale, the local correspondent may be a representative who performs services for more than one accounting firm. A very loose operating relationship may exist. At the other end of the scale, a very strong correspondent relationship may exist in which the local firm performs services exclusively for one foreign public accounting firm. Whether an auditing firm expands abroad through strong or weak correspondent relationships, the partners in other countries remain separate, autonomous organizations. Unlike a corporation, which retains equity control over its far-flung operations, these partnerships are built on mutual benefit and service. These are situations in which an auditing firm in one country owns operations in other countries, but those are the exception rather than the rule.

A stronger presence abroad is to be part of a global alliance of firms that share technology, clients, and sometimes staff. These alliances may be separate legal entities that use the parent firm's name or a derivative thereof. The partnership in individual countries remains its separate identity, but a more cohesive cooperative effort exists among the firms through the international partnership. With one exception, all the global audit firms operated in this manner until the mid-1990s and still do so in many countries. Ernst & Young, for example, trades as Ernst & Young in the United States, Canada, and other large English-speaking countries but becomes Ernst & Young—Henry Martin, Lisdero y Asociados in Argentina and Ernst & Young—Punongbayan & Araullo in the Philippines. This arrangement allows for local knowledge plus global clients, but without the tight control of a single firm.

The strongest presence for any global firm would be a single entity with common equity holdings. This can be achieved by expanding outward through branches of the original firm or by the merging of previously independent entities. Home office personnel often fill the important positions in foreign branches until domestic personnel can be trained to take over. In some cases, local firms are acquired; in others, new firms are established. The branch concept, coupled with strong central management, provides for tighter control over services. Arthur Andersen, for example, has always operated as a single entity, expanding as and when required by new branches. KPMG, by contrast, is the descendant of a number of very strong local firms and has only relatively recently established a common presence and brand name globally.

Audit Challenges: Audit Impediments from Cross-National Diversity, Availability, and Training of Auditors

If the audit firm should choose to open a branch rather than rely on correspondents, it faces the challenge of getting staff on the ground that it is satisfied with. These challenges include problems of reciprocity for its expatriate staff being transferred in, lack of local audit staff, and a variety of training models for preparing staff for the audit function. We now examine the profession and the firms that it serves.

Supply of Auditors   The number of accountants also depends on barriers to entry to the profession, such as strict educational and testing requirements. In Table 10.2 we compare the number of accountants in a country by computing a ratio of the number of accountants in the country to the population, that is, accountants per capita. It is interesting to note that the emerging market countries such as Kenya and Korea have a small number of accountants per capita compared with the high-income countries. Also, countries with a tradition of standards designed to service the government (Code Law countries) have a relatively smaller number of accountants. For example, the United Kingdom, with roughly the same population as France, has eight times France's number of accountants.

Cross-National Differences in Training of Practicing Auditors   Not only do numbers of accountants vary between countries but also the training of potential audit professionals can vary considerably. In some countries, such as the United States, a high value is placed on the university experience in the education of students, and firms that recruit at universities are familiar with the background students will have when they graduate. The education system might also be influenced by the role an

Table 10.2   Accounting Professionals

Country	Population 1994 (millions)	Number of Accountants	Number of Accountants Per 000 of Population
Canada	29.141	101,800	3.49
Egypt	61.636	384	0.006
France	57.747	26,200	0.45
Germany	81.278	21,225	0.26
Hong Kong	5.838	6,559	1.12
India	918.570	77,700	0.08
Italy	57.157	63,000	1.1
Japan	124.815	12,559	0.1
Kenya	27.343	1,500	0.05
Korea, Republic of	44.563	3,100	0.07
Mexico	91.858	13,700	0.15
Netherlands	15.397	8,000	0.52
Nigeria	108.467	7,339	0.07
South Africa	40.555	14,598	0.36
United Kingdom	58.091	205,458	3.54
United States	260.631	439,000	1.68

Source: International Federation of Accountants; United Nations.

accountant is expected to play. In Germany, for example, there is a high premium on managerial accounting and tax accounting. In the Netherlands, there is a high premium on economics rather than accounting.

Like many of the learned professions, preparation to become a practicing accountant includes the time elements of formal education, experience, and examination. There are essentially three different models of accounting education leading to certification:

1. The *apprenticeship* approach, patterned after the British experience, which does not require specific university training in accounting
2. The *university-based* model for certification, similar to the approaches used in the United States and Germany
3. The *dual-track* model, found in the Netherlands and France, which permits either approach

While each model has its strength, auditors may be unfamiliar with the competence level of staff in all countries. In the apprenticeship model, even after several years of study, staff with significant experience may not yet be qualified, in a professional sense. One may often get staff that are relatively junior for many years. In the university model, staff may be qualified and yet not as fully experienced as one would like. One solution for the global firm is to concentrate on developing a strong human capital base through common global training and internship or foreign residency programs. It is common to find accountants in various stages of their careers, usually from the managerial level up, working in foreign offices to learn the challenges of audits in those countries and to train local accountants in the ways of the international firm. When these accountants return to their home countries, they can more effectively perform local subsidiary audits that comply with the requirements in countries where the client's parent company is located. This in turn allows the engagement partner for the parent to express an opinion.

Reciprocity   As we saw earlier, the number of accountants available in any particular country varies significantly. It would therefore seem natural that if international business activity grows in a country with relatively few accountants, auditors would move from relative surplus countries such as the United States and United Kingdom to countries in need. Even between surplus countries, it would often seem to be reasonable that such intracountry flows would speed up the global audit process. However, as the International Federation of Accountants noted in a 1995 *Statement of Policy:*

> National professional institutes and national regulatory authorities have been reluctant to accept the professional qualifications of foreign accountants for regulated services. Conditions of residence, citizenship, special educational criteria and examinations have been set, conditions which are, in many cases, impossible to meet. Moreover, some of these criteria do not pertain to the professional qualifications. Given the international scope of the accountancy profession, professionally qualified accountants, both as individuals and firms, are increasingly seeking to be recognized in foreign countries, and often see these barriers as unreasonable.
>
> The demand for recognition of foreign accountancy qualifications has been given special impetus by the successful completion of the Uruguay Round of trade negotiations, and the General Agreement on Trade in Services (GATS). The GATS addresses regulatory obstacles to international trade and foreign investment in service industries, including the cross-border practice of accountancy and other professions. It sets out a series of rules to discipline government intervention in the marketplace, to ensure that foreign or internationally-affiliated service providers, firms and professionals enjoy the same privileges as their domestic counterparts or competitors with respect to government regulation and to remove discriminatory obstacles to market entry and practice by persons from other countries. Signatories to the GATS and its provisions bind their national and sub-national regulatory authorities. (*Recognition of Professional Accountancy Qualifications Statement of Policy of Council,* para. 3–4).

Reciprocity has varied. At one time, British accountants could and did have a valid global certificate to practice. This changed most dramatically in the United States but also in Canada and Australia in the 1970s. In the 1990s, regional economic integration has begun a return to reciprocity. The free trade agreement signed between the United States and Canada in 1989 initiated a closer degree of economic cooperation between the two largest trading partners in the world, and it also created closer cooperation in accounting. On September 1, 1991, a memorandum of understanding entitled "Principles for Reciprocity" was signed between the AICPA, the NASBA (National Association of State Boards of Accountancy), and the Canadian Institute of Chartered Accountants (CICA). According to the agreement, a professionally qualified accountant in one country could ask for the other country's qualification, subject to taking an exam on the local tax and legal framework. This special exam eliminated the need for Canadian accountants, for example, to take the Uniform CPA exam. This short-term exam has been extended to members of the Institute of Chartered Accountants of Australia, who similarly take the short-form IQEX exam. IQEX is an acronym for the International Uniform Certified Public Accountant Qualification Examination. The examination is one of the requirements used to assess the professional competence of Australian and Canadian chartered accountants who wish to obtain the CPA certificate.

In a similar regional reciprocity situation, the European Union issued a series of directives that must be incorporated into national law in each country. The Eighth Directive was adopted by the Council of Ministers of the European Union in 1984, and it deals with the qualifications of statutory auditors. Within the EU, auditors from one country are allowed to practice in another member country if the following two conditions are met:

1. The auditor must have obtained qualifications that are deemed to be equivalent to the reviewing authorities' in the host country.

2. The auditor must demonstrate that it understands the laws and requirements for conducting statutory audits in the host country.

The rules for reciprocity are relatively flexible in several other countries. In the Netherlands, for example, the Ministry of Economic Affairs may issue a license to a foreign accountant on the grounds of proof of suitable qualifications obtained abroad and satisfactory moral standing. The French recognize foreign diplomas from countries that grant reciprocal treatment once the candidate has passed an oral examination administered by the Ministry of Education covering French law, tax and accounting, and ethics. However, the Germans and British are as strict as the United States in not easily granting reciprocity. In the early 1990s, there were discussions between the United States and the European Union about granting reciprocity, but as of 2000 there were still too many challenges to resolve. As a result, the British and American professions were discussing a bilateral reciprocity that would involve requiring knowledge of local laws before accountants are allowed to practice.

GLOBAL AUDIT FIRMS

Introduction

As noted earlier, there are wide differences in the backgrounds and abilities of public accountants around the world. However, the need for auditing services extends beyond national borders. If a British corporation acquires a Swedish firm and needs to have the financial statements of that firm audited, can it rely on the services of the Swedish auditors? There are no generally accepted worldwide auditing standards or uniform requirements for becoming certified, but these differences have to be dealt with in a global auditing environment.

Strategies of the Global Audit Firm

As a global MNE as well as global service provider, public accounting firms have traditionally expanded abroad to better service their clients and to provide a line of defense against other global accounting firms that might be tempted to encroach on their client base. Companies that have switched from small or medium-size auditors to more international auditors often give the following two reasons for the switch:

1. The need to reflect the increasing size of their overseas business

2. The need to have one firm auditing all companies within the group

A good example of global strategy was the battle over the expanding Varity audit. In 1990, KPMG took over the audit engagement of Varity Corporation, which had three business groups: Massey-Ferguson, a tractor manufacturer; Perkins, a diesel engine manufacturer; and Kelsey-Hayes, a wheel and brake components manufacturer. When Varity acquired Kelsey-Hayes in 1989, it decided to submit its audit work to open bid, and KPMG won out over Deloitte & Touche, Ernst & Young, and Price Waterhouse. As KPMG developed its bid, the partner chosen to coordinate the engagement visited thirty Varity locations throughout the world and prepared a bid based on KPMG's strength worldwide. The partner felt that his global experience, especially his work with British clients, given Varity's significant British operations, was a key factor in the decision.

One of the major reasons for the mergers discussed below is the increasing globalization of business. The *Big Five* audit firms have increasingly become multinational firms in the mold of Unilever or GM rather than a loose alliance of related service providers. This has been especially true in Europe, where the implementation of the Fourth Directive has required more firms to be audited than previously had been the case. Further, the European Union's expansion and elimination of most of the remaining barriers to free trade and investment by the end of 1992 caused these firms to look more closely at their ability to service clients outside their home markets.

Many other markets were opening up to mergers and acquisitions and to new foreign investment in the early and mid-1990s. In 1991, for example, India decided to open up its market and allow foreign firms to have a majority equity position in Indian companies, something that had been restricted in the past. This international expansion also opens up the market to the auditing firms. The 1993 NAFTA treaty and its predecessor, the U.S./Canada Free Trade Agreement, also opened continent-wide markets. It was clear at that point that the auditors had to follow the lead of their clients to provide adequate service. Given that most of the large corporations in the world are in the United States and Canada, Europe, and Asia, the auditing firms began to look at ways to strengthen their presence in each of those major markets.

Structure of the Audit Industry

As in business generally, there are large and small audit firms. In the United States alone, there are more than 45,000 CPA firms. However, the world's largest public accounting firms conduct the audits of most of the world's largest corporations. Figure 10.1 identifies the top five firms in 1999 by revenues and provides the revenue data of those firms in the United States.

A major development since the early 1980s with respect to the competitive position of the major public accounting firms is merger activity. In 1989, in rapid succession, Deloitte Haskins & Sells and Touche Ross announced they would merge into a new U.S firm, Deloitte & Touche (DT), and Ernst & Whitney and Arthur Young announced the formation of a new U.S. firm, Ernst & Young (EY). Although discussions were taking place between Arthur Andersen (AA) and Price Waterhouse, a merger did not result. It is very difficult for such large firms to mesh together, especially where there are significant differences in organizational culture. In 1998, Price Waterhouse successfully merged with Coopers & Lybrand to form PricewaterhouseCoopers (PWC). Attempts to merge Ernst & Young and KPMG were stymied by regulators.

Another trend for public accounting firms is to organize around industry. For example, in 1995 KPMG announced it was going to organize the firm around five national integrated industry-focused teams. Each team consists of assurance (auditing), tax, and consulting professionals and each team focuses on one of the five industries,

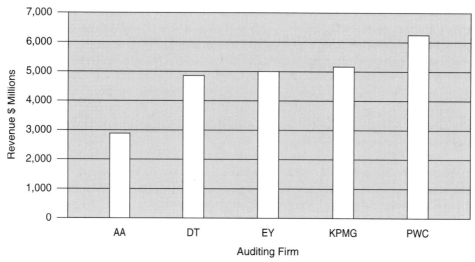

Figure 10.1 U.S. Revenues of Global Audit Firms 1999

with a shared top- and bottom-line. Thus, bottom-line responsibility would no longer rest on the traditional functional and geographical organizations. This model of organizational structure is similar to the *global product organization* discussed in Chapter 3. The teams are health care and life sciences; information, communications, and entertainment; public services; financial services; and manufacturing, retailing, and distribution. The result is more of a matrix form of organization, with the industry as the primary focus and functional organizations as a secondary focus.

From a manager's point of view both the strategy and structure of audit firms indicate that they have in many ways achieved a textbook-like level of success. On

---

Who We Are Is What We Do
Arthur Andersen is a global, multidisciplinary professional services organization that provides clients, large and small, all over the world, the thing they need most to succeed; knowledge. Our work is to acquire knowledge and to share knowledge—knowledge of how to improve performance in management, business processes, operations, information technology, finance, and change navigation—so that our clients can grow and profit. This knowledge comes from three sources: experience, education, and research. In all three, Arthur Anderson excels.

Who We Are Is How We Work
Arthur Andersen is a global organization, with 382 offices in 81 countries. But for us, global is more than a worldwide presence; it's also an attitude. With a unique organizational structure, common methods, and shared values, Arthur Andersen is able to serve its clients, wherever they are located, as "one firm." Our team of over 70,000 people work together—across boundaries of competencies, functions, and geographies—to deliver to each client a multidisciplinary, complete solution.

Who We Are Is Where We Came From
When Mr. Arthur Andersen founded the firm in 1913, he said, "We want to measure our contribution more by the quality of the service rendered than by whether we are making a good living out of it." Today, quality is still our number one focus, as we strive continuously to understand, accept, meet, and ExCEED our clients' needs and expectations.

Figure 10.2 A Mission Statement from a Global Audit Firm—Arthur Andersen

Source: http://www.arthurandersen.com

the one hand, they provide value to their clients, and yet, unlike many other service agencies, they do this through a structure and strategy that is suitable to their role as global corporations and from which they no doubt learn how to better serve their clients. All of this has been achieved in an industry that is nationally and sub-nationally regulated and where the supply of skills in no way matches the pattern of global growth. The mission statement of Arthur Andersen provides an interesting insight into the strategy and organization of the global audit firm (see Figure 10.2).

IFAC AND THE EXTERNAL AUDITOR

While multinationals, audit firms, and governments attempt to standardize their practices and permit the cross-national transfer of audit services there will still be obstacles to auditing. Much as the IASC is attempting to harmonize financial reporting practices, the International Federation of Accountants (IFAC) is attempting to harmonize audit services and audit professions globally. More information on IFAC is contained in International Bulletin 10.1.

International Bulletin 10.1

International Federation of Accountants (IFAC)

Organization Overview.   IFAC is an organization of national profession accountancy organizations that represent accountants employed in public practice, business and industry, the public sector, and education, as well as some specialized groups that interface frequently with the profession. Currently, it has 143 member bodies in 104 countries, representing 2 million accountants. Full membership in IFAC automatically includes membership in the International Accounting Standards Committee (IASC). Click here for information on IFAC's organization and structure. For a brief summary of IFAC's historical background click here.

Objective.   IFAC strives to develop the profession and harmonize its standards worldwide to enable accountants to provide services of consistently high quality in the public interest. IFAC will fulfill this objective within the framework of its Constitution.

Primary Activities.   IFAC's leadership, its committees and task forces work with member bodies to achieve this objective by:

Serving as international advocates. IFAC develops and promotes high quality technical, professional and ethical publications and guidance for use by accountants employed in every sector.

- **Acting as agents for change.** IFAC provides leadership on emerging issues, the impetus for the liberalization of accountancy services, and a universal voice for the world's accountants on issues of pubic and professional concern. Much of this is accomplished through outreach to numerous organizations that rely on or have an interest in the activities of the international accountancy profession.
- **Facilitating the development of a harmonized worldwide accountancy profession.** IFAC fosters the advancement of strong national accountancy organizations. It works closely with regional accountancy organizations and development agencies to accomplish this.

Source: http://www.ifac.org.

CONCLUSIONS

The role of the auditor, both internal and external, is to assist management with carrying out its strategic goals. In the case of external auditors there is the second role of providing independent information to indicate to those financing the MNE that the corporation continues to be viable. In carrying out these tasks the auditor faces many of the problems of culture and currency faced by their clients. In addition, the global audit firm itself must adopt a multinational strategic process, which is a classic example of a service firm in global competition.

SUMMARY

1. The quality of the auditing profession is a function of several factors, such as the reputation of the accounting and auditing profession, the quality of the education system, and the certification process. The certification or licensing process for an auditor is a function of several factors, such as the identity of the candidate, educational requirements, experience requirements, and examination.

2. An important worldwide issue for the auditing profession is reciprocity or the ability of a certified accountant in one country to practice in another.

3. The European Union issued the Eighth Directive, which attempts to harmonize the requirements leading to certification of auditors and which also establishes conditions for countries to consider in granting reciprocity to accountants from other EU member countries.

4. The Big Five, the world's largest auditing firms, are responsible for auditing most of the largest MNEs. A major development in the global strategies of the world's largest auditing firms in recent years has been the merger of firms such as Deliotte Haskins & Sells with Touche Ross, and Arthur Young with Ernst & Whitney, to form larger auditing firms better able to audit global corporations.

5. Auditors can service their global clients by sending staff from the home office to foreign locations; by establishing correspondent relationships with foreign auditing firms; and by investing in a foreign auditing practice through a branch office, a joint venture with a local auditing firm, or a wholly owned company.

6. It is the responsibility of the engagement partner of the audit of a global company to determine the scope of the audit, taking into consideration such factors as the countries where the client has subsidiaries; the materiality of each subsidiary vis-à-vis the corporation as a whole; the existence of a branch, subsidiary, or correspondent of the auditor in the country or city of each major subsidiary; and so on.

7. The ability of the auditor to perform a good audit depends on factors that are specific to each country's environment (e.g., business practices and customs, foreign currency, language, and distance; restrictions on the use of the firm's name; restrictions on rights of establishment and association; restrictions on scope of practice; restrictions on repatriation of fees, royalties, and profits; tax discrimination; and quality control).

8. The development of audit standards in a given country, which can take place in the public or private sector, is a complex interrelationship of cultural, legal-political, and economic variables, which leads to wide differences in standards and practices from country to country.

9. Audit opinions contain useful information to help one identify which accounting statements are being audited, what is the basis for accounting standards being used by the corporation, and what is the basis for the auditing standards or practices that are being followed.

10. Some of the unique challenges that arise from conducting an audit in a foreign environment are local accounting practices, foreign currency, local legal and business practices, language and customs, and distance.

11. The International Federation of Accountants (IFAC) is attempting to harmonize auditing standards and practices so financial statement users worldwide can be confident of the accuracy and reliability of the underlying financial statements.

DISCUSSION QUESTIONS

1. In this chapter, we discussed the personal qualifications, educational requirements, and experience requirements of different countries. Develop a matrix that includes countries down one side and the three dimensions just described across the top so you can compare and contrast the different countries.

2. The U.S. system leans toward a heavy education requirement mixed with practice, and the British system leans more toward a heavy experience requirement bordering on apprenticeship. Which system is more effective and why? Which system would you recommend for a country like Mozambique?

3. If you were a certified accountant in your home country and wanted to practice as an auditor in another country, you would most likely not be allowed to practice. Why do these barriers to entry exist? What strategies could you pursue to service your clients in markets where you are not allowed to practice?

4. What is the purpose of the Eighth Directive of the European Union? What do you think some of these challenges hindering its total implementation might be?

5. Why are the audits of most of the largest global companies done by the Big Five auditing firms?

6. In 1989, Price Waterhouse considered merging with Arthur Andersen, but the merger fell apart. What are some of the reasons why those two firms might have considered merging in the first place? What are some of the possible reasons why they didn't go through with their merger plans? What might be the consequences of their failure to merge?

7. What are some different ways auditing firms can service their global clients? What are the strengths and weaknesses of each approach?

8. What are some of the challenges global auditing firms face in trying to service their clients?

9. The IFAC is attempting to harmonize auditing standards and practices. What do you think are some of the barriers to this harmonization? What are the benefits of their work being successful?

10. You have the opportunity to work on an internship in a foreign country for an audit firm with an office in that country. What would be the pros and cons of such an experience, and what would you do to prepare for that experience?

11. It was mentioned in the chapter that KPMG has reorganized itself around five national industry-focused teams that consist of assurance, tax, and consulting professionals concentrating on each industry. Why do you think KPMG moved to this type of organizational structure rather than remain organized by service (assurance, tax, and consulting services)? What do you think some of the challenges might be in switching to this type of structure? Given that KPMG is a global company, are there any unique global challenges to this structure?

12. What does a global public accounting firm need to do to prepare its professionals to be competitive in a global environment?

CASE

Bell Canada Enterprises

BCE (Bell Canada Enterprises) is a household name in Canada and is well known around the world. It is a descendant of Bell Telephone Company of Canada, which was formed in 1880 for the original purpose of operating Canada's entire telephone system by employing the patented inventions of AT&T, the mammoth U.S. firm founded in 1877 with the patent of Alexander Graham Bell. The firm of Philip S. Ross was appointed to audit and certify the company's first financial statements. This firm later affiliated itself with the accounting firm of Touche, taking the name Touche Ross in Canada. The relationship between the auditor and company has continued unbroken since 1880.

By 1970, revenues for the Bell Canada group reached $936 million while assets topped $3.3 billion. The group consisted of Northern Electric (now known as Northern Telecom) and Bell Canada. In 1983, Bell Canada Enterprises (known as BCE) superseded Bell Canada as the parent company of the group.

By 1988, the BCE group was the largest of Touche Ross's Canadian clients and one of its largest worldwide. In 1988, its revenues exceeded $15 billion, and assets exceeded $28 billion. This would have placed BCE in twenty-first place in the Fortune 500. Moreover, these figures do not include BCE's 49 percent interest in Trans Canada Pipe Lines Limited's (TCPL) $3.5 billion in revenues and $6 billion in assets. BCE's investment in TCPL was accounted for on the equity basis. Net income for BCE in 1985, 1986, and 1987 exceeded $1 billion but fell to $882 million in 1988.

In 1988, BCE employed over 116,000 employees worldwide in businesses ranging from telecommunications operations to real estate development and international consulting. The operations included many industry and geographic segments. Central to BCE's business are their telecommunications operations and telecommunications equipment manufacturing. Other operations include R&D, international consulting, and communication and information services, such as the publishing of telephone directories and the Canadian domestic satellite network.

BCE Client Engagement

In 1988, Touche Ross audited every substantive BCE subsidiary (more than 50 percent owned) in the world and also many of their related companies. In cases where other auditors were responsible, the audit team had to be totally knowledgeable about all business, financial reporting, and audit issues. Each operation has different problems and is managed by different executives, and the audit team has to be responsive to management in each operation.

In 1988, for financing or regulatory reasons, Touche Ross also undertook a quarterly review of most of the major companies in BCE. The audit team was present in many client engagements. In addition, BCE uses Touche Ross to provide additional services beyond the statutory audit requirements, such as providing information to securities regulators and the capital markets. The Canadian regulator of Bell Canada's telephone arm also requires an annual price study of the $1 billion in goods and services Northern Telecom supplies to Bell Canada. The CRTC requires that the transactions be extensively reviewed because the two companies are related. In addition, Touche Ross must audit the $7.5 billion in BCE's pension funds, the largest private pool of funds in Canada. Dozens of funds and the real estate ventures in which these funds have been invested must be audited annually. Other audit functions include opinions on royalty agreements and accounting opinions in foreign countries. For example, in the audit of Northern Telecom, offshore revenues represent only 10 percent of total revenues. However, offshore is a larger element in the audit effort because of local statutory requirements.

The BCE client service team also provides income tax and consulting services. Touche Ross was the principal tax advisor to BCE in 1988, providing corporate tax services to over

120 company groups and personal tax services to over 250 executives and senior managers. It also provided financial counseling and exit interviews. Touche Ross is also involved in the purchase investigation of every investment BCE makes and performs valuations of business segments. Consulting engagements encompass anything from information systems to personnel recruitment.

Each subsidiary and sub-business within the BCE group is operated as an individual corporation or division. Lines of authority and responsibility on the audit engagement team generally parallel those of BCE's business structure. There are about two dozen operational audit committees within the group.

The BCE engagement is organized around the core team, a small group of partners responsible for each major component of the BCE engagement. This group uses five principles as guidelines for providing services:

1. Quality service delivered on budget and on time to all companies.
2. Continuous dialogue with executives and managers of all companies.
3. Prompt identification and resolution of client and technical issues and service difficulties for all companies.
4. Consistency throughout the group in the total relationship.
5. Practice development through the sale of appropriate extended services where required.

Those charged with managing the entire engagement have the responsibility to influence team selection for each subsidiary and each special assignment in all locations around the world. The capacity of core team partners to determine team selection is essential if an international engagement is to be property serviced. Part of the team consists of affiliate accounting firms who are not members of the Touche family. Team selection ultimately becomes the foundation on which the entire client relationship flows.

Team selection for the BCE group takes place as if the individual company were a standalone client and not just another subsidiary obtained as a matter of right. Each company must believe that the most appropriate professionals have been assigned to its account. A matching process involving knowledge level, skills, age, language, cultural background, and personality must be employed, and a team of auditors and tax specialists is selected based on these characteristics and the size and complexity of the company. A service team for a single engagement or special assignment is frequently drawn from multiple offices.

The task of the core team is to ensure that the local service team will provide BCE with quality, timely, and friendly service. The core team and service team must agree on basic issues in the engagement, which are the following:

1. *Understand the task:* Know what is to be done, by whom, by when, and for how much, and know how the service team will manage itself.
2. *Understand the client culture:* A telephone company is generally more conservative than a real estate company. Boundaries in each subsidiary must be agreed upon.
3. *Special requirements:* A tough CEO may require special care, or poor profits may suggest a more careful review.
4. *Client interface:* Work with client personnel who are handling the engagement.
5. *Special assignments:* Assess and communicate areas where Touche can assist management.

As we have previously noted, the linkages structured into the audit attempt to parallel linkages in the business. For example, the audit partner in charge of Tele Direct Publication reports to the audit partner responsible for Bell Canada, just as the CEO of Tele Direct reports to the CEO of Bell Canada. This process winds its way up to the core partners, and the international structure of the firm allows these relationships to function throughout the world. Linkages must be minimized when establishing internal interfaces so nothing gets lost in the communication process. In addition, it is not uncommon for partners to be involved in dual or multiple activities within the group (i.e., two different companies in the same city being served by the same engagement team).

The purpose of these linkages is to ensure that each partner in the BCE engagement ends up with a clearly defined service role and an understanding of the expectations for internal interface requirements. Team selection, team operation, and team structure must be planned because these roles can be comprised of many elements. Planning is critical to ensure that the overall engagement meets its objectives.

The strength of communications before and during any client service function determines the success of the assignment. The first rule of Touch Ross is to talk—communication between audit partner and tax partner, between the audit partner responsible for the subsidiary and the audit partner responsible for the parent, and between partners and client. The core team insists on regular planning and progress meetings. Talking ensures that everybody is kept up to date and that problems are identified and resolved. Interactive, ongoing, continual dialogue is critical to service in an international engagement such as BCE.

Talk alone cannot run a client engagement, however. Written communication, such as memos of instructions, memos on results, and memos on problems, is encouraged. The writers of these memos are directed to send copies to other team members who may have an interest in the subject. These are sent via fax, telex, and e-mail. In addition, a newsletter directed to the key partners servicing the BCE team is published twice a year. It gives each partner some idea of what's going on in the group and lets everyone know who's who on both the Touche side and the BCE side of the engagement. This newsletter is circulated to some of the 225 partners worldwide who are involved with the BCE service team.

Questions

1. What are some of the major problems Touche Ross might have encountered in performing the audit of BCE in 1988?

2. What are the major elements in the audit process that Touche Ross followed during its audit of BCE?

3. In 1989, Touche Ross merged with Deloitte Haskins & Sells to form Deloitte & Touche. What kinds of concerns might BCE have had when the merger was announced?

REFERENCES AND FURTHER READING

American Institute of Certified Public Accountants and National Association of State Boards of Accountancy. (1994). *Digest of State Accountancy Law and State Board Regulations.* New York: AWPA and NASBA, pp. vii, 81–82, and 103–105.

Arens, A. and J. Loebbecke. (1994). *Auditing: An Integrated Approach,* 6th ed. Englewood Cliffs, NJ: Prentice-Hall.

"International Accounting Firms Consolidate Worldwide: A Study of a Multinational Service Industry." (1980). *Multinational Business* 3: 5, 7.

International Federation of Accountants. (1995). *Statement of Policy of Council: Recognition of Professional Accountancy Qualifications.* New York: IFAC, June, Appendix 1.

Needles, Jr., B., T. McDermott, and R. Ternkin. (1991). "Taxonomy of Auditing Standards." In *Handbook of International Accounting,* chap. 6, F.D.S. Choi, Ed. New York: Wiley.

Nobes, C. (1989). *Interpreting European Financial Statements: Towards 1992.* London: Butterworths, pp. 54–55.

"North American Trade Parts and CE Free Trade Given Recognition Bonus." (1992). *World Accounting Report* (April): 2, 6.

Office of the U.S. Trade Representative. (1983). *U.S. National Study on Trade in Services.* Washington, DC: GPO, pp. 231–233.

Smith, A. (1995). "The United States–Canada Bilateral Agreement on Reciprocity from a U.S. Perspective." *IFAC Newsletter,* 19(1, March): 1–3.

Stamp, E. and M. Moonitz. (1978). *International Auditing Standards.* Englewood Cliffs, NJ: Prentice-Hall.

SOME USEFUL INTERNET WEB SITES

The following are the Web sites of the Big Five global auditing firms:
1. Arthur Anderson and Co: *www.arthurandersen.com*
2. Ernst & Young: *http://www.eyi.com*
3. Deloitte Touche Tohmatsu: *http://www.deloitte.com*
4. KPMG International: *http://www.kpmg.com*
5. PricewaterhouseCoopers: *http://www.pwcglobal.com*

Other useful web sites:
1. BDO (a large regional firm): *http://www.bdo-international.com/aboutBDO.html*
   The firm was founded in 1963, and has a long history of commitment to service excellence and client satisfaction, which has contributed to its leadership position. In 2000, it is securely positioned as the world's sixth-largest international accounting and consulting organization.
2. IFAC: *http://www.ifac.org*
   IFAC is an organization of national professional accountancy organizations that represent accountants employed in public practice, business and industry, the public sector, and education, as well as some specialized groups that interface frequently with the profession. Currently, it has 143 member bodies in 104 countries, representing 2 million accountants. A subpage *http://www.ifac.org/FactsAndFigures/MemberBodies.html* has links to all IFAC members.
3. ACAUS: *http://www.acaus.org/info/ca.html*
   An organization of chartered accountants (non-U.S. auditors). This page has links to all the major English-speaking auditors

INDEX

Abdallah, W., 53
Acceptable quality level (AQL), 85
Accounting. *See also* management accounting
    and centralization vs. decentralization, 33–34
    cycle of corporate exposure to international aspects, 7–9
    and firm structure, 33–35
    impact of differences in practice, 127–129
    measurement basis for financial statements, 125–126
    types of issues for multinational enterprises, 6–7
Accounting Standards Committee, U.K., 182–183
Adhikari, A., 149
Aloha Company, 171
American options, 18
Ameripill Company case, 59–68
Antweiler, Werner, 13
APEC companies
    and budgeting, 56, 58
    and objective setting, 54–55
Appleyard, A., 53
Appraisal costs, 86
Arthur Andersen, 38, 208
Asia, 49, 55, 56–57, 58. *See also* Confucian dynamism; East Asia
Assada, Takayuki, 53, 54, 57, 58
Auditing, global
    Bell Canada Enterprises case, 212–214
    currency issues, 201
    distance as factor, 202–203
    firm organization options, 202–203
    firm strategies, 206–207
    and IFAC, 209
    industry structure, 207–209
    language and culture issues, 201

    legal issues, 201–202
    and local business practice issues, 200–201
    overview, 199
    and Procter & Gamble, 200
    sample mission statement, 208
    services of firms, 199–200
    staffing issues, 203–206
    taxonomy, 199, 200
Australia, 55, 56, 58, 131, 159

Bailes, Jack C., 53, 54, 57, 58
Barings Bank case, 23–24
Bartlett, Christopher, 30, 32, 34, 35, 37
Bell Canada Enterprises case, 212–214
Blaxill, Mark, 83
BMW, 2
Bond, M., 49
Branches, foreign, 105
British pounds, in foreign exchange example, 12, 13, 14, 15–16, 17, 18, 19–20. *See also* United Kingdom
British Telecom
    case study, 137–139
    financial statements, 123–124
    as reporting example, 123–124
Brownell, P., 55
Bryant, S.M., 130, 133
Budgeting
    APEC multinationals, 58
    capital, 80
    as control issue, 72–74
    cross-national studies, 55–56
    and culture, 50
    currency considerations, 72–74
    foreign exchange in process, 74–79
    issues across countries, 55
    in multinational enterprises, 72–74
    re-engineering, 89
    U.S. vs. Japan, 57–58

Business. *See* global economy; international trade; multinational enterprises
Business culture. *See* culture

Calvert, A., 5
Canada
  Bell Canada Enterprises case, 212–214
  foreign currency translation process,
    183–184
  segmental disclosure requirements, 159
  Yarmouth Woolens case, 186–197
Canadian Bank of Montreal, 13
Capital budgeting, 80
Cases
  Ameripill Company, 59–68
  Barings Bank, 23–24
  Bell Canada Enterprises, 212–214
  British Telecom, 137–139
  Midwest Uniforms, 109–112
  Nestlé, 165–167
  Niessen Apparel, 92–93
  Piparo International, 186
  Procter & Gamble, 41–43
  Yarmouth Woolens, 186–197
Cassells, Olivia. *See* Ameripill Company
Caterpillar, 84
Centralization
  and accounting function, 33–34
  vs. decentralization, 30–33
  and global imperatives, 32–33
CFCs. *See* controlled foreign corporations
Chicago Mercantile Exchange, 18, 19
China, 7, 49, 50, 84, 131, 159
Choi, F.D.S., 141
Chow, Chee W., 51, 54
Chrysler, 2. *See also* DaimlerChrysler
Closing exchange rates, 175
Coca-Cola, 7, 34, 202
Collaborative arrangements. *See* strategic
  alliances
Collectivism vs. individualism, 49, 50, 51
Comparative advantage, 3
Competition
  and need for information disclosure,
    144–145
  in taxes, 101
Confucian dynamism, 49, 50, 56–57
Conservatism, defined, 126
Controlled foreign corporations (CFCs),
  102
Corning, 2, 3
Corporate culture. *See* culture
Corporate income tax
  classic vs. integrated systems, 95

defining taxable income, 96–97
  and expenses, 97
  overview, 95–96
  ways to integrate, 95–96
  withholding, 97
Corporate reviews
  detailed contents list, 150–151, 152, 154
  overview, 148, 150
  sample environmental disclosure, 152,
    153
  sample mission statement, 151, 152
  sample value-added statement, 151, 152
Corporations
  extent of international trade, 1, 2
Cost accounting. *See* management accounting
Costing
  overview, 83–84
  vs. price, 83–85
  and quality, 85–86
  standard, 84
  target, 84–85
Costing, standard, 84
Culture
  and budgeting, 50
  dimensions of, 49
  and management control, 49–52
  overview, 48–49
  and performance measurement, 51
  rules for developing global orientation,
    34–35
Currency. *See* foreign exchange
Current exchange rates, 175
Current rate translation method
  overview, 175–176
  process, 179–181
  Yarmouth Woolens case, 187, 191, 192,
    193

Daimler-Benz, 2
DaimlerChrysler, 151, 152
Decentralization
  and accounting function, 33–34
  vs. centralization, 30–33
Defects. *See* quality
Demirag, I., 54, 79
Derivatives
  forward contracts, 16–18
  futures contracts, 18
  options, 18–20
  overview, 15–16
  role in foreign exchange transactions,
    172–173
  swaps, 18

U.K. approach to accounting, 174
U.S. approach to accounting, 173–174
Direct investment. *See* foreign direct investment (FDI)
Disclosure
    as competitive disadvantage, 144–145
    and East Asian financial crisis, 142–143
    importance of, 143
    international regulation and reporting trends, 146–155
    managerial attitudes toward voluntary reporting, 145–146, 147
    managerial incentives for, 143–144
    overview, 141
    segmental requirements, 155–163
    varying stock exchange requirements, 148, 149
Dollars. *See* exchange rates
Double taxation, 98–100

East Asia
    company budgeting processes, 58
    corporate objective setting, 54–55
    role of accounting in financial crisis, 142–143
Economic exposure, 21
Economic profit. *See* economic value added (EVA)
Economic value added (EVA), 89–90. *See also* value-added statements
Egelhoff, W.G., 36
Electrolux, 6, 151, 152
Electronic data interchange (EDI), 35
Ernst & Young, 202, 203
Euro, 14–15
European options, 18
European Union. *See also* Euro
    and corporate income taxes, 95–96, 98
    and corporate reviews, 150–154
    and disclosure regulation, 145, 148, 158
    and exports, 102
    and foreign currency translation process, 182
    number of multinational corporations, 5, 6
    role in global trade and accounting, 3, 129
    segmental disclosure requirements, 158, 159
    and tax competition, 101
    and VAT, 102
EVA (economic value added), 89–90. *See also* value-added statements

Exchange rates. *See also* foreign exchange
    in budgeting process, 74–79
    current or closing, 175
    defined, 12
    and derivatives markets, 15–16
    historical, 175
    spot market, 12
    U.S. dollar rates, 13
Expatriates, and taxation, 102
Expenses
    cross-national allocation, 82–83
    tax treatment, 82–83, 97
Exports. *See also* international trade
    and financial statements, 114
    and foreign exchange problems, 12–15
    servicing, 105
Exposure
    economic, 21
    transaction, 20–21
    translation, 21
    types of, 20–21
External failure costs, 86

Farmer, R., 6
FDI. *See* foreign direct investment (FDI)
Femininity vs. masculinity, 49
Financial Accounting Standards Board (FASB), 157
Financial reporting
    accounting diversity, 125–126
    classifying of systems, 118–121
    competitive disadvantage of disclosure, 144–145
    costs of information production, 144
    defining system parameters, 121–122
    differences among countries, 122–126
    disclosure in reports, 141–146
    format issues, 122–124
    Gray model, 119–121
    importance of information disclosure, 143
    international disclosure regulation and reporting trends, 146–155
    managerial attitudes toward voluntary disclosure, 145–146, 147
    managerial incentives for disclosure, 143–144
    Nobes model, 118–119
    varying global stock exchange requirements, 148, 149
Financial reviews, 155

Financial statements. *See also* financial reporting
  environmental influences, 116–117
  foreign exchange translation process, 175–181
  format issues, 122–124
  measurement of accounting items, 125–126
  models for financial reporting, 118–121
  overview, 114–115, 116
Financial Times, 12
Foreign branches, 105
Foreign direct investment (FDI)
  country-specific advantages, 4
  and financial statements, 114–115
  firm-specific advantages, 4–5
  as method of international business involvement, 4–5
  overview of accounting and control issues, 8–9
  reasons for, 4–5
  role in global economy, 2–3
Foreign exchange. *See also* exchange rates
  in budgeting process, 74–79
  and derivative products, 15–18
  and exporting problems, 12–15
  and exposure, 20–21
  functional vs. reporting currencies, 175
  locking in rate, 16
  and MNE budgeting, 72–74
  obtaining exchange rate quotes, 12–14
  and risk, 20–21
  role of hedging and derivatives in transactions, 172–174
  transaction accounting, 169–174
  translation risk, 174–181
  U.S. dollar rates in foreign currency units, 13
Foreign Sales Corporations (FSCs), 102
Foreign subsidiaries, 106
Forward contracts, 16–18
Forward rate, 16, 17
Foster, G., 46
France, in Ameripill case, 63, 66–67
Francis, J., 21
Fraser, Robin, 89
Free trade zones, 3
Frucot, V., 55, 56
Functional currency, 175, 176–177, 179
Futures contracts, 18

GAAP. *See* generally accepted accounting principles (GAAP)
General Electric, 83

Generally accepted accounting principles (GAAP)
  in British Telecom case, 137–139
  role of parent company, 34
  U.S. vs. U.K., 126–129, 137–139
General Motors, 7, 97
Germany
  in Ameripill case, 63, 64–65, 68
  and corporate income taxes, 95, 97
  foreign exchange transaction example, 171
  segmental disclosure requirements, 159
  stock exchanges, 131
Ghoshal, Sumantra, 30, 32, 34, 35, 37
Global, defined, 32
Global audits. *See* auditing, global
Global economy. *See also* multinational enterprises
  choosing among business involvement methods, 3–5
  role of direct foreign investment, 2–3, 4
  role of portfolio investment, 2–3
  role of strategic alliances, 2, 3–4
  role of trade, 1–2, 3
Global innovators, 39, 86, 88
Goizueta, Roberto, 90
Goods and services taxes, 98
Govindarajan, Vijay, 38, 71, 86, 87–88
Gray, S.J., 49, 119–121, 122, 123, 126, 127, 128, 129, 130, 133, 143, 144–145, 146, 147, 157
Gray financial reporting model, 119–121
Greenfield sites, 2
Group accounts, 123
Gupta, Anil K., 38, 71, 86, 87–88

Haka, Susan F., 59
Hamel, G., 32
Harrell, A., 55
Harrison, G., 51, 56, 58
Harrison, P., 55
Hedges
  role in foreign exchange transactions, 172–173
  U.K. approach to accounting, 174
  U.S. approach to accounting, 173–174
Heterogeneous networks, 36
Hiromoto, T., 83
Historical exchange rates, 175
Hitachi, 83
H.J. Heinz, 123–124
Hofstede, G., 48, 49, 51–52, 119
Hong Kong, 55, 56, 58, 96, 131
Hope, Jeremy, 89

Horngren, G., 46
Hout, Thomas, 31, 83
Hungary, 112, 159

IAS. *See* international accounting standards
IASC. *See* International Accounting Standards Committee (IASC)
IBM, 82
IFAC (International Federation of Accountants), 209
Implementers, 39, 86, 88
Importing. *See* international trade
Income, taxable, defining, 96–97
Income tax, corporate, 95–97
India, 33, 159
Indirect taxes, 98
Individualism vs. collectivism, 49, 50, 51
Indonesia, 50, 56
Information processing, 36
Innovators, global vs. local, 39, 86, 88
Integrated players, 39, 86, 88
Internal failure costs, 86
Internal pricing. *See* transfer pricing
International accounting standards, 130, 132, 174, 184
International Accounting Standards Committee (IASC)
    and IOSCO, 134–135
    overview, 117, 129–130
    reporting requirements, 158–163
    standard for accounting for hedges and derivatives, 174
International Federation of Accountants (IFAC), 209
International Financial Performance System (IFPS), 65–66
International trade
    extent of, 1–2
    importance of, 1–2
    as method of business involvement in global economy, 3
    overview of accounting and control issues, 7–8
Internet, 36
Intracorporate transfer pricing. *See* transfer pricing
Investment, foreign. *See* foreign direct investment (FDI); portfolio investment, international
IOSCO (International Organization of Securities Commissions), 130, 131, 134–135

IPS (International Financial Performance System), 65–66

Japan, 5, 53–54, 57, 58, 83, 85, 132

Kaplan, R., 86
Keller, D., 53
Koblenz Chemie Company, 64–65
Korea, 2, 3

Lambertson, Barbara A., 59
LANs (local area networks), 35
Leeson, Nick, 23–24
Lessard, Donald, 74, 75
Levitt, Arthur, 142
Line-of-business (LOB) segments, 155
Local innovators, 39, 86, 88
Locus of control, 55
Long-term orientation, 49
Lorange, Peter, 74, 75

Malaysia, 4, 56, 132
Management accounting. *See also* accounting
    vs. management control, 47–48
    overview, 46–47
    purposes of, 46–47
Management control
    and budgeting, 72–74
    and culture, 49–52
    cycle of corporate exposure to international aspects, 7–9
    vs. management accounting, 47–48
    overview, 48
    process issues, 47
    types of issues for multinational enterprises, 6–7
    value chain illustration, 47, 48
Management information systems
    and global firms, 35–39
    types of processes, 36
Martz, Larry, 103
Masculinity vs. femininity, 49
Matrix organizational structure, 29–30, 34
Meek, G.K., 143, 145, 147
Merchant, K., 54
MERCOSUR, 3
Mexican companies, 55–56
Microsoft financial statements, 115, 116
Middleware, 36
Midwest Uniforms case, 109–112

Montreal Stock Exchange, 131
Morsicato, H., 53, 79
Multidomestic vs. global firms, 31, 33, 37
Multinational enterprises
    auditing, 200–215
    avoiding double taxation, 98–100
    budgeting issues, 72–74
    corporate reviews, 148, 150–154
    countries with most, 5
    disclosure in corporate reports,
        141–146
    financial reviews, 155
    and financial statements, 115–133
    firm-specific advantages, 4
    and foreign exchange risk, 20–21
    intracorporate transfer pricing, 80–83,
        102–105
    list of largest, 6
    and management information systems,
        35–39
    operations reviews, 154–155
    organizational structure, 26–30
    overview, 5–6
    and performance evaluation, 86–89
    product-name problems, 7
    setting objectives, 52–58
    strategic control process, 71–72
    tax planning, 105–106
    and transborder data flows, 37
    types of accounting and control issues,
        6–7
Murdoch, Rupert, 101

NAFTA (North American Free Trade
    Agreement), 3
Nakagawa, Yu, 54
Nestlé, 6, 133, 165–167
News Corporation, 6, 101
Nichols, N., 157
Niessen Apparel case, 92–93
Nissan, 2
Niswander, F., 49, 120, 121
Nobes, C.W., 118–119
Nobes financial reporting model,
    118–119
Nonroutine information, 36

Objectives, setting, 52–58, 72, 73
OECD, 96, 100, 101, 145
Offshore production, 83–84
Operations reviews, 154–155
Options
    American vs. European, 18

calculating cost of, 18–20
    defined, 18
Organizational structure
    and accounting function, 33–35
    domestic, 27
    global, 28–30
    and global imperatives, 32–33
    international division, 27–18
    matrix, 29–30, 34
    overview, 26–27
    transnational, 33
Overhead, allocating, 82–83

PepsiCo, 29
Performance evaluation
    basis of measurement, 87, 88
    and culture, 51
    and economic value added, 89–90
    emerging trends, 88–89
    managerial vs. subsidiary, 87–88
    measurement in Ameripill Company
        case study, 59–68
    in multinational enterprises, 86–89
    and ROI, 88
    and strategic business units, 88
Philips
    financial statements, 123–124
    as multinational corporation, 6
    as reporting example, 123–124
    segmental disclosures, 158, 160–162
Pillai Auto example, 179–181
Piparo International case, 186
Planning, tax, 105–106
Porter, M.E., 31
Portfolio investment, international, 3
Power distance, large vs. small, 49, 50
Prahalad, C.J., 32
Prevention costs, 86
Price Waterhouse Coopers, 36
Pricing
    vs. cost, 83–85
    internal, 80–83, 102–105
    and market conditions, 81–82
    tax considerations, 80, 103–105, 106
    transfer, 80–83, 102–105
    U.S. rules, 103–105
Private branch exchanges (PBXs), 35
Procter & Gamble
    case study, 41–43
    centralized structure, 31
    extent of international business, 1, 2
    and global auditing, 200
    Organization 2005 strategic initiative,
        41–43

Public accounting firms
  audit industry structure, 207–209
  strategies, 206–207
Puerto Rico, 110–112

Quality, impact on costs, 85–86

Radebaugh, L.H., 129, 144–145, 146
Rahman, Zabaidur, M., 143
Reciprocal information, 36
Re-engineering, budget, 89
Regulation. *See also* European Union; Se-
    curities and Exchange Commission
    (SEC)
  IASC reporting requirements, 158–163
  international reporting and disclosure
    trends, 146–155
Reporting currency, defined, 175
Return on investment (ROI), 53, 54, 81, 88
Richman, B., 6
Ricks, David A., 7
Risk, and foreign exchange, 20–21. *See also*
    translation, in foreign exchange ac-
    counting
Robbins, S., 52, 79
Roberts, C.B., 144–145, 146, 147
Roget, Gene. *See* Ameripill Company
ROI (return on investment), 53, 54, 81, 88
Routine information, 36
Rudden, E., 31
Rugman, Alan, 4
Russian Radiators example, 176–178

Salter, S., 34, 49, 51, 120, 121
Samsung, 2, 3
Satellite technology, 35
SEC. *See* Securities and Exchange Commis-
    sion (SEC)
Securities and Exchange Commission
    (SEC)
  and disclosure regulation, 148
  and East Asian financial crisis, 142
  Form 20-F, 127–129
  and non-U.S. corporations, 127–129
  segmental disclosure requirements, 157
Segmental information
  benefits of reporting, 156
  costs of reporting, 156–157
  defined, 155
  global requirements, 158
  IASC requirements, 158–163
  U.K. requirements, 157–158

U.S. requirements, 157
uses and users, 155–156
Sekaran, U., 57, 58
Sequential information, 36
Sharp, D., 34, 51
Shearon, W., 55, 56
Shields, Michael, 53, 54
Singapore, 55, 56, 58, 132, 159. *See also*
    Barings Bank case
Sinning, Kathleen E., 109
SmithKline Beecham, 152, 153
Sollenberger, Harold M., 59
Spot rate
  defined, 12
  vs. forward rate, 16–17
Standard costing, 84
Stein, Collen. *See* Ameripill Company
Sterling Software, 36
Stobaugh, R., 52, 79
Stock exchanges. *See also* Securities and Ex-
    change Commission (SEC)
  and international accounting standards,
    130, 131–132
  variations in disclosure requirements,
    148, 149
Stopford and Wells, 30, 31
Strategic alliances
  as method of international business in-
    volvement, 3–4
  role in global economy, 2
Strategic business units (SBUs), 88
Strategic control process, 71–72
Street, D.L., 130, 133, 157
Strong, N., 53
Subsidiaries, foreign, 106
Swaps, currency, 18

Taiwan, 54, 56
Tang, R.Y.W., 103
Target costing, 84–85
Taxable income, defining, 96–97
Tax competition, 101
Tax credits, 99
Taxes
  avoiding double taxation, 98–100
  corporate income tax, 95–97
  credits and deductions, 98–99
  on goods and services, 98
  impact on location of foreign opera-
    tions, 106
  indirect, 98
  planning for, 105–106
  and transfer pricing, 80, 103–105, 106
  value-added, 98, 102

Tax havens, 100–101
Tax incentives, 101–102
Tax treaties, 100
TBF. *See* transborder data flows
Tearney, M., 21
Temporal translation method, 175, 176–179, 187
Texas Instruments, 86
Thailand, 56, 132, 159
Tondkar, R.H., 149
Total quality management (TQM), 85–86
Toyota Motor Company, 85
TQM. *See* total quality management (TQM)
Trade. *See* international trade
Transaction exposure, 20–21
Transborder data flows, 37
Transfer pricing
 matching to market conditions, 81–82
 overview, 80, 102–103
 tax considerations, 80, 103–105, 106
 U.S. rules, 103–105
Translation, in foreign exchange accounting
 current rate method, 175–176, 179–181
 functional vs. reporting currency, 175
 methodology overview, 175–176
 process in Canada, 183–184
 process in Europe, 182
 process in United Kingdom, 182–183
 process in United States, 181–182
 risk and exposure overview, 21, 174–175
 temporal method, 175, 176–179
 Yarmouth Woolens case, 187–196
Transnational organizational structure, 33
Transparency, 141, 142. *See also* disclosure
Treaties, tax, 100
Two-transaction exchange rate approach, 170–171

Ueno, S., 57, 58
Uncertainty avoidance, strong vs. weak, 49
Unilever, 6, 31
United Kingdom. *See also* British Telecom
 in Ameripill case, 62, 65, 66, 67–68
 British pounds in foreign exchange example, 12, 13, 14, 15–16, 17, 18, 19–20
 and conservatism in international accounting, 126–129
 and corporate income taxes, 96, 98
 foreign currency translation process, 182–183
 Japanese companies in, 54, 79, 85
 London Stock Exchange, 132
 segmental reporting requirements, 157–158, 159
United Nations, 129, 145, 159
United States. *See also* Securities and Exchange Commission (SEC)
 accounting for hedges and derivatives, 173–174
 vs. Australia, 58
 and conservatism in international accounting, 126–129
 foreign currency translation process, 181–182
 vs. Japan, 57–58
 number of multinational corporations, 5, 6
 rules for transfer pricing, 103–105
 segmental reporting requirements, 157, 159
 stock exchanges, 132
 U.S. dollar exchange rates, 13
University of British Columbia, 13

Valencia, Juan, 92
Value-added statements, 151, 152. *See also* economic value added (EVA)
Value-added taxes, 98, 102
VAT. *See* value-added taxes
Voluntary disclosure, 145–146, 147

Wadia, Jim, 38
Wall Street Journal, 12
Walton, P., 53
Wanandi, Jussuf, 50
WANs (wide area networks), 36
Weetman, P., 128, 129
Whitrow, G.J., 50
Wide area networks (WANs), 36
Withholding tax, 97
Wolfensohn, James D., 143
Wolk, H., 21
World Bank, 143
World trade. *See* international trade
World Trade Organization (WTO), 3
Wu, A., 54

Yarmouth Woolens case, 186–197